Ethics After Poststructuralism

Ethics After Poststructuralism

A Critical Reader

Edited by LEE OLSEN,
BRENDAN JOHNSTON *and*
ANN KENISTON

ETHICS AND CULTURE
Series Editor James M. Okapal

McFarland & Company, Inc., Publishers
Jefferson, North Carolina

ALSO OF INTEREST AND FROM MCFARLAND

*The New American Poetry of Engagement:
A 21st Century Anthology* (Ann Keniston
and Jeffrey Gray, 2012)

This book has undergone peer review.

ISBN (print) 978-1-4766-7687-6
ISBN (ebook) 978-1-4766-3907-9

LIBRARY OF CONGRESS AND BRITISH LIBRARY
CATALOGUING DATA ARE AVAILABLE

Library of Congress Control Number 2020002054

On the cover: "Hearing the News," mixed media (oil and transfer)
painting, 12"h × 9"w, artist Brenda Steinberg

Printed in the United States of America

*McFarland & Company, Inc., Publishers
Box 611, Jefferson, North Carolina 28640
www.mcfarlandpub.com*

Table of Contents

Section 3: Decoloniality and Ethics

Section 4: Posthuman Ethics

Acknowledgments

We gratefully acknowledge the University of Nevada, Reno Office for Research Innovation, the College of Liberal Arts, and the CLA Scholarly and Creative Activities Grants Program for permissions, and the English Department for its support of graduate research assistants. We also thank our research assistants, who performed work in locating and previewing chapters, preparing the manuscript, and obtaining permissions, including Aaron Schneeberger, Craig Charbonneau, Sarah Johnson, Nathan Lachner, and Tian Dubelko; special thanks to Shelby Grauberger, Elsa De Jong, and Stefanie Pressesky for their sustained and careful efforts in preparing the final manuscript. Thanks to colleagues Diane Perpich, Deborah Achtenberg, and Michael Koontz for their specific suggestions and general encouragement. We are grateful to the two anonymous readers of the manuscript and to our editor at McFarland, Gary Mitchem, and series editor, Jim Okapal, for their enthusiasm, recommendations, and patience.

We also thank the following for permission to reprint the chapters and essays that compose this volume:

Agamben, Giorgio. "Introduction." From *Homo Sacer: Sovereign Power and Bare Life*, by Agamben, Giorgio, translated by Daniel Heller-Roazen. © 1998 by the Board of Trustees of the Leland Stanford Jr. University. All rights reserved. Used by permission of the publisher, Stanford University Press, sup.org.

Braidotti, Rosi. "Affirmation versus Vulnerability: On Contemporary Ethical Debates." *Symposium: Canadian Journal of Connental Philosophy,* Volume 10, Issue 1, Spring 2006, pp. 235–254. DOI: 10.5840/symposium 200610117. Used by permission of the author.

Bunch, Mary. "Posthuman Ethics and the Becoming Animal of Emmanuel Levinas." *Culture, Theory and Critique,* Vol. 55:1, pp. 34–50 (2013). Reprinted by permission of the publisher, Taylor & Francis Ltd.

Butler, Judith. "Precarious Life." From *Precarious Life: The Powers of Mourning and Violence* (Verso Books, 2006), pp. 128–152. Used by permission of Verso Books.

Derrida, Jacques. "The Animal That Therefore I Am (More to Follow)." Translated by David Wills. From *The Animal That Therefore I Am* (Fordham University Press, 2008), pp. 1–51. Used by permission of Fordham University Press.

Derrida, Jacques. "Hospitality, Justice, and Responsibility: A Dialogue with Jacques Derrida." *Questioning Ethics: Contemporary Debates in Philosophy,* Ed. Richard Kearney and Mark Dooley, Routledge, 1999, pp. 65–83. Used by permission of Taylor & Francis Books.

Dussel, Enrique. "'Sensibility' and 'Otherness' in Emmanuel Levinas." *Philosophy Today,* Volume 43, Issue 2, Summer 1999, pp. 126–134. DOI: 10.5840/philtoday199943224. Used by permission of the Philosophy Documentation Center.

Dussel, Enrique, with Eduardo Ibarra-Colado. "Globalization, Organization, and the Ethics of Liberation." *Sage Journals*, Volume 13(4): pp. 489–508, copyright © 2006 by Sage Publications. Reprinted by permission of SAGE Publications, Ltd.

Foucault, Michel. "Right of Death and Power over Life" from *The History of Sexuality: Volume I: An Introduction* by Michel Foucault, translated by Robert Hurley, translation copyright © 1978 by Penguin Random House LLC. Used by permission of Pantheon Books, an imprint of the Knopf Doubleday Publishing Group, a division of Penguin Random House LLC. All rights reserved.

Levinas, Emmanuel. "Responsibility for the Other." Translated by Richard A. Cohen. *Ethics and Infinity: Conversations with Philippe Nemo.* © 1985 by Duquesne University Press. Used by permission of Duquesne University Press.

Maldonado-Torres, Nelson. "Levinas's Hegemonic Identity Politics, Radical Philosophy, and the Unfinished Project of Decolonization." *Levinas Studies*, Volume 7, 2012, pp. 63-94. DOI: 10.5840/levinas201276. Used by permission of the Philosophy Documentation Center.

Plonowska Ziarek, Ewa. "Feminist Reflections on Vulnerability: Disrespect, Obligation, Action." *SubStance* 42:3 (2013), 67–84. © Johns Hopkins University Press and SubStance, Inc. Reprinted with permission of Johns Hopkins University Press.

Ruti, Mari. "Is Autonomy Unethical? Trauma and the Politics of Responsibility." From *The Ethics of Remembering and the Consequences of Forgetting.* Edited by Michael O'Loughlin. Copyright © 2014. Used by permission of Rowman & Littlefield Publishing Group. All rights reserved.

Smith, Mick. "Articulating Ecological Ethics and Politics," in *Against Sovereignty: Ethics, Biopolitics, and Saving the Natural World* (University of

Minnesota Press, 2011) pp. 159–192. Copyright © 2011 by the Regents of the University of Minnesota.

Tlostanova, Madina V., and Walter D. Mignolo. "On Pluritopic Hermeneutics, Trans-modern Thinking, and Decolonial Philosophy," *Encounters* (2009). Used by permission of Zayed University.

Yegenoglu, Meyda. "Liberal Multiculturalism and the Ethics of Hospitality in the Age of Globalization." © 2003 Meyda Yegenoglu. Used by permission of the author.

Introduction

LEE OLSEN *and* BRENDAN JOHNSTON

Even in socially and politically fraught contemporary times, ethical discourse eludes us. While ethical questions saturate the news, we struggle to invoke any universally applicable ethics to address our moment. Ethical imperatives, while always bound to moral and existential questions, are overused and their effectiveness is largely lost, especially when applied to current events. Partisan politicians use the terms *ethics* and *morals* to obfuscate ideology. Right-wing nationalists, fighting for a mythological heritage of Western exceptionalism, often appropriate Aristotle, Marcus Aurelius, and Immanuel Kant to help justify calls for cultural insularity and ethnic exclusion. Left-wing proponents of identity politics—the "social justice warriors" of academia and grass-roots movements like Occupy Wall Street, Black Lives Matter, and #MeToo—at times speak back to this "heritage" in moralistic terms, arguing for the recognition of oppressed minorities and against socio-economic injustice and white-male privilege. While the long tradition of ethics might exonerate the latter position more readily than the former, it is hard to ignore—especially in today's climate of moral outrage, political self-righteousness, and blatant hypocrisy—the fact that invocations of ethics from all sides often muddy the waters more than they clarify possibilities for positive action. In 2018, a state senator in Illinois likened her state's Ethical Oversight Committee to a "fox guarding the hen house." Indeed, it seems to be a fact universally acknowledged that whenever someone invokes the word *ethics* it would be wise to check the coop. This seems to be especially true in the era of whistle-blowers like Reality Winner, Michael Cohen, Julian Assange, and Edward Snowden.

Despite the apparent and widespread misuse of *ethics*, the need for comprehensible and useful ethical frameworks has grown more urgent than ever. Recent years have witnessed morally charged yet increasingly polarized debates about immigration, border control, and the exclusion of certain

1

groups in the interest of national security; arguments for isolationism and Western exceptionalism; arguments about identity politics and prevalent use of xenophobic rhetoric for political leverage; and discussions and denials of climate change alongside empirically demonstrable ecological devastation and mass extinction. The daily news contributes to this ever-growing list of ethically compelling issues, yet even the news media are subject to partisan analysis and ideological "spin" such that the same images and sound-bites can be used to prove opposing ideological positions.

These debates suggest the limits of traditional conceptions of ethics, which have focused variously on civic virtue, rationality, moral behavior, and self-care—all conceptual starting-points for universal ethical impulses and imperatives. Many of these debates hinge on conceptions of the Self in relation to Others who are different from the Self, from the majority, and from those in power. These vulnerable Others—if we can indeed conceive of them as Other—may include those of nondominant ethnic origins and religious beliefs, women, children, the poor, the disenfranchised, the disabled, immigrants, and refugees from the global South—other humans who have been dehumanized and silenced by political rhetoric, perpetual marginalization, economic exploitation, and physical violence. Some Others are so culturally and politically marginalized that we fail to recognize them in the first place: other-than-human animals, the more-than-human biosphere, and even (in)organic entities like mountaintop coal deposits and deep-sea trenches we treat merely as resources or dumps. It is difficult to acknowledge these defamiliarized entities, much less to respond to them, to take responsibility for them, or to speak on their behalf. Suffice it to say we inherit a long history of systematic Othering, dehumanization, and externalization—an unfortunate human legacy which presumably precedes recorded history. This legacy has not only justified but facilitated the treatment of both human and non-human Others as inferior, as means not ends, and as external to and separate from our own intrinsic systems of valuation.

As coeditors of this volume, we suggest that it is crucial in our present social and political moment to reappraise our ethical conceptions of and commitments to other peoples, communities, and ecologies. We see radical implications in interrogating the frameworks by which we have conceived, or more often misconceived, the Other. We wish to explore notions of Otherness, shared vulnerability, and a radical praxis grounded in responsibility and universal hospitality. For this reason, we draw attention to a tradition of ethical thought founded on responsibility to the vulnerable Other, formulated first by Emmanuel Levinas (1906–1995), a Lithuanian-French Jewish philosopher. Having survived combat against and internment by Nazi Germany (most of his immediate family were murdered in Lithuania by the Nazis), Levinas dedicated his life to theorizing the Holocaust and how it was that

Germany, in the heart of enlightened modern Europe, could commit such atrocities under the banner of a "final solution." Levinas studied under the German philosopher Martin Heidegger, an influential early–twentieth-century phenomenologist and, unfortunately, a Nazi sympathizer. Though Levinas later distanced himself from his teacher, Heideggerian phenomenology remained central to his existential thinking. (Hannah Arendt, another student of Heidegger who is frequently mentioned in this reader, followed a similar path, going on to publish extensively on Nazism, fascism, authoritarianism, totalitarianism, and "the banality of evil," or the tendency of indifferent, complacent humans to commit atrocious acts.) After surviving the concentration camps of Vichy France, Levinas went on to become one of the most influential figures in continental philosophy and early poststructuralist politics and ethics in the twentieth century. His major works include *Totality and Infinity* (1961) and *Otherwise than Being* (1974). The readings collected here respond to and extend his revolutionary approach to ethics as articulated in these major works and others.

But what was so revolutionary about Levinas's conception of ethics? Philosophers before him, such as René Descartes and Immanuel Kant, imagined that the source of morality, or the ethical *ought*, resided within the Self, the bounded individual of Enlightenment thinking. Levinas insisted, alternately, that an ethics established through rationality, as in Kant, was too detached from lived, embodied experience, and that any "categorical imperative" should precede rational thought. He theorized that the source of the ethical *ought*, indeed the source of all ethical behavior, resides not in the Self but, in fact, in the vulnerable Other—or, more precisely, in the Self's corporeal, sensible, pre-rational relationship to the Other. This ethics of the Other entails a mode of subjectivity in which Selfhood is predicated on a proximal, face-to-face interaction with, responsibility to, and substitution for the Other. The immediate ethical obligation is subsumed by the face of the Other, and the Other's vulnerability becomes one's chief responsibility. In fact, this vulnerability becomes radically substituted for or incorporated into the Self. It is a moment of infinite substitution and sacrifice—or, as some have argued, a moment of almost masochistic self-extinction. By apprehending the face of the Other, the Self becomes not host but hostage. In this way, Levinas spawned a novel mode of theorizing ethics, politics, and subjectivity. We as editors have sought to illustrate the influence of this radical strain of thought insofar as it has developed organically into a tradition of its own.

To be more specific, *Ethics After Poststructuralism* features prominent continental philosophers—primarily from Western Europe—including Levinas, Michel Foucault, Jacques Derrida, and Giorgio Agamben. Until recently, these contributors received little attention from American and British readers other than those scholars interested in poststructuralism as such.[1] We hope to bring them to a broader audience by excerpting some of their important yet more accessible writings on ethics. This reader also includes recent responses to and applications of these influential theorists by Judith Butler, Mari Ruti, Ewa Plonowska Ziarek, Enrique Dussel, Walter D. Mignolo and Madina V. Tlostanova, Nelson Maldonado-Torres, Mary Bunch, Mick Smith, and Rosi Braidotti. These theorists focus on multidisciplinary work in post–9/11 global politics, postcolonialism, decoloniality, animal studies, ecology, and posthumanism. They demonstrate the continued relevance of ethics insofar as they extend, challenge, and even supplant poststructuralist-inflected thought in response to the contemporary challenges of an ethically complex world.

By tracing a Levinasian strand of contemporary ethics through a range of disciplines, this reader emphasizes the always vulnerable status of an Other who can never be fully known or articulated. The essays explore issues of subjectivity, difference, hospitality, responsibility, sovereignty, power, and control, all of which underlie recent discussions of marginalization, appropriation, inclusion, and the priority of the human. They question the reliability of language, the legacy of Enlightenment humanism, the Cartesian separation of body and mind, the notion of universal truths, and the possibility of standing outside ideology. Ultimately, the volume affirms the continued influence of Levinas's notion of the Other in contemporary ethical discourse, although, to be clear, *Ethics After Poststructuralism* does not argue for the primacy of Levinasian ethics nor does it advocate any one correct way to conceive of or respond to Others. As much as this reader turns on Levinasian ethics, many of the readings we include radically reimagine Levinas's ethical injunction. By delineating a strand of ethics concerned with the Other, the volume engenders more questions than it answers, thus underscoring the crucial task of constantly challenging traditional and culturally accepted conceptions of ethics.

Our volume's consideration of contemporary ethical dilemmas entails a reevaluation of poststructuralism's capacity to enrich interdisciplinary investigations of ethics. The stakes of constantly reexamining ethical debates in social, political, and academic spheres are, we feel, enormous. As scholars trying to make sense of these ongoing debates, we inherit a late–twentieth-century legacy of indeterminacy—the sense there is no ground on which to anchor knowledge, belief, or practice—that this volume seeks to better understand. The opening up to free play advocated by poststructuralists including Jacques Derrida, Jacques Lacan, and others became a productive moment in ethical thought—especially after the modernist grand narratives and ideology sometimes associated with Hitler's fascism, Stalin's totalitarianism, and the subsequent ascendency of American imperialism/exceptionalism at midcentury. Poststructuralism is often depicted as apart from and less productive than other, more "empirical" approaches to ethics, including analytic philosophy, an Anglo-American strain that jettisons unfalsifiable questions of Being and Truth in its rigorous pursuit of logic and linguistic clarity. This particular depiction suggests that continental philosophy's poststructural models of ethics and social justice, while concerned with historically marginalized subjects (the Other), hierarchy, logocentrism, and economically hegemonic ideologies, still tend toward skepticism, indeterminacy, and unfeasible utopian frameworks at odds with practical ethics. On the other hand, analytic philosophy is often portrayed as divorced from metaphysical gesturing and grounded in more logical, practical, and empirically discernible areas of human action. Rather than entering into these already tired debates within contemporary philosophy, we as editors suggest the value of engaging continental philosophy with analytic philosophy as a means of overcoming the unproductive historical feud between these at-times productive approaches.

Granted, to engage these two traditions we must traffic in tensions and accusations, and we as editors find it necessary to defend our return to poststructuralism. It is important to note that Levinas never aligned himself with the poststructuralist movement as such. Rather, poststructuralists, including Derrida, as well as later historical apologists such as Simon Critchley, brought Levinas into this conversation. Indeed, how does one create a concrete, applicable ethical framework in the absence of concrete or rational foundational frameworks, one that resists grand narratives, even grand ethical narratives? Critics also note that poststructuralism's critique of social construction has been readily appropriated by ideologues who advance decidedly retrograde agendas. Proponents of deregulated free-market capitalism, for example, use a distorted version of social constructivism to undermine mounting scientific evidence of climate change, suggesting that this evidence has been manipulated by radical socialists who celebrate intrusive government regulation. This distortion says that, if we cannot prove that our actions are affecting the planet, we should not be held responsible when others face the dire consequences of our actions, as in the case of faceless others living in island nations facing displacement by tropical storms and rising oceans. Indeterminacy can be dangerous, as this example suggests.

Acknowledging the limitations of radical indeterminacy, we ask if it is possible to construct an ethics, consistent with lived and shared experiences, that accounts for the detriments of structure and universalism? In a globalized yet fragmented world, can humans devise an ethics with planetary applicability? Do we want such a widely applicable ethics, considering such drawbacks as false universalisms and erasure of difference across ethically diverse cultures? As a starting point, we might consider an ethics based on responsibility in face-to-face, contextualized experiences. This ethics has the potential to transcend any ethics predicated on a rational Platonic or Aristotelian self-centered notion that happiness is an ultimate goal achievable through virtue and moral discipline. It moves beyond a Kantian ideal, where reason dictates what we *ought* to do and prescribes our duty with a categorical imperative, an absolute rule about what *must* be done. This ethics also moves beyond John Stuart Mill's utilitarian ethics, which holds that rational beings behave ethically for the greater communal good. And it compels us to consider that historic notions of ethics have, at times, been used to facilitate clearly unethical behavior. For example, attempts to quantify the "greater good" of ethics necessarily create states of exception and sacrifice, in the most violent sense of those words. As the essays in this volume suggest, Levinas's being-for-the-Other may offer a useful foundation for an ethics not based on virtue, rationality, duty, utilitarianism, or pragmatism. They also suggest that it is crucial to reinterrogate, modify, extend, or even reject Levinas's ethical injunction despite its potentially universal implications.

In fact, Levinas himself revealed the limitations, ignorance, and insensibility of his own notions of the non–Western subject and the nonhuman animal Other—issues taken up explicitly in the third and fourth sections of our reader. In a late interview, "Dialogue on Thinking-of-the-Other," Levinas addressed such limitations with regard to the finite nature of the law and the notion that even our most cherished principles must be continually interrogated and reinterpreted—this after the interviewer challenged Levinas's ethics for being "extravagantly" generous and problematically unspecific. The interviewer asked: "In comparison with (and I quote you) 'the extravagant generosity of the for-the-other'—aren't politics and, in a more precise sense, law, the only means of instituting society? Moreover, isn't this necessity of the Law, this limitation of an infinite right, one of the political lessons of the Talmud?" To this Levinas replied:

> I wasn't challenging law or politics—I even tried to deduce the necessity for them—I have also shown their ethical limits. What you say about the Talmud is correct, but the Talmud never limits itself to the concept, which, however, is important to it. When it uses concepts, it never forgets the examples from which the concept was drawn. "Here is the law—it is perfectly good, but what will happen if…." This "what will happen if…" is a particular case. The discussion never drops it, and often the concept is reversed and reveals a completely different meaning than the one it "pretended to be" at the beginning.[2]

The interviewer, in invoking the Talmud (the codified laws of early Jewish faith) rather than the Torah, which references the divine text as a whole, challenges Levinas's insistence on infinite responsibility to the Other by arguing that this impossible and perhaps excessively generous imperative cannot be codified in formal law nor into any practical, universalized politics. But Levinas highlights the usefulness and eternal benefit of leaving open this unchangeable command for an infinite arbitration or adjudication. In Jewish thought, the Torah—or rather the Talmud, or compendium of laws—is always preserved in unaltered form, yet it endures constant reinterpretation for specific contexts. Levinas affirms the law and insists that ethics, likewise, remain open to interpretation.

This insistence is undoubtedly a response to the "final solutions" of the twentieth century, which Levinas experienced directly: rigid, idealist solutions which engendered unspeakable evil. Further, this insistence clarifies *Ethics After Poststructuralism* insofar as it illustrates an enduring yet problematic legacy through texts that affirm, extend, and counter Levinas's contribution to ethics. Like Levinas, the volume's editors highlight the importance of ongoing arbitration, interpretation, and situational determinacy. Rather than grant infallible primacy to Levinas, this reader actually highlights the vulnerability of Levinas's legacy in contemporary thought: as its chapters demonstrate, even some of his most central ideas are problematic, specifically his overt Eurocentrism ("only the Bible and the Greeks"), his hierarchical notions of the animal, and his concept of bad animalities within human nature. As Levinas suggests in relation to the Talmud, interpretations change and often have to change. They get recast to fit situations which demand difficult, even exceptional adjudication. The essays collected here ask how we might reinterpret Levinas's ideas, how we might reconcile self-sacrifice with the practical demands of individual, socio-political, and environmental justice, and how we might extend Levinas's Eurocentric ethics to a planetary scale.

Section Overviews

The volume's first section, "Hospitality and Responsibility for the Other," introduces and responds to Levinas's influential association of ethics with unconditional responsibility. The readings reveal the centrality of Levinasian ideas to contemporary thinking about ethics and the problematic elements of these ideas, especially in relation to actual political situations, including recent immigration and refugee crises. In an interview from *Ethics and Infinity: Conversations with Philippe Nemo* (1985), Levinas summarizes the essential features of his thinking about responsibility, otherness, and the threat and prohibition of violence that he elaborated in *Otherwise than Being* (1974). Levinas's association of ethics with "responsibility for the Other" links responsibility to subjectivity itself. Here Levinas also reinforces his most radical and controversial notion that, even if the Other persecutes the I, the I remains responsible for the Other and, implicitly, for those persecutions. This is reiterated so strongly that his interviewer Phillipe Nemo claims to be astounded, even incredulous. For Levinas, unconditional responsibility entails turning from the host into the hostage of the Other. True hospitality is not limited to friends, family, and familiars, but includes the radical Other, the Other who might do us harm. The remaining chapters in the section counter and extend these radical propositions.

In "Hospitality, Justice, and Responsibility: A Dialogue" (1999), Jacques Derrida extends Levinas's notions of prerational ethics to interrogate Western conceptions of justice and the law. These conceptions, Derrida argues, are grounded in rationality and codification and thus are overdetermined and sclerotic insofar as they cannot account for infinitely heterogenous material-discursive realities, such as recent mutations in state power and corporate governance (themes that resound in Section Two). Derrida, following Levinas, suggests that justice and law must be informed by an ethical responsibility that originates in the possibility of decision and subsequently considers the particularities of every event. The chapter is at once a challenge to historic conceptions of justice and law and a response to those who claim poststructuralism generally and deconstruction specifically are rendered ineffectual and ethically void because they are mired in undecidability and indeterminacy. Derrida suggests the exact opposite: deconstruction, itself strongly inflected by Levinasian ethics, illuminates the limitations of juridical determination and affirms the value of infinite undecidability. Derrida insists here that the impetus that drives his deconstruction is in principle Levinasian. And that his later, more explicitly political writings are indebted to, if not themselves captivated under, the Levinasian notion of the radical Other.

Judith Butler, in "Precarious Life" (2004), explores Levinas's compressed and seemingly contradictory claims about the face of the Other, considering these ideas in relation to a contemporary political environment that has repeatedly and uncritically reproduced images of Others (of Afghanis and Iraqis, for example). Here Butler articulates the challenges of responding to what she calls the Other's "demand" or address. This obligation to respond, Butler claims, evokes Levinas's notion of vulnerability, or precariousness, and the biblical injunction "Thou shalt not kill," an injunction complicated by the notions that precariousness itself incites violence and that murder should never be committed as self-preservation.

Drawing from psychoanalysis and its contemporary applications in the work of Slavoj Žižek, Mari Ruti also considers Levinas in relation to precariousness and specifically sexual violence. In "Is Autonomy Unethical?" (2015), she challenges Butler's influential reading of Levinas, noting that Butler conflates Levinas's notion of ethics with his notion of justice, notions that Ruti argues are in fact separate insofar as justice demands an outside arbitrator, whereas the Levinasian ethical moment is always one-to-one and prerational. Through a detailed discussion of the ways that Butler reconciles Levinasian notions of the Other with psychoanalysis—especially the notions of precarity and grievability, and the principle that "the other dwells within the self"— Ruti challenges Butler's underlying assumptions and the gendered power dynamics occluded by Levinasian abstractions. Ultimately Ruti celebrates individuation and autonomy, as when the Self resists conscription into violence enacted by clearly unethical aggression, as in the case of women resisting sexual violence.

In an affirmative mode similar to Ruti, Ewa Plonowska Ziarek, in "Feminist Reflections on Vulnerability: Disrespect, Obligation, Action" (2013), extends Levinas, Butler, Arendt, and French feminists such as Luce Irigaray with a feminist analysis grounded in vulnerability and focused on domination, struggles for freedom, and ethical obligation. Attending to negative manifestations of biopolitics and liberal individualism, and distinguishing between negative and positive connotations of vulnerability, Plonowska Ziarek argues that contesting domination, political exclusion, and excessive, paranoid assessments of risk necessitates an abiding attention to ethical responsibility. Plonowska Ziarek challenges liberal individualism's tendency to make embodied subjects suspicious of their own (positive) vulnerability and, thus, its inability to foster empathy and productively undermine domination.

In Section Two, "States of Exception," recognition of and responsibility for the Other remain central, though political rather than individual issues of sovereignty, power, representation, and exclusion are more clearly foregrounded, and the always political nature of the Other is engaged directly. Like Derrida, Plonowska Ziarek, Ruti, and Butler, the authors in this section suggest that notions of ethics and responsibility must be modified to account for manipulations of state power and corporate governance and for evolving ideas of multiculturalism, subjectivity, identity, and dehumanization. In the first selection, "Right of Death and Power over Life," Part Five of *The History of Sexuality: Volume I* (1978), Michel Foucault introduces what he terms the modern emergence of *biopolitics* or *biopower*—the institutional techniques of organization, regularization, and control of people and populations that greatly exceed and envelop any instantiation of individual agency. He argues that the traditional notions of the sovereign, which entailed the right to decide life and death, have shifted from the right to "take life and let live" to a system of biopolitical control that "makes live and lets die." This new iteration of the sovereign, while masked by the trappings of Western democracy and the Enlightenment principles of individual liberty, succeeds in maintaining and policing all aspects of human life. These technologies of regulation, rather than evoking the traditional sovereign ruler, have been inculcated into the self-regulation of the population as a whole.

Giorgio Agamben's *Homo Sacer: Sovereign Power and Bare Life* (1997) extends Foucault's notion of biopower, recasting its relevance at the turn of the last century. In his work's Introduction, included here, Agamben, drawing on not only Foucault but also the work of Hannah Arendt and Carl Schmitt, introduces the concept of "the state of exception," where marginalized human bodies are disavowed yet simultaneously exploited to the sovereign's benefit. Some contemporary legacies of this notion include places like Guantánamo Bay or immigrant detention facilities at the southern U.S. border, where political and human rights are suspended and often openly violated. Agamben identifies modern power as a new iteration of the archaic notion of sovereignty, which produces the *homo sacer*, or the sacred man: one who can be killed, though never sacrificed, without penalty. The *homo sacer* is both disposable and vitally necessary to sustain the rest of the officially recognized population. Foucault and Agamben both question what ethics might mean when biopolitics transforms democracy into totalitarianism, thus instrumentalizing the increasingly non-agential, disposable, but secretly necessary Other.

In "Liberal Multiculturalism and the Ethics of Hospitality in the Age of Globalization" (2003), Meyda Yegenoglu troubles the ideas underlying liberal multiculturalism and tolerance inherent in supposedly "progressive" Eurocentric thought, arguing that multiculturalism actually reinscribes Western sovereign power inasmuch as it enacts a subtle racism—associated with the idea of conditional hospitality—and imposes borders, limitations, and foreclosure, especially on non–Western subjects. Echoing the affirmative approach to ethico-politics of Ruti, Plonowska Ziarek, and Derrida, and countering the negative biopolitical power examined in Foucault and Agamben, Yegenoglu proposes that unconditional hospitality may allow for more productive ethical and political engagement. This vulnerable yet affirmative, expansive notion of hospitality is taken up in very specific decolonial and nonhuman instances in the reader's third and fourth sections.

The third section, "Decoloniality and Ethics," employs one of the most recent, and arguably the most radical, responses to Levinasian ethics: a decolonial ethics that emerged from postcolonial and anticolonial theory. Whereas postcolonial theory—in the vein of Homi Bhabha, Gayatri Spivak, and Edward Said—spoke back to the colonizer in the language of the colonizer, decoloniality—exemplified by Frantz Fanon, Aimé Césaire, and Édouard Glissant—speaks back in the language of the oppressed. The authors in this section move past a Eurocentric orientation, trying to think beyond an oppressive European "colonial matrix of power" (Aníbal Quijano's term) by deploying non–Eurocentric ethics, epistemologies, and philosophies. They challenge Levinasian ethics with decolonial (specifically Central, South American, and African) perspectives and non–Western methodologies and illustrate how decolonial ethics help us think beyond the oppressive and exploitative ten-

dencies of European modernity, evident in such atrocities as economic imperialism, slavery, genocide, epistemological violence, and cultural homogenization.

Decolonial Levinasian ethics (itself a problematic but surprisingly productive synthesis) takes as its point of radical departure a conversation
between Emmanuel Levinas and liberation theorist Enrique Dussel in which
Levinas charged Dussel and other decolonial theorists with the task of theorizing colonialism, slavery, and genocide in a mode similar to his, a mode
that he applied primarily to Jews in a European context. Thus, we as editors
chose to begin this section with "'Sensibility' and 'Otherness' in Emmanuel
Levinas" (1999), the essay in which Dussel discusses the influence of Levinas
on his own work and his encounter with Levinas. In the next chapter, "Globalization, Organization, and the Ethics of Liberation," Dussel and Eduardo
Ibarra-Colado challenge the asymmetrical development and violence of Eurocentric modernity by theorizing an ethics of liberation that hinges on responsibility to the Other. Decolonial liberation ethics acknowledge a "transmodern"
moment in which all cultures contribute to global development in a more
diverse, democratic mode.

In the next chapter, "On Pluritopic Hermeneutics, Trans-modern Thinking, and Decolonial Philosophy" (2009), Madina V. Tlostanova and Walter
D. Mignolo push back against the very notion of Same and Other and the
construction of "otherness" on which that dichotomy relies. Unlike Dussel,
they interrogate the violence of that dichotomy insofar as it has been deployed
in European colonialism and Eurocentric philosophy. Like Dussel, Tlostanova
and Mignolo also challenge the Eurocentric construc of "modernity," and its
reliance on the construction of "otherness," a construction that tends to portray the Other as less-than-human (*anthropos*) and the Same as fully human
(*humanitas*). The authors propose decolonizing interhuman relations by
embracing "the convivial pluri-versality" of human life and thus mitigating
the violence of constructing people as Other and subsequently less-than-
human.

In the section's final chapter, "Levinas's Hegemonic Identity Politics,
Radical Philosophy, and the Unfinished Project of Decolonization" (2012),
Nelson Maldonado-Torres fully acknowledges some of Levinas's more problematic assertions, specifically Levinas's privileging of "the Bible and the
Greeks," and he works to redeem his ethics from accusations of obscurantism
and Eurocentrism. Reading Levinas against Frantz Fanon and other decolonial philosophers, Maldonado-Torres argues for the ongoing value of explor-
ing Levinasian ethics in relation to political and juridical issues without, however,
discounting such ethics from the grounds of uncritical identity politics and
multiculturalism. Like Dussel and Tlostanova and Mignolo, Maldonado-Torres
exemplifies a decolonial, Fanonian approach to ethics and politics, an approach

which attends to alterity, materiality, and political economic violence in a transmodern present.

Section Four, "Posthuman Ethics," extends Levinasian ethical considerations to a global ecology in which ethics is enacted not by humans separate from nature but by humans embedded in larger ecologies and alongside other-than-human subjectivities. This section's readings cohere around posthumanist thinking, which challenges anthropocentric humanist thought by decentering the human in critical inquiry and political praxis. This section pays greater ethical attention to the material, to physical bodies, and complex, more-than-human ecologies. Themes of embodiment, difference, sentience, physical pain, and biopolitics recur. Like the previous section, this section attends to the implications of casting ethically compelling beings as Other, this time in the context of a tangled world of which humans are only one embedded part.

The section begins with Derrida's early championing of "the animal question" in an excerpt from "The Animal That Therefore I Am (More to Follow)" (2002). Here, Derrida considers a literal and figurative situation in which the naked Self, having met the gaze of a nonhuman animal Other—in this case his pet cat—feels ashamed. Derrida implicitly challenges or extends Levinas's thought by suggesting that the face of the animal Other disrupts his own ego, compelling him to acknowledge the animal's radical alterity. Upon tracing an anthropocentric philosophical treatment of "the animal," through many of philosophy's central figures, Derrida returns to Jeremy Bentham's question "Can the animal suffer?" (1789), which he suggests "changes everything" insofar as it impels us to acknowledge animals as ethically compelling beings. Derrida also considers the accelerated transformation of human-animal relations over the past two centuries, which resulted at least in part from the biopolitical developments discussed by Foucault and Agamben in Section Two.

The subsequent chapters move well beyond Derrida's rereading of Levinas and his more capacious conception of ethical subjectivity. By advocating ethical attention to the nonhuman, Mary Bunch's "Posthuman Ethics and the Becoming Animal of Emmanuel Levinas" (2013) offers a corrective to the unapologetic anthropocentrism of Western philosophy, modifying Levinas's own pejorative treatment of the animal and his notion of the bad "animalities" within human nature. Addressing Levinas, the biopolitical theories of Michel Foucault and Giorgio Agamben, and Gilles Deleuze and Félix Guattari's concept of "becoming animal," Bunch reconsiders Levinas's ethics of the face in the context of the radical dehumanization of the contemporary biopoliticized world. Taking seriously the conception of becoming animal, Bunch suggests, is a first step in extending Levinasian ethics into the political realm but also beyond the constrained, anthropocentric realm of the human. Such an extension, she suggests, is necessary for understanding and addressing biopolitical forces, which cut across not only the human but the nonhuman as well.

Mick Smith's "Articulating Ecological Ethics and Politics" (2011) champions an ethics that addresses responsibility for the nonhuman Other, which includes the ecologies that surround humans. Smith's political and philosophical concerns recall Agamben and Foucault's notions of sovereignty and Derrida and Levinas's concerns with the problem of articulating the "wholly Other." Smith distinguishes morality from ethics and ethics from politics. Extending Levinas's notion of ethics and Hannah Arendt's notion of politics, he advocates for a political approach to ecology that both rejects traditional notions of sovereignty and reiterates the importance of responsibility. While Smith's work hearkens back to the first section, it also links the second with the third by broadening the category of the Other.

Like Bunch, Rosi Braidotti, in "Affirmation versus Vulnerability: On Contemporary Ethical Debates" (2006), theorizes an affirmative ethics—one explicitly indebted to ideas from Baruch Spinoza, Friedrich Nietzsche, Levinas, Foucault, Agamben, and Derrida—that amends previous approaches to Eurocentric liberalist and humanist ethics that have focused negatively on violence, injustice, mourning, and so on. A posthumanist and "nomadic" conception of ethical subjectivity, Braidotti argues, allows for greater attention to immanence, connection, affirmation, and the positive connotations of vulnerability. Like Spinoza before her, Braidotti suggests that the purpose of ethics is to discover what the body, and bodies together, can do, and what manifestations of creativity and freedom they can enable, rather than how bodies can be constrained and delimited.

Suggested Further Reading

Many essays in this reader have been condensed, though we encourage readers to consult the complete versions. It would be impossible to include here a thorough list of useful texts on ethics generally and Levinas specifically. However, we note that this volume extends several important texts, which we encourage interested readers to consult. A useful starting point is Diane Perpich's *The Ethics of Emmanuel Levinas* (2008), a thorough overview of Levinasian ethics, especially in relation to environmental ethics and social movements. As Mari Ruti notes in her essay in this reader, Tina Chanter's edited collection *Feminist Interpretations of Emmanuel Levinas* (2001) offers a comprehensive collection of feminist engagements with Levinas. Nelson Maldonado-Torres's essay included in the present volume was first published in a special decolonial issue of *Levinas Studies* (Vol. 7, 2012), edited by John Drabinski, and we encourage interested readers to consult that issue and Drabinski's other work, including *Levinas and the Postcolonial: Race, Nation, Other* (2011). We recommend the collection *Radicalizing Levinas* (2010), and we have sought to elaborate on what editors Matthew Calarco and Peter Atterton call the third wave of Levinas scholarship, "an explicit attempt to situate and explore Levinas's work within the context of the most pressing sociopolitical issues of our time."[3] Our third and fourth sections overlap similarly with Calarco and Atterton's third-wave application of Levinasian ethics, though in distinctly decolonial and posthumanist modes. We echo our fellow editors in one case: like them, we view Judith Butler as one of the most useful contemporary explicators of Levinas. Yet, as our selections from Ruti and Plonowska Ziarek attest, Butler's thought deserves further adjudication as well.

We also recommend another firmly Levinasian politics reader, Asher Horowitz and Gad Horowitz's *Difficult Justice: Commentaries on Levinas and Politics* (University of Toronto Press, 2006). This collection opens with a seminal essay from Levinas, "Reflections on the Philosophy of Hitlerism" (1934) (first published in *Esprit* and later reprinted in *Critical Inquiry* [1990]), and illustrates how Levinasian politics relates to contemporary political thought, especially conversations on liberalism's inability to achieve a political theory "absolutely opposed to oppression" (*Otherwise than Being* 177).

We also direct readers to several quite different collections not focused on Levinasian ethics. Todd Davis and Kenneth Womack's collection *Mapping the Ethical Turn* (University of Virginia Press, 2001) and Marjorie Garber, Beatrice Hanssen, and Rebecca Walkowitz's *The Turn to Ethics* (Routledge, 2000) include valuable writings on ethics, especially ethics at the beginning of the twentieth century. Similarly, in a properly philosophical vein, *The Continental Ethics Reader* (Routledge, 2003) and *The Ethical Turn: Otherness and Subjectivity in Contemporary Psychoanalysis* (Routledge, 2016) reveal continued interest in ethics, although both offer a narrower approach than *Ethics After Poststructuralism*. *The Continental Ethics Reader* reviews ethics in continental philosophy from Kant through French feminism in the 1970s and '80s. *The Ethical Turn: Otherness and Subjectivity in Contemporary Psychoanalysis* mirrors our own explicitly Levinasian approach, though it is written for readers with strong interests in philosophy and psychoanalysis. Finally, we note two field-specific collections: *Biopolitics: A Reader* (Duke University Press, 2013) deals, in ways that resemble the second and third sections of our reader, with issues of globalization, biopolitics, and necropolitics, and will appeal to those working in history, sociology, and literary cultural studies. *The Ethics of Remembering and the Consequences of Forgetting: Essays on Trauma, History, and Memory* (Rowman & Littlefield, 2014) will appeal to those working in psychoanalysis and trauma studies.

NOTES

1. Levinas never aligned himself with the poststructuralist movement as such. Rather, poststructuralism's important practitioners like Derrida and its later historical apologists like Simon Critchley brought Levinas into that movement. See, for example, Derrida's essays in the present volume and Critchley's *The Ethics of Deconstruction: Levinas and Derrida* (Edinburgh: Edinburgh University Press, 2014).

2. Emmanuel Levinas, *Entre Nous: Thinking-of-the-Other*, trans. Michael B. Smith and Barbara Harshav (New York: Columbia University Press, 2000).

3. Peter Atterton and Matthew Calarco, Introduction to *Radicalizing Levinas*, ed. by Peter Atterton and Matthew Calarco (New York: SUNY Press, 2010), x.

Hospitality and Responsibility for the Other

Responsibility for the Other

Emmanuel Levinas

Conversation with Philippe Nemo

Philippe Nemo: *In your last great book published,* Otherwise than Being or Beyond Essence, *you speak of moral responsibility. Husserl had already spoken of responsibility, but of a responsibility for the truth; Heidegger had spoken of authenticity; as for yourself, what do you understand by responsibility?*

    Emmanuel Levinas: In this book I speak of responsibility as the essential, primary, and fundamental structure of subjectivity. For I describe subjectivity in ethical terms. Ethics, here, does not supplement a preceding existential base; the very node of the subjective is knotted in ethics understood as responsibility.

    I understand responsibility as responsibility for the Other, thus as responsibility for what is not my deed, or for what does not even matter to me; or which precisely does matter to me, is met by me as face.

P.N.: *How, having discovered the Other in his face, does one discover him as he to whom one is responsible?*

    E.L.: In describing the face positively, and not merely negatively. You recall what we said: meeting the face is not of the order of pure and simple perception, of the intentionality which goes toward adequation. Positively, we will say that since the Other looks at me, I am responsible for him, without even having *taken* on responsibilities in his regard; his responsibility *is incumbent on me.* It is responsibility that goes beyond what I do. Usually, one is responsible for what one does oneself. I say, in *Otherwise than Being,* that responsibility is initially a *for the Other.* This means that I am responsible for his very responsibility.

P.N.: What in this responsibility for the Other defines the structure of subjectivity?

E.L.: Responsibility in fact is not a simple attribute of subjectivity, as if the latter already existed in itself, before the ethical relationship. Subjectivity is not for itself; it is, once again, initially for another. In the book, the proximity of the Other is presented as the fact that the Other is not simply close to me in space, or close like a parent, but he approaches me essentially insofar as I feel myself—insofar as I am—responsible for him. It is a structure that in nowise resembles the intentional relation which in knowledge attaches us to the object—to no matter what object, be it a human object. Proximity does not revert to this intentionality; in particular it, does not revert to the fact that the Other is known to me.

P.N.: I can know someone to perfection, but this knowledge will never by itself be a proximity?

E.L.: No. The tie with the Other is knotted only as responsibility, this moreover, whether accepted or refused, whether knowing or not knowing how to assume it, whether able or unable to do something concrete for the Other. To say: here I am [*me voici*].[1] To do something for the Other. To give. To be human spirit, that's it. The incarnation of human subjectivity guarantees its spirituality (I do not see what angels could give one another or how they could help one another). Dia-chrony before all dialogue: I analyze the inter-human relationship as if, in proximity with the Other—beyond the image I myself make of the other man—his face, the expressive in the Other (and the whole human body is in this sense more or less face), were what *ordains* me to serve him. I employ this extreme formulation. The face orders and ordains me. Its signification is an order signified. To be precise, if the face signifies an order in my regard, this is not in the manner in which an ordinary sign signifies its signified; this order is the very signifyingness of the face.

P.N.: You say at once "it orders me" and "it ordains me." Is this not a contradiction?

E.L.: It orders me as one orders someone one commands, as when one says: "Someone's asking for you."

P.N.: But is not the Other also responsible in my regard?

E.L.: Perhaps, but that is *his* affair. One of the fundamental themes of *Totality and Infinity* about which we have not yet spoken is that the intersubjective relation is a non-symmetrical relation. In this sense, I am responsible for the Other without waiting for reciprocity, were I to die for it. Reciprocity is *his* affair. It is precisely insofar as the relationship between the Other and me is not reciprocal that I am subjected to the Other; and I am "subject" essentially in this sense. It is I who support all. You know that sentence in

Dostoyevsky: *"We are all guilty of all and for all men before all, and I more than the others."*[2] This is not owing to such or such a guilt which is really mine, or to offenses that I would have committed; but because I am responsible for a total responsibility, which answers for all the others and for all in the others, even for their responsibility. The I always has one responsibility *more* than all the others.

P.N.: *That means that if the others do not do what they ought to do, it is owing to me?*

E.L.: I have previously said elsewhere—I do not like mentioning it for it should be completed by other considerations—that I am responsible for the persecutions that I undergo. But only me! My "close relations" or "my people" are already the others and, for them, I demand justice.

P.N.: *You go that far!*

E.L.: Since I am responsible even for the Other's responsibility. These are extreme formulas which must not be detached from their context. In the concrete, many other considerations intervene and require justice even for me. Practically, the laws set certain consequences out of the way. But justice only has meaning if it retains the spirit of dis-inter-estedness which animates the idea of responsibility for the other man. In principle, the I does not pull itself out of its "first person"; it supports the world. Constituting itself in the very movement wherein being responsible for the other devolves on it, subjectivity goes to the point of substitution for the Other. It assumes the condition—or the unconditon—of hostage. Subjectivity as such is initially hostage; it answers to the point of expiating for others.

One can appear scandalized by this utopian and, for an I, inhuman conception. But the humanity of the human—the true life—is absent. The humanity in historical and objective being, the very breakthrough of the subjective, of the human psychism in its original vigilance or sobering up, is being which undoes its condition of being: dis-inter-*estedness*. This is what is meant by the title of the book: *Otherwise than Being*. The ontological condition undoes itself, or is undone, in the human condition or unconditon. To be human means to live as if one were not a being among beings. As if, through human spirituality, the categories of being inverted into an "otherwise than being." Not only into a "being otherwise"; being otherwise is still being. The "otherwise than being," in truth, has no verb which would designate the event of its un-rest, its *dis-inter-estedness,* its putting-into-question of this being—or this *estedness*—of the being.

It is I who support the Other and am responsible for him. One thus sees that in the human subject, at the same time as a total subjection, my primogeniture manifests itself. My responsibility is untransferable, no one could replace me. In fact, it is a matter of saying the very identity of the human I starting from responsibility, that is, starting from this position or deposition of the sovereign I in self consciousness, a deposition which is precisely its responsibility for the Other. Responsibility is what is incumbent on me exclusively, and what, *humanly,* I cannot refuse. This charge is a supreme dignity of the unique. I am I in the sole measure that I am responsible, a non-interchangeable I. I can substitute my-self for everyone, but no one can substitute himself for me. Such is my inalienable identity of subject. It is in this precise sense that Dostoyevsky said: *"We are all responsible for all for all men before all, and I more than all the others."*

NOTES

1. Genesis 22, lines 1, 7, and 11, and Isaiah 6, line 8 (Hineni). See also Emmanuel Levinas, "God and Philosophy," *Philosophy Today* 22, no. 2 (1978): 127–145.—Trans.

2. Fyodor Dostoyevsky, *The Brothers Karamazov*, trans. Constance Garnett (New York: New American Library, 1957), 264.

From "Hospitality, Justice, and Responsibility: A Dialogue"

Jacques Derrida

Question: *Allow me to begin with a simple question: after deconstruction, what is to be done? How do we act? Let me try and formulate this more thoroughly.*

If there is nothing outside of the text—a much misunderstood phrase—how do we move from the text, understood in the broad sense, to action? If there is a deconstructive logic of undecidability, where an event or an action can be both/and, neither/nor, or in ethical terms both good and evil, neither good nor evil, how do we make a decision on the basis of undecidability? If we take key concepts like "law," "truth," and "lie," and submit them to the subtlety of 100 qualifications and close readings, how can we prevent conscience making cowards of us all?

In a nutshell, how do we discriminate between good and bad actions? How do we decide? How do we know what is the legitimate other that calls us to act and what is the fraud, the impostor?

Jacques Derrida: Your question started with the phrase "after deconstruction," and I must confess I do not understand what is meant by such a phrase. Deconstruction is not a philosophy or a method, it is not a phase, a period, or a moment. It is something which is constantly at work and was at work before what we call "deconstruction" started, so I cannot periodize. For me there is no "after" deconstruction—not that I think that deconstruction is immortal—but for what I understand under the name deconstruction, there is no end, no beginning, and no after.

The next step in your question is about deconstruction and ethics, and the relation between text and action. As you well know, what I call the "text" is not distinct from action or opposed to action. Of course, if you reduce a text to a book or to something that is written on pages, then perhaps there will be a problem with action. Although even a text in the form of a book, in the classical sense of something written on pages, is already something like an action. There is no action, even in the classical sense of the word, no political or ethical action which could be simply dissociated from, or opposed to, discourse. There is no politics without discourse, there is no politics without the book in our culture. So the general frame of the question needs a re-elaboration.

I would include what we call "action," or "praxis," or "politics," within the general space of what I call "the trace." Within this general space, we have to distinguish between a number of determinate agencies, such as, of course, the book, the text in the narrow sense, and action. Once this has been undertaken, the question of "undecidability" emerges. Many of those who have written about deconstruction understand undecidability as paralysis in face of the power to decide. That is not what I would understand by "undecidability." Far from opposing undecidability to decision, I would argue that there would be no decision, in the strong sense of the word, in ethics, in politics, no decision, and thus no responsibility, without the experience of some undecidability. If you don't experience some undecidability, then the decision would simply be the application of a program, the consequence of a premise or of a matrix. So a decision has to go through some impossibility in order for it to be a decision. If we knew what to do, if I knew in terms of knowledge what I have to do before the decision, then the decision would not be a decision. It would simply be the application of a rule, the consequence of a premise, and there would be no problem, there would be no decision. Ethics and politics, therefore, start with undecidability. I am in front of a problem and I know that the two determined solutions are as justifiable as one another. From that point, I have to take responsibility, which is heterogeneous to knowledge. If the decision is simply the final moment of a knowing process, it is not a decision. So the decision first of all has to go through a terrible process of undecidability, otherwise it would not be a decision, and it has to be heterogeneous to the space of knowledge. If there is a decision, it has to go through undecidability and make a leap beyond the field of theoretical knowledge. So when I say "I don't know what to do," this is not the negative condition of decision. It is, rather, the possibility of a decision.

Not knowing what to do does not mean that we have to rely on ignorance and to give up knowledge and consciousness. A decision, of course, must be prepared as far as possible by knowledge, by information, by infinite analysis. At some point, however, for a decision to be made, you have to go beyond knowledge, to do something that you don't know, something which does not belong to, or is beyond, the sphere of knowledge. That is why the distinction between good and evil doesn't depend on knowledge; that is why we should not know, in terms of knowledge, what is the distinction between good and evil. To have to make such a distinction, which depends precisely on responsibility, is, I confess, both a terrible and tragic situation in which to find oneself. Without this terrible experience, however, there would be no decision, there would simply be a serene application of a program of knowledge and then we could delegate decisions to scientists and theoreticians.

Q: *So is every decision one of fear and trembling, as in the case of Abraham?*

JD: Of course, if there is a decision. That is why Kierkegaard's *Fear and Trembling* is a major text, however we interpret it. It is the moment when the general categories have to be overcome, when I am alone facing a decision. A decision is something terrible.

Now I would not claim that I am sure that there is such a thing as decision. The sentence "I decide," or "I made a decision," or "I assume a responsibility," is a scandal; it's just good conscience. I am never sure that "I" made a decision in terms of a determinant judgment. It is not a theoretical judgment; I cannot be certain that "I" made a decision. Not only should I not be certain that I made a good decision, but I shouldn't even be certain that I made a decision. A decision *may* have happened. That is why, as I often say, and it sounds a little provocative, that "I" never decide, that "I" never make a decision in my own name, because as soon as I claim that "I" have made a decision, you can be sure that is wrong. For a decision to be a decision, it must be made by the other in myself, which doesn't exonerate me from responsibility. On the contrary, I am passive in a decision, because as soon as I am active, as soon as I know that "I" am the master of my decision, I am claiming that I know what to do and that everything depends on my knowledge which, in turn, cancels the decision.

At some point, and perhaps you were trying to provoke me, you said that if we practice close reading we will never act. On the contrary, I would assume that political, ethical, and juridical responsibility requires a task of infinite close reading. I believe this to be the condition of political responsibility: politicians should read. Now, to read does not mean to spend nights in the library. To read events, to analyze the situation, to criticize the media, to listen to the rhetoric of the demagogues, that's close reading, and it is required more today than ever. So I would urge politicians and citizens to practice close reading in this new sense, and not simply to stay in the library.

In the case of Hamlet, I try to show in *Specters of Marx* that the responsibility in front of the father's call, for it to be a responsibility, demands that choices be made; that is, you cannot remember everything for a fact; you have to filter the heritage and to scrutinize or make a close reading of the call. This means that to inherit, or to keep memory for a finite being implies some selection, some choice, some decision. So the son has to make a decision;

even if he wants to be true to the father or to remember the father, as a finite being he has to select within the heritage, and that is again the question of undecidability. Of course, that is the classical interpretation of Hamlet as a victim of undecidability: he doesn't know, and he gets paralyzed. Nevertheless, if we assume that Hamlet is a figure of paralysis or neurosis because of undecidability, he might be also a paradigm for action: he understands what action should be and he undergoes the process of undecidability at the beginning.

"How do we know?" was your last question and my answer is simply "we don't know!" Of course, we have to know as much as possible, but when we make a decision—if we make a decision—we don't know and we shouldn't know. If we knew, there would be no decision.

Q: *Your presentation of "Two Sources of Religion at the Limits of Mere Reason," in Capri in 1994, uncovers those sources, as far as I understood it, as "faith" and "the holy." In the Book of Job, Job undergoes the loss of this faith and of his experience of the holy as these are conventionally understood. It appears to me that he loses faith and the holy at the first level. Through that, it seems, Job achieves a new experience of the holy beyond all manipulability, as well as a faith in a relationship with an other, in this case a "You" to whom he now adheres for the sake of the "You" alone. I would like to ask whether you find in Job any echoes of your own articulation of the religious?*

JD: First of all, how could we find an echo in Job, but also how could we not find an echo? Let me improvise with reference to Levinas who mentions Job at some points.

While teaching Levinas on the theme of "hospitality" recently, I made reference to Job in the following situation. As you know, in *Totality and Infinity* Levinas describes the ethical relationship as religious; religion and ethics imply a face to face: you alone, face to face with the absolute other, the infinite other, and this face to face (*visage*) is the original ethics. This is described as a dual situation: you and I. Levinas, however, has to take into account "the third one": when the third appears, and when the demand of the third appears, then the call for justice appears also. But Levinas insists on the fact that the third one does not appear after the other two as someone else—one, two, and then three—but is already involved in the face to face relation as a call for justice. At this point we encounter a terrible situation: in order to be just, by taking into account the third one, I have to betray in some way my pure asymmetrical—but dual—relation with the other. This is followed by a complaint in Levinas, a complaint which sounds very much like Job's complaint: "What should I have to do with justice, because justice is unjust?" For Levinas, justice implies comparison, rationality; that is, because the third one is like the second other, I have to compare, I have to use concepts, I have to refer to resemblance, everything which implies ontology in the Greek sense and is divorced from ethics in the Levinasian sense. So I have to go back to philosophy, to Greek philosophy, in order to be just. There is a cry in many passages in Levinas: "What do I have to do with justice? Why justice?" There is some impatience with justice because justice is unjust. Nevertheless, we cannot, we should not, avoid justice.

So what does Job say? He feels that he is innocent and he protests against injustice. This is the terrible situation in which the unjust is not simply the contrary of justice, in which decision is not simply the contrary to undecidability. This looks terrible, and negative, and tragic, but it is also a chance, it is the condition of a decision. This terrible situation of two and three which I have just described is not simply a trap, it is a condition of justice. If there is a justice, it has to go through this terrible situation where there are two and three: I have a relation to the other in his/her singularity or uniqueness, and, at the same time, the third one is already in place. The second one is a third one. "You are a third one"—that is the condition of justice.

Q: Since Glas *you have been working on the notion of what you call "the gift," or that which escapes the circular motion of spirit or reason in the Hegelian sense. Recently, you have attempted to define more directly the nature of this quite central motif in works such as* Given Time *and* The Gift of Death, *while endeavoring to relate it to themes such as hospitality, community, and the political. There seems, in other words, to be a direct relationship between the notion of the gift and many of your current preoccupations. In brief, therefore, could you tell us how you actually go about applying the idea of the gift to the aforementioned notions which are becoming predominant in your work?*

JD: In fact, it is the same logic which is at work in both cases. How could we relate briefly the gift and hospitality? Of course, it is obvious that hospitality is supposed to consist in giving something, offering something. In the conventional scene of hospitality, the guest gives something in gratitude. So there is this scene of gratitude among hosts and guests. In the same way that I have tried to show that the gift supposes a break with reciprocity, exchange, economy, and circular movement, I have also tried to demonstrate that hospitality implies such a break; that is, if I inscribe the gesture of hospitality within a circle in which the guest should give back to the host, then it is not hospitality but conditional hospitality. That is the way hospitality is usually understood in many cultures, such as the Greek and Islamic cultures. The host remains the master in the house, the country, the nation. He controls the threshold, he controls the borders, and, when he welcomes the guest, he wants to keep the mastery. "I am the master of the house, the city, the nation"—that is what is implied in this form of conditional hospitality. This conditionality, which is also the conditionality of the gift as exchange, finds a number of examples in the history of our cultures. The one which interests me most, however, is Kant's example in "Perpetual Peace,"[1] in which he advocates universal hospitality as the condition of perpetual peace. To summarize very briefly, he says that peace must be perpetual; if you make peace only provisionally in order to resume the war, this would not be peace but armistice or cease-fire. For a peace really to be a peace, a promise of eternal peace must be at work.

Such a concept of peace implies, therefore, universal hospitality; that is, all the nation-states should guarantee hospitality to the foreigner who comes, but only under certain conditions: first, being a citizen of another nation-state or country, he must behave peaceably in our country; second, he is not granted the right to stay, but only the right to visit. Kant has a number of sharp distinctions about this. I would call this "conditional hospitality," and I would oppose it to what I call "unconditional" or "pure" hospitality, which is without conditions and which does not seek to identify the newcomer, even if he is not a citizen.

Today this is a burning issue: we know that there are numerous what we call "displaced persons" who are applying for the right of asylum without being citizens, without being identified as citizens. It is not for speculative or ethical reasons that I am interested in unconditional hospitality, but in order to understand and to transform what is going on today in our world.

So unconditional hospitality implies that you don't ask the other, the newcomer, the guest, to give anything back, or even to identify himself or herself. Even if the other deprives you of your mastery or your home, you have to accept this. It is terrible to accept this, but that is the condition of unconditional hospitality: that you give up the mastery of your space, your home, your nation. It is unbearable. If, however, there is pure hospitality, it should be pushed to this extreme.

I try to dissociate the concept of this pure hospitality from the concept of "invitation." If you are the guest and I invite you, if I am expecting you and prepared to meet you, then this implies that there is no surprise, everything is in order. For pure hospitality or a pure gift to occur, however, there must be an absolute surprise. The other, like the Messiah, must arrive whenever he or she wants. She may even not arrive. I would oppose, therefore, the traditional and religious concept of "visitation" to "invitation": visitation implies the arrival of someone who is not expected, who can show up at any time. If I am unconditionally hospitable I should welcome the visitation, not the invited guest, but the visitor. I must be unprepared, or prepared to be unprepared, for the unexpected arrival of *any* other. Is this possible? I don't know. If, however, there is pure hospitality, or a pure gift, it should consist in this opening without horizon, without horizon of expectation, an opening to the newcomer, whoever that may be. It may be terrible because the newcomer may be a good person, or may be the devil; but if you exclude the possibility that the newcomer is coming to destroy your house—if you want to control this and exclude in advance this possibility—there is no hospitality. In this case, you control the borders, you have customs officers, and you have a door, a gate, a key, and so on. For unconditional hospitality to take place you, have to accept the risk of the other coming and destroying the place, initiating a revolution, stealing everything, or killing everyone. That is the risk of pure hospitality and pure gift, because a pure gift might be terrible too. That is why exchange and controls and conditions try to make a distinction between good and evil. Why did Kant insist on conditional hospitality? Because he knew that, without these conditions, hospitality could turn into wild war, terrible aggression. Those are the risks involved in pure hospitality, if there is such a thing, and I am not sure that there is.

[...]

Q: *How do you envisage the connection between "justice," on the one hand, and what you define as "the moment of strategy, of rhetoric, of ethics, and of politics" (Limited Inc....) which seems to give rise to a process in your work, one which takes the form of the injunction "one must" assume responsibility?*

JD: Let me, very awkwardly, try to approach these difficulties. In your question you located the "we must" on the side of strategy, politics, ethics. Yes, and no: the "we must" has no process; it is foreign to the process. When I feel that "I must," on the one hand, of course, I enter a process, but in the name of something which doesn't tolerate the process. It's immediate. For instance, I must answer the call of the other: it's something which has to be absolute, unconditional, and immediate; that is, foreign to any process.

Now, of course, if I want to be responsible to the "I must," to the immediate imperative, the unconditional "I must," then in the name of this just response I have to engage myself in a process; that is, to take into account conditions, strategy, rhetoric, and so on. That is a great dilemma. I have no solution to that. If I told you that I have a solution, I would be lying. I think there is no solution, no rules or norms for that.

The response, not the solution, should be invented each time, at each moment in the singular situations. This, of course, doesn't exclude the process, but at some point when I respond, if I want to respond in the name of justice, I have to invent singularly, to sign, so to speak, the response.

Now, you know that I began using the name or the word "justice" very late in my process, and I try to distinguish between "justice" and "right" (*le droit*); that is, I try to make a sharp distinction between "justice" and "the law" or the "right." On the side of the right you would put what you called, a little hastily, politics, ethics, rhetoric (ethics and politics, for me, are also on the other side). Now, when I made this distinction I knew we should not oppose justice to the law, to the history of right. Of course, the history of right can be deconstructed, can be transformed. There is the history of the law, of legal concepts, and because of that the legality can be transformed, deconstructed, criticized, improved. This is an infinite process within the legal space. But this process unfolds itself *in the name of justice:* justice requires the law. You can't simply call for justice without trying to embody justice in the law. So justice is not simply outside the law; it is something which transcends the law, but which, at the same time, requires the law; that is, deconstruction, transformations, revolutions, reformations, improvement, perfectibility—all that is a process. So even if justice is foreign to the process, it nevertheless requires the process, it requires political action, rhetoric, strategies, etc. What is foreign to strategy requires strategy. That is the double-bind which causes the difficulty.

So, to repeat, when we talk of this "we must," of this responsibility, the "we must" is always foreign to the process. However, in the name of this "we must" we have to enter the process, and to analyze and to transform infinitely. This is a strange logic indeed. But I would not simply oppose, on the one side, the field of politics, ethics, and rhetoric, and, on the other side, justice. We have to pay attention to their heterogeneity, I would insist on that. They are heterogeneous and, because of this, one calls for the other: they are indissociable. If I wanted to formalize, in a very abstract, empty, or formal way, this situation, I would say that there is at the same time heterogeneity, radical heterogeneity, between two terms; but, at the same time, the two terms are indissociable. Decision, an ethical or a political responsibility, is absolutely heterogeneous to knowledge. Nevertheless, we have to know as much as possible in order to ground our decision. But, even if it is grounded in knowledge, the moment I take a decision, it is a leap; I enter a heterogeneous space, and that is the condition of responsibility.

This is not only a problem, but the *aporia* we have to face constantly. For me, however, the *aporia* is not simply paralysis, but the *aporia* or the *non-way* is the condition of walking: if there was no *aporia*, we wouldn't walk, we wouldn't find our way; path-breaking implies *aporia*. This impossibility to find one's way is the condition of ethics.

[...]

Q: Deconstruction is concerned with a critique of centers of control, as was the work of Michel Foucault. As a method, what can deconstruction offer to advance our ethical understanding of power beyond the analysis already proposed by Foucault?

JD: I don't know. But I don't think deconstruction "offers" anything *as* deconstruction. That is sometimes what I am charged with: saying nothing, not offering any content or any full proposition. I have never "proposed" anything, and that is perhaps the essential poverty of my work. I never offered anything in terms of "this is what you have to know" or "this is what you have to do." So deconstruction is a poor thing from that point of view.

Now, perhaps using the strategy of deconstruction, you may for yourself understand, not what power is, but what powers may be in such and such a context. Of course, if I wanted to justify at any cost what I am doing, I would say that everything that I do is concerned with the question of power everywhere. The question of power is so pervasive, however, that I could not isolate the place where I deal with *just* the question of power.

What interests me in what Foucault says about power is not the claim that everything is power, or will to power, in society, but his proposition or assumption that there is no such thing as "*the* Power," and that today power is in fact dispersed and not concentrated in the form of the state. There are rather only micro-powers. This is a more useful approach that is not to rely on a homogeneous and centralized concept of power. From that point of view, I think this is the condition of a new politics, a new approach to politics. I think this is very necessary and useful.

Nevertheless, my concern will be this one: of course we have to pay attention to micro-powers, to invisible or new forms of power, larger or smaller than the state, or foreign to the logic of the state. We should not, however, forget the state: the state is still very strong, the logic of the state is still very strong. It is today undergoing an unprecedented process. What one calls "globalization," or *mondialization*—the constitution of new powers in the form of capitalistic corporations, which are stronger than states and do not depend on states—relativizes the authority of states. Nevertheless, the international law, everything which rules the market today, is in the hands of so-called sovereign states; the international law, the United Nations, GATT, and so on are today dependent on states. So the question of the state is not behind us. We have to pay attention to the two logics: on the one hand, the deconstruction of the state, and, on the other hand, the survival of the state.

I want to say that the state has both good aspects and bad aspects, and I mention, among its bad aspects, repression and authority. However, if we want to resist *some* forces in the world, economic forces, for example, perhaps the good old state might be useful! So I am not for or against the state. It depends on the situation: in some contexts, I am for the state, and in other contexts I am against the state, and I want to retain the right to decide depending on the context.

[...]

Q: May I start by saying that I have great difficulty with your philosophical position: I am alarmed, and yet pleased, that you now think it possible to talk about ethical issues and, in particular, truth—a truth which seems to be objective, or which can be objectively verified with reference to facts. Ethics seems to me to be a form of metalanguage which calls not for deconstruction but reconstruction. This is so because ethics talks about moral experience, which I think is concerned with codes of behavior. Can you confirm for me that, with your recent work, you have begun this process of reconstruction? If so, is it correct to assume that we can juxtapose an "early Derrida" to a "late Derrida," the latter having abandoned deconstruction?

Lastly, I am not convinced of the merits of your privileging absence over presence, of difference over unity, as you attempt—if this is what you are doing—to overcome Hegel. In particular, I am not satisfied with your assertion that discourse, knowledge, and, therefore, moral practice, is a process of endless dif-férance: what has been called "hallucinatory thinking." Perhaps you can help me with this?

JD: You said at the beginning that you have some difficulty reading me—this I can confirm! First of all, deconstruction is not opposed to reconstruction. Furthermore, I have always insisted that deconstruction is not destruction, is not annihilation, is not negative. As soon as you realize that deconstruction is not something negative, you cannot simply oppose it to reconstruction. How could you reconstruct anything without deconstruction?

What I say about truth would require many precautions and implies a long itinerary. Nevertheless, I never confuse truth with fact—truth is not a fact. Truth has nothing to do with a fact. Truth is the quality of a statement, a judgment, or an intuition related to something which you might call a fact, but truth is not reality. The distinction between truth and reality is absolutely elementary, as is the distinction between truth and veracity; that is, to say something true does not mean that you say something real. You may say something true without being sincere, you may lie by telling the truth. So there is a distinction between veracity, truth, and fact which must be taken seriously.

Turning to the subject of "endless difference": it is commonplace today to understand *différance* with an "a" as simply postponement which neutralizes decision. This is something which—had some attention been paid to the text in the beginning—could have been overcome. If *différance* was simply infinite postponement, it would be nothing. If I played on the "a" of *différance,* it is in order to keep in a single word two logics: one of the delay, the detour, which implies a process, a strategy, or a postponement; and difference with an "e," which implies heterogeneity, alterity, and so on. Now, because there is alterity and the other, for example, this cannot wait. There is an unconditional commandment, so to speak, not to wait, and it is because there is this possibility of postponing that we can, and we must, make decisions. If there was no possibility of delay, there would be no urgency either. *Différance,* therefore, is not opposed to ethics and politics, but is their condition: on the one hand, it is the condition of history, of process, strategy, delay, postpone-ment, mediation, and, on the other hand, because there is an absolute dif-ference or an irreducible heterogeneity, there is the urge to act and respond immediately and to face political and ethical responsibilities.

So this is far from being hallucinatory thinking, although I am very interested in hallucinations and I think this is a serious problem. If I am interested in spectrality, and if I think the concept of spectrality difficult to overcome, it is because I think some hallucination is irreducible, even here now. But is there a better way of overcoming hallucination than to pay atten-tion to the other? For me, the other is "the real thing," and reference to the other is what breaks with hallucination, if such a break is possible. In order to respect the transcendence or the heterogeneity of the other, we have to pay attention. Sometimes, however, attention is not sufficient to surmount hallucination. But, in order to overcome hallucination, we have to pay atten-tion to the other—that is, to listen to the other and to closely read the other. Reading, in the broad sense which I attribute to this word, is an ethical and political responsibility. In attempting to overcome hallucinations, we must decipher and interpret the other by reading. We cannot be sure that we are not hallucinating by saying simply "I see" ("I see" is, after all, just what the hallucinating person says). No, in order to check that you are not hallucinat-ing, you have to read in a certain way. I have no rule for that. Who can decide what counts as the end of hallucination? It is difficult, and I have difficulties with my own work also.

Q: Several commentators have criticized you for becoming ultimately a rela-tivist, primarily a cognitive relativist, but, as a consequence, also an ethical rel-ativist in your emphasis on the question of undecidability—or what I would call indeterminacy of meaning. One such commentator is Putnam, who says strangely enough that both Quine and Derrida arrive at the same point, namely indeterminacy of meaning. Quine has a way of avoiding relativism because he can appeal to the crude behaviorist notion that he has, but Derrida has no resource for getting out of the relativist dilemma. Do you think, first, that this is a misunderstanding of your work? And, second, what is your position on rel-ativism?

JD: If I wanted to be brutal, I would say yes, this is a radical misunder-standing. I am shocked by the debate around this question of relativism. What is relativism? Are you a relativist simply because you say, for instance, that the other is the other, and that every other is other than the other? If I want to pay attention to the singularity of the other, the singularity of the sit-uation, the singularity of language, is that relativism? If I say that there is the English and the French language, and I have to pay attention to these differ-ences, is the attention paid to these differences relativism? No, relativism is a doctrine which has its own history in which there are only points of view with no absolute necessity, or no references to absolutes. That is the opposite to what I have to say. Relativism is, in classical philosophy, a way of referring to the absolute and denying it; it states that there are only cultures and that there is no pure science or truth. I have never said such a thing. Neither have I ever used the word relativism.

To take the case of Sokal: here is a man who wants to charge a number of mostly French people, including me, with being relativists, with threatening science, with threatening everything which shouldn't be threatened. How does he handle this regarding myself? He took a sentence which I improvised at a conference thirty years ago, the only time I referred to science in the strict sense. I was responding to a question from Hyppolite in 1966, in which he asked what was the relation between what I said in my paper "Structure, Sign and Play" and the constant in Einsteinian relativity. In my answer, referring to what I had said, I quoted Hyppolite's reference to the constant, and this man now charges me with being a relativist and contesting science. This is totally arbitrary. This is relativism: someone, who, because he is a scientist, presumes to say anything. I take into account differences, but I am no relativist.

If I say that there are two zero points here and there, that you cannot reduce the difference, and if this is interpreted as being relativism, then I am a relativist, and who is not? This, of course, does not mean that I deny scientificity: indeed, I ask, in [the Introduction to Edmund Husserl's] *The Origin of Geometry,* how is it possible that from perception we constitute ideal objects and a community of truth? So this charge against me amounts to obscurantism, and is issued by people who don't read. My concern would be this: what is their interest and motivation? What do they want?

In the same way, I never said that there is indeterminacy of meaning. I think there are interpretations which determine the meaning, and there are some undecidabilities, but undecidability is not indeterminacy. Undecidability is the competition between two determined possibilities or options, two determined duties. There is no indeterminacy at all; a word in a text is always determined. When I say that there is nothing outside the text, I mean there is nothing outside the context; everything is determined. Now, because there are contexts and singularities, there are movements, processes, and transformations, and, for transformations to occur, something has to be determined, something is determinable. Determinability is not indeterminacy; to take into account determinability, you must assume that what is determinable is still undetermined regarding the coming determination, but it is not undetermined. Let me take an example: if I say I have to make a decision and I shall tell you what that decision is tomorrow, this is determinable. Of course, what I shall do tomorrow is undetermined, but this indeterminacy is not an empty something. Everything is totally determined. There is, however, the future, what is to come, and I would say there is indeterminacy of the coming of the future. But that is not relativity of meaning.

Usually they charge me with saying that the text means anything, a charge made even in academic circles, not only in the media. If I were saying such a stupid thing, why would that be of any interest? Who would be interested in that, starting with me? There must be something else. Why are they anxious about their own interpretation of what I say? They are anxious that a text *may* call for interpretation, that there may be some complication in a text. I would say that a text is complicated, there are many meanings struggling with one another, there are tensions, there are overdeterminations, there are equivocations; but this doesn't mean that there is indeterminacy. On the contrary, there is too much determinacy. That is the problem. So these charges really have to be interpreted.

[...]

Q: *Professor Derrida, I am interested in the continuity of your thinking because I do not think that there is anything like the* Kehre *or Heideggerian turning in your thought. I would like you to comment, therefore, on your relationship to a certain aspect of Husserl whom you discuss in your early work, namely the* epoché. *Husserl recommends in his radical revision of philosophical practice that we should involve ourselves in* epoché, *which for him means to suspend what he terms the "natural attitude" through a process of bracketing or parenthesizing—terms, I believe, which are rather similar to some of the deconstructive strategies which you employ. In particular, Husserl talks of "undecidability," meaning that the very notion of putting things in brackets can make some things undecidable. I was wondering if the notion of undecidability in your work has its source in Husserl, and whether you see deconstruction as essentially a radicalization of Husserl's* epoché.

JD: First of all, I am grateful that you don't want to cut me in two; I do wish to be cut, but in more than two places! It is true that, for me, Husserl's work, and precisely the notion of *epoché*, has been and still is a major indispensable gesture. In everything I try to say and write, *epoché* is implied. I would say that I am constantly trying to practice this whenever I am thinking and writing. I think it is the condition for thinking and speaking. This does not mean that I think the *epoché* is the last word. I do have questions about it, but I think that the suspension of the thesis, of the judgment, and the attention paid to phenomenality is the elementary and indispensable condition of every step that I take. So it is correct to say that I am true to Husserl from this point of view.

The word, if not the concept, "undecidability" comes not from Husserl but from Gödel, whose notion of "indecidables" I came across when writing the Introduction to *The Origin of Geometry*. Now, of course, what I mean by "undecidability" does not correspond to Gödel's "indecidables," but the word comes from here, and I try to displace the word in other fields. Even at the time when I wrote this first text on Husserl, there was, on the one hand, a certain passage referring to Gödel's discourse on undecidability, but throughout the Introduction, the logic of undecidability was at work without the name or the noun. It was only when I began to take some distance from Husserl that I developed the logic of undecidability, which is not compatible, I would argue, with the strictest practice of phenomenology. On the one hand, I drew undecidability from some interest in Husserl, but, on the other hand, I was interested in undecidability to the extent that I was taking a distance from Husserl. When, in reply to a previous question, I said that it was thanks to Husserl that we can formulate the alterity of the alter-ego, I was implying that he sought to interrupt the principle of principles (the *ego cogito*). This is the moment of undecidability in Husserl.

Levinas says at some point that, when phenomenology addresses the question of the other, it interrupts itself. What does that mean? Is it possible to interrupt yourself? That is what undecidability means, and that is what my relation to Husserl is founded on—self-interruption. Levinas meant by this that it is in order to describe the things in themselves that we have to abandon the principle of intuition; it is because the other is *the* other that I must describe my relation to him/her ethically and not in a purely phenomenological fashion. But I do this in the name of phenomenology: in order to be a phenomenologist to the end, I have to interrupt phenomenology. That is what is meant by self-interruption, which is another name for *différance*. Just as there would be no responsibility or decision without some self-interruption, neither would there be any hospitality; as master and host, the self, in welcoming the other, must interrupt or divide himself or herself. This division is the condition of hospitality.

[...]

Q: Is there a logic of ethical testimony at work in deconstruction?

JD: Yes, it is absolutely central to it. Testimony, which implies faith or promise, governs the entire social space. I would say that theoretical knowledge is circumscribed within this testimonial space. It is only by reference to the possibility of testimony that deconstruction can begin to ask questions concerning knowledge and meaning.

Q: Do you have an absolute definition of the "human being?"

JD: There can be no acontextual definition of a human being.

NOTE

1. Immanuel Kant, "To Perpetual Peace: A Philosophical Sketch," in *Perpetual Peace and Other Essays on Politics, History, and Morals*, trans. Ted Hu (Hackett, 1983).

Precarious Life

Judith Butler

… the surplus of every sociality over every solitude.
—Levinas

At a recent meeting, I listened to a university press director tell a story. It was unclear whether he identified with the point of view from which the story was told, or whether he was relaying the bad news reluctantly. But the story he told was about another meeting, where he was listening, and there a president of a university made the point that no one is reading humanities books anymore, that the humanities have nothing more to offer or, rather, nothing to offer for our times. I'm not sure whether he was saying that the university president was saying that the humanities had lost their moral authority, but it sounded like this was, in fact, someone's view, and that it was a view to take seriously. There was an ensuing set of discussions at the same meeting in which it was not always possible to tell which view was owned by whom, or whether anyone really was willing to own a view. It was a discussion that turned on the question, Have the humanities undermined themselves, with all their relativism and questioning and "critique," or have the humanities been undermined by all those who *oppose* all that relativism and questioning and "critique"? Someone has undermined the humanities, or some group of people has, but it was unclear who, and it was unclear who thought this was true. I started to wonder whether I was not in the middle of the humanities quandary itself, the one in which no one knows who is speaking and in what voice, and with what intent. Does anyone stand by the words they utter? Can we still trace those words to a speaker or, indeed, a writer? And which message, exactly, was being sent?

Of course, it would be paradoxical if I were now to argue that what we really need is to tether discourse to authors, and in that way we will reestablish both authors and authority. I did my own bit of work, along with many of you, in trying to cut that tether. But what I do think is missing, and what I would like to see and hear return is a consideration of the structure of address itself. Because although I did not know in whose voice this person was speaking, whether the voice was his own or not, I did feel that I was being addressed, and that something called the humanities was being derided from some direction or another. To respond to this address seems an important obligation during these times. This obligation is something other than the rehabilitation of the author-subject *per se*. It is about a mode of response that follows upon having been addressed, a comportment toward the Other only after the Other has made a demand upon me, accused me of a failing, or asked me to assume a responsibility. This is an exchange that cannot be assimilated into the schema in which the subject is over here as a topic to be reflexively interrogated, and the Other is over there, as a theme to be purveyed. The structure of address is important for understanding how moral authority is introduced and sustained if we accept not just that we address others when we speak, but that in some way we come to exist, as it were, in the moment of being addressed, and something about our existence proves precarious when that address fails. More emphatically, however, what binds us morally has to do with how we are addressed by others in ways that we cannot avert or avoid; this impingement by the other's address constitutes us first and foremost against our will or, perhaps put more appropriately, prior to the formation of our will. So if we think that moral authority is about finding one's will and standing by it, stamping one's name upon one's will, it may be that we miss the very mode by which moral demands are relayed. That is, we miss the situation of being addressed, the demand that comes from elsewhere, sometimes a nameless elsewhere, by which our obligations are articulated and pressed upon us.

Indeed, this conception of what is morally binding is not one that I give myself; it does not proceed from my autonomy or my reflexivity. It comes to me from elsewhere, unbidden, unexpected, and unplanned. In fact, it tends to ruin my plans, and if my plans are ruined, that may well be the sign that something is morally binding upon me. We think of presidents as wielding speech acts in willful ways, so when the director of a university press, or the president of a university speaks, we expect to know what they are saying, and to whom they are speaking, and with what intent. We expect the address to be authoritative and, in that sense, to be binding. But presidential speech is strange these days, and it would take a better rhetorician than I am to understand the mysteriousness of its ways. Why should it be, for instance, that Iraq is called a threat to the security of the "civilized world" while missiles flying from North Korea, and even the attempted hostage-taking of U.S. boats, are called "regional issues"? And if the U.S. President was urged by the majority of the world to withdraw his threat of war, why does he not seem to feel obligated by this address? But given the shambles into which presidential address has fallen, perhaps we should think more seriously about the relation between modes of address and moral authority. This may help us to know what values the humanities have to offer, and what the situation of discourse is in which moral authority becomes binding.

I would like to consider the "face," the notion introduced by Emmanuel Levinas, to explain how it is that others make moral claims upon us, address moral demands to us, ones that we do not ask for, ones that we are not free to refuse. Levinas makes a preliminary demand upon me, but his is not the only demand that I am bound to follow these days. I will trace what seem to me the outlines of a possible Jewish ethic of non-violence. Then I will relate this to some of the more pressing questions of violence and ethics that are upon us now. The Levinasian notion of the "face" has caused critical consternation for a long time. It seems to be that the "face" of what he calls the "Other" makes an ethical demand upon me, and yet we do not know which demand it makes. The "face" of the other cannot be read for a secret meaning, and the imperative it delivers is not immediately translatable into a prescription that might be linguistically formulated and followed.

Levinas writes:

> The approach to the face is the most basic mode of responsibility.... The face is not in front of me (*en face de moi*), but above me; it is the other before death, looking through and exposing death. Secondly, the face is the other who asks me not to let him die alone, as if to do so were to become an accomplice in his death. Thus the face says to me: you shall not kill. In the relation to the face I am exposed as a usurper of the place of the other. The celebrated "right to existence" that Spinoza called the *conatus essendi* and defined as the basic principle of all intelligibility is challenged by the relation to the face. Accordingly, my duty to respond to the other suspends my natural right to self-survival, *le droit vitale*. My ethical relation of love for the other stems from the fact that the self cannot survive by itself alone, cannot find meaning within its own being-in-the-world.... To expose myself to the vulnerability of the face is to put my ontological right to existence into question. In ethics, the other's right to exist has primacy over my own, a primacy epitomized in the ethical edict: you shall not kill, you shall not jeopardize the life of the other.[1]

Levinas writes further:

> The face is what one cannot kill, or at least it is that whose meaning consists in saying, "thou shalt not kill." Murder, it is true, is a banal fact: one can kill the Other; the ethical exigency is not an ontological necessity.... It also appears in the Scriptures, to which the humanity of man is exposed inasmuch as it is engaged in the world. But to speak truly, the appearance in being of these "ethical peculiarities"—the humanity of man—is a rupture of being. It is significant, even if being resumes and recovers itself.[2]

So the face, strictly speaking, does not speak, but what the face means is nevertheless conveyed by the commandment, "Thou shalt not kill." It conveys this commandment without precisely speaking it. It would seem that we can use this biblical command to understand something of the face's meaning, but something is missing here, since the "face" does not speak in the sense that the mouth does; the face is neither reducible to the mouth nor, indeed, to anything the mouth has to utter. Someone or something else speaks when the face is likened to a certain kind of speech; it is a speech that does not come from a mouth or, if it does, has no ultimate origin or meaning there. In fact, in an essay entitled "Peace and Proximity," Levinas makes plain that "the face is not exclusively a human face."[3] To explain this, he refers to Vassili Grossman's text *Life and Fate,* which he describes as:

> the story … of the families, wives, and parents of political detainees traveling to the Lubyanka in Moscow for the latest news. A line is formed at the counter, a line where one can see only the backs of others. A woman awaits her turn: [she] had never thought that the human back could be so expressive, and could convey states of mind in such a penetrating way. Persons approaching the counter had a particular way of craning their neck and their back, their raised shoulders with shoulder blades like springs, which seemed to cry, sob, and scream.[4]

Here the term "face" operates as a catachresis: "face" describes the human back, the craning of the neck, the raising of the shoulder blades like "springs." And these bodily parts, in turn, are said to cry and to sob and to scream, as if they were a face or, rather, a face with a mouth, a throat, or indeed, just a mouth and throat from which vocalizations emerge that do not settle into words. The face is to be found in the back and the neck, but it is not quite a face. The sounds that come from or through the face are agonized, suffering. So we can see already that the "face" seems to consist in a series of displacements such that a face is figured as a back which, in turn, is figured as a scene of agonized vocalization. And though there are many names strung in a row here, they end with a figure for what cannot be named, an utterance that is not, strictly speaking, linguistic. Thus the face, the name for the face, and the words by which we are to understand its meaning—"Thou shalt not kill"— do not quite deliver the meaning of the face, since at the end of the line, it seems, it is precisely the wordless vocalization of suffering that marks the limits of linguistic translation here. The face, if we are to put words to its meaning, will be that for which no words really work; the face seems to be a kind of sound, the sound of language evacuating its sense, the sonorous substratum of vocalization that precedes and limits the delivery of any semantic sense.

At the end of this description, Levinas appends the following lines, which do not quite accomplish the sentence form: "The face as the extreme precariousness of the other. Peace as awakeness to the precariousness of the other."[5] Both statements are similes, and they both avoid the verb, especially the copula. They do not say that the face *is* that precariousness, or that peace *is* the mode of being awake to an Other's precariousness. Both phrases are substitutions that refuse any commitment to the order of being. Levinas tells us, in fact, that "humanity is a rupture of being" and in the previous remarks he performs that suspension and rupture in an utterance that is both less and more than a sentence form. To respond to the face, to understand its meaning, means to be awake to what is precarious in another life or, rather, the precariousness of life itself. This cannot be an awakeness, to use his word, to my own life, and then an extrapolation from an understanding of my own precariousness to an understanding of another's precarious life. It has to be an understanding of the precariousness of the Other. This is what makes the face belong to the sphere of ethics. Levinas writes, "the face of the other in its precariousness and defenselessness, is for me at once the temptation to kill and the call to peace, the 'You shall not kill.'"[6] This last remark suggests something quite disarming in several senses. Why would it be that the very precariousness of the Other would produce for me a temptation to kill? Or why would it produce the temptation to kill *at the same time* that it delivers a demand for peace? Is there something about my apprehension of the Other's precariousness that makes me want to kill the Other? Is it the simple vulnerability of the Other that becomes a murderous temptation for me? If the Other, the Other's face, which after all carries the meaning of this precariousness, at once tempts me with murder and prohibits me from acting upon it, then the face operates to produce a struggle for me, and establishes this struggle at the heart of ethics. It would seem that it is God's voice that is represented by the human voice, since it is God who says, through Moses, "Thou shalt not kill." The face that at once makes me murderous and prohibits me from murder is the one that speaks in a voice that is not its own, speaks in a voice that is no human voice.[7] So the face makes various utterances at once: it bespeaks an agony, an injurability, at the same time that it bespeaks a divine prohibition against killing.[8]

Earlier in "Peace and Proximity," Levinas considers the vocation of Europe, and wonders whether the "Thou shalt not kill" is not precisely what one should hear in the very meaning of European culture. It is unclear where his Europe begins or ends, whether it has geographical boundaries, or whether it is produced every time the commandment is spoken or conveyed. This is, already, a curious Europe whose meaning is conjectured to consist in the words of the Hebrew God, whose civilizational status, as it were, depends upon the transmission of divine interdictions from the Bible. It is Europe in which Hebraism has taken the place of Hellenism, and Islam remains unspeakable. Perhaps Levinas is telling us that the only Europe that ought to be called Europe is the one that elevates the Old Testament over civil and secular law. In any case, he seems to be returning to the primacy of interdiction to the meaning of civilization itself. And though we might be tempted to understand this as a nefarious Eurocentrism, it is probably also important to see that there is no recognizable Europe that can be derived from his view. In fact, it is not the existence of the interdiction against murder that makes Europe Europe, but the anxiety and the desire that the interdiction produces. As he continues to explain how this commandment works, he refers to Genesis, chapter 32, in which Jacob learns of his brother and rival Esau's imminent approach. Levinas writes, "Jacob is troubled by the news that his brother Esau—friend or foe—is marching to meet him 'at the head of four hundred men.' Verse 8 tells us: 'Jacob was greatly afraid and anxious.'" Levinas then turns to the commentator Rashi to understand "the difference between fright and anxiety," and concludes that "[Jacob] was frightened of his own death but was anxious he might have to kill."[9]

Of course, it is unclear still why Levinas would assume that one of the first or primary responses to another's precariousness is the desire to kill. Why would it be that the spring of the shoulder blades, the craning of the neck, the agonized vocalization conveying another's suffering would prompt in anyone a lust for violence? It must be that Esau over there, with his four hundred men, threatens to kill me, or looks like he will, and that in relation to that menacing Other or, indeed, the one whose face represents a menace, I must defend myself to preserve my life. Levinas explains, though, that murdering in the name of self-preservation is not justified, that self-preservation is never a sufficient condition for the ethical justification of violence. This seems, then, like an extreme pacifism, an absolute pacifism, and it may well be. We may or may not want to accept these consequences, but we should consider the dilemma they pose as constitutive of the ethical anxiety: "Frightened for his own life, but anxious he might have to kill." There is fear for one's own survival, and there is anxiety about hurting the Other, and these two impulses are at war with each other, like siblings fighting. But they are at war with each other in order *not* to be at war, and this seems to be the point. For the nonviolence that Levinas seems to promote does not come from a peaceful place, but rather from a constant tension between the fear of undergoing violence and the fear of inflicting violence. I could put an end to my fear of my own death by obliterating the other, although I would have to keep obliterating, especially if there are four hundred men behind him, and they all have families and friends, if not a nation or two behind them. I could put an end to my anxiety about becoming a murderer by reconciling myself to the ethical justification for inflicting violence and death under such conditions. I could bring out the utilitarian calculus, or appeal to the intrinsic rights of individuals to protect and preserve their own rights. We can imagine uses of both consequentialist and deontological justifications that would give me many opportunities to inflict violence righteously. A consequentialist might argue that it would be for the good of the many. A deontologist might appeal to the intrinsic worth of my own life. They could also be used to dispute the primacy of the interdiction on murder, an interdiction in the face of which I would continue to feel my anxiety.

Although Levinas counsels that self-preservation is not a good enough reason to kill, he also presumes that the desire to kill is primary to human beings. If the first impulse towards the other's vulnerability is the desire to kill, the ethical injunction is precisely to militate against that first impulse. In psychoanalytic terms, that would mean marshaling the desire to kill in the service of an internal desire to kill one's own aggression and sense of priority. The result would probably be neurotic, but it may be that psychoanalysis meets a limit here. For Levinas, it is the ethical itself that gets one out of the circuitry of bad conscience, the logic by which the prohibition against aggression becomes the internal conduit for aggression itself. Aggression is then turned back upon oneself in the form of super-egoic cruelty. If the ethical moves us beyond bad conscience, it is because bad conscience is, after all, only a negative version of narcissism, and so still a form of narcissism. The face of the Other comes to me from outside, and interrupts that narcissistic circuit. The face of the Other calls me out of narcissism towards something finally more important.

Levinas writes:

> The Other is the sole being I can wish to kill. I can wish. And yet this power is quite the contrary of power. The triumph of this power is its defeat as power. At the very moment when my power to kill realizes itself, the other has escaped me…. I have not looked at him in the face, I have not encountered his face. The temptation of total negation … this is the presence of the face. To be in relation with the other face to face is to be unable to kill. It is also the situation of discourse.[10]

It is also the situation of discourse…

… this last is no idle claim. Levinas explains in one interview that "face and discourse are tied. It speaks, it is in this that it renders possible and begins all discourse."[11] Since what the face "says" is "Thou shalt not kill," it would appear that it is through this primary commandment that speaking first comes into being, so that speaking first comes into being against the backdrop of this possible murder. More generally, discourse makes an ethical claim upon us precisely because, prior to speaking, something is spoken to us. In a simple sense, and perhaps not quite as Levinas intended, we are first spoken to, addressed, by an Other, before we assume language for ourselves. And we can conclude further that it is only on the condition that we are addressed that we are able to make use of language. It is in this sense that the Other is the condition of discourse. If the Other is obliterated, so too is language, since language cannot survive outside of the conditions of address.

But let us remember that Levinas has also told us that the face—which is the face of the Other, and so the ethical demand made by the Other—is that vocalization of agony that is not yet language or no longer language, the one by which we are wakened to the precariousness of the Other's life, the one that rouses at once the temptation to murder and the interdiction against it. Why would it be that the inability to kill is the situation of discourse? Is it rather that the tension between fear for one's own life and anxiety about becoming a murderer constitutes the ambivalence that is the situation of discourse? That situation is one in which we are addressed, in which the Other directs language towards us. That language communicates the precariousness of life that establishes the ongoing tension of a non-violent ethics. The situation of discourse is not the same as what is said or, indeed, what is sayable. For Levinas, the situation of discourse consists in the fact that language arrives as an address we do not will, and by which we are, in an original sense, captured, if not, in Levinas's terms, held hostage. So there is a certain violence already in being addressed, given a name, subject to a set of impositions, compelled to respond to an exacting alterity. No one controls the terms by which one is addressed, at least not in the most fundamental way. To be addressed is to be, from the start, deprived of will, and to have that deprivation exist as the basis of one's situation in discourse.

Within the ethical frame of the Levinasian position, we begin by positing a dyad. But the sphere of politics, in his terms, is one in which there are always more than two subjects at play in the scene. Indeed, I may decide *not* to invoke my own desire to preserve my life as a justification for violence, but what if violence is done to someone I love? What if there is an Other who does violence to another Other? To which Other do I respond ethically? Which Other do I put before myself? Or do I then stand by? Derrida claims that to try and respond to every Other can only result in a situation of radical irresponsibility. And the Spinozists, the Nietzscheans, the utilitarians, and the Freudians all ask, "Can I invoke the imperative to preserve the life *of the Other* even if I cannot invoke this right of self-preservation for myself?" And is it really possible to sidestep self-preservation in the way that Levinas implies? Spinoza writes in *The Ethics* that the desire to live the right life requires the desire to live, to persist in one's own being, suggesting that ethics must always marshal some life drives, even if, as a super-egoic state, ethics threatens to become a pure culture of the death drive. It is possible, even easy, to read Levinas as an elevated masochist and it does not help us to avert that conclusion when we consider that, when asked what he thought of psychoanalysis, he is said to have responded, *is that not a form of pornography?*

But the reason to consider Levinas in the context of today is at least twofold. First, he gives us a way of thinking about the relationship between representation and humanization, a relationship that is not as straightforward as we might like to think. If critical thinking has something to say about or to the present situation, it may well be in the domain of representation where humanization and dehumanization occur ceaselessly. Second, he offers, within a tradition of Jewish philosophy, an account of the relationship between violence and ethics that has some important implications for thinking through what an ethic of Jewish non-violence might be. This strikes me as a timely and urgent question for many of us, especially those of us supporting the emergent moment of post–Zionism within Judaism. For now, I would like to reconsider first the problematic of humanization if we approach it through the figure of the face.

When we consider the ordinary ways that we think about humanization and dehumanization, we find the assumption that those who gain representation, especially self-representation, have a better chance of being humanized, and those who have no chance to represent themselves run a greater risk of being treated as less than human, regarded as less than human, or indeed, not regarded at all. We have a paradox before us because Levinas has made clear that the face is not exclusively a human face, and yet it is a condition for humanization.[12] On the other hand, there is the use of the face, within the media, in order to effect a dehumanization. It would seem that personification does not always humanize. For Levinas, it may well evacuate the face that does humanize; and I hope to show, personification sometimes performs its own dehumanization. How do we come to know the difference between the inhuman but humanizing face, for Levinas, and the dehumanization that can also take place through the face?

We may have to think of different ways that violence can happen: one is precisely *through* the production of the face, the face of Osama bin Laden, the face of Yasser Arafat, the face of Saddam Hussein. What has been done with these faces in the media? They are framed, surely, but they are also playing to the frame. And the result is invariably tendentious. These are media portraits that are often marshaled in the service of war, as if bin Laden's face were the face of terror itself, as if Arafat were the face of deception, as if Hussein's face were the face of contemporary tyranny. And then there is the face of Colin Powell, as it is framed and circulated, seated before the shrouded canvas of Picasso's *Guernica:* a face that is foregrounded, we might say, against a background of effacement. Then there are the faces of the Afghan girls who stripped off, or let fall, their burkas. One week last winter, I visited a political theorist who proudly displayed these faces on his refrigerator door, right next to some apparently valuable supermarket coupons, as a sign of the success of democracy. A few days later, I attended a conference in which I heard a talk about the important cultural meanings of the burka, the way in which it signifies belonging-ness to a community and religion, a family, an extended history of kin relations, an exercise of modesty and pride, a protection against shame, and operates as well as a veil behind which, and through which, feminine agency can and does work.[13] The fear of the speaker was that the destruction of the burka, as if it were a sign of repression, backwardness or, indeed, a resistance to cultural modernity itself, would result in a significant decimation of Islamic culture and the extension of U.S. cultural assumptions about how sexuality and agency ought to be organized and represented. According to the triumphalist photos that dominated the front page of the *New York Times,* these young women bared their faces as an act of liberation, an act of gratitude to the U.S. military, and an expression of a pleasure that had become suddenly and ecstatically permissible. The American viewer was ready, as it were, to see the face, and it was to the camera, and for the camera, after all, that the face was finally bared, where it became, in a flash, a symbol of successfully exported American cultural progress. It became bared to us, at that moment, and we were, as it were, in possession of the face; not only did our cameras capture it, but we arranged for the face to capture our triumph, and act as the rationale for our violence, the incursion on sovereignty, the deaths of civilians. Where is loss in that face? And where is the suffering over war? Indeed, the photographed face seemed to conceal or displace the face in the Levinasian sense, since we saw and heard through that face no vocalization of grief or agony, no sense of the precariousness of life.

So we seem to be charting a certain ambivalence. In a strange way, all of these faces humanize the events of the last year or so; they give a human face to Afghan women; they give a face to terror; they give a face to evil. But is the face humanizing in each and every instance? And if it is humanizing in some instances, in what form does this humanization occur, and is there also a dehumanization performed in and through the face? Do we encounter those faces in the Levinasian sense, or are these, in various ways, images that, through their frame, produce the paradigmatically human, become the very cultural means through which the paradigmatically human is established? Although it is tempting to think that the images themselves establish the visual norm for the human, one that ought to be emulated or embodied, this would be a mistake, since in the case of bin Laden or Saddam Hussein the paradigmatically human is understood to reside outside the frame; this is the human face in its deformity and extremity, not the one with which you are asked to identify. Indeed, the disidentification is incited through the hyperbolic absorption of evil into the face itself, the eyes. And if we are to understand ourselves as interpellated anywhere in these images, it is precisely as the unrepresented viewer, the one who looks on, the one who is captured by no image at all, but whose charge it is to capture and subdue, if not eviscerate, the image at hand. Similarly, although we might want to champion the suddenly bared faces of the young Afghan women as the celebration of the human, we have to ask in what narrative function these images are mobilized, whether the incursion into Afghanistan was really in the name of feminism, and in what form of feminism did it belatedly clothe itself. Most importantly, though, it seems we have to ask what scenes of pain and grief these images cover over and derealize. Indeed, all of these images seem to suspend the precariousness of life; they either represent American triumph, or provide an incitement for American military triumph in the future. *They are the spoils of war or they are the targets of war.* And in this sense, we might say that the face is, in every instance, defaced, and that this is one of the representational and philosophical consequences of war itself.

It is important to distinguish among kinds of unrepresentability. In the first instance, there is the Levinasian view according to which there is a "face" which no face can fully exhaust, the face understood as human suffering, as the cry of human suffering, which can take no direct representation. Here the "face" is always a figure for something that is not literally a face. Other human expressions, however, seem to be figurable as a "face" even though they are not faces, but sounds or emissions of another order. The cry that is represented through the figure of the face is one that confounds the senses and produces a clearly improper comparison: that cannot be right, for the face is not a sound. And yet, the face can stand for the sound precisely because it is *not* the sound. In this sense, the figure underscores the incommensurability of the face with whatever it represents. Strictly speaking, then, the face does not represent anything, in the sense that it fails to capture and deliver that to which it refers.

For Levinas, then, the human is not *represented by* the face. Rather, the human is indirectly affirmed in that very disjunction that makes representation impossible, and this disjunction is conveyed in the impossible representation. For representation to convey the human, then, representation must not only fail, but it must *show* its failure. There is something unrepresentable that we nevertheless seek to represent, and that paradox must be retained in the representation we give.

In this sense, the human is not identified with what is represented but neither is it identified with the unrepresentable; it is, rather, that which limits the success of any representational practice. The face is not "effaced" in this failure of representation, but is constituted in that very possibility. Something altogether different happens, however, when the face operates in the service of a personification that claims to "capture" the human being in question. For Levinas, the human cannot be captured through the representation, and we can see that some loss of the human takes place when it is "captured" by the image.[14]

An example of that kind of "capture" takes place when evil is personified through the face. A certain commensurability is asserted between that ostensible evil and the face. This face *is* evil, and the evil that the face *is* extends to the evil that belongs to humans in general—generalized evil. We personify the evil or military triumph through a face that is supposed to be, to capture, to contain the very idea for which it stands. In this case, we cannot hear the face through the face. The face here masks the sounds of human suffering and the proximity we might have to the precariousness of life itself.

The face over there, though, the one whose meaning is portrayed as captured by evil is precisely the one that is not human, not in the Levinasian sense. The "I" who sees that face is not identified with it: the face represents that for which no identification is possible, an accomplishment of dehumanization and a condition for violence.

Of course, a fuller elaboration of this topic would have to parse the various ways that representation works in relation to humanization and dehumanization. Sometimes there are triumphalist images that give us the idea of the human with whom we are to identify, for instance the patriotic hero who expands our own ego boundary ecstatically into that of the nation. No understanding of the relationship between the image and humanization can take place without a consideration of the conditions and meanings of identification and disidentification. It is worth noting, however, that identification always relies upon a difference that it seeks to overcome, and that its aim is accomplished only by reintroducing the difference it claims to have vanquished. The one with whom I identify is not me, and that "not being me" is the condition of the identification. Otherwise, as Jacqueline Rose reminds us, identification collapses into identity, which spells the death of identification itself.[15] This difference internal to identification is crucial, and, in a way, it shows us that disidentification is part of the common practice of identification itself. The triumphalist image can communicate an impossible overcoming of this difference, a kind of identification that believes that it has overcome the difference that is the condition of its own possibility. The critical image, if we can speak that way, works this difference in the same way as the Levinasian image; it must not only fail to capture its referent, but *show* this failing.

The demand for a truer image, for more images, for images that convey the full horror and reality of the suffering has its place and importance. The erasure of that suffering through the prohibition of images and representations more generally circumscribes the sphere of appearance, what we can see and what we can know. But it would be a mistake to think that we only need to find the right and true images, and that a certain reality will then be conveyed. The reality is not conveyed by what is represented within the image, but through the challenge to representation that reality delivers.[16]

The media's evacuation of the human through the image has to be understood, though, in terms of the broader problem that normative schemes of intelligibility establish what will and will not be human, what will be a livable life, what will be a grievable death. These normative schemes operate not only by producing ideals of the human that differentiate among those who are more and less human. Sometimes they produce images of the less than human, in the guise of the human, to show how the less than human disguises itself, and threatens to deceive those of us who might think we recognize another human there, in that face. But sometimes these normative schemes work precisely through providing no image, no name, no narrative, so that there never was a life, and there never was a death. These are two distinct forms of normative power: one operates through producing a symbolic identification of the face with the inhuman, foreclosing our apprehension of the human in the scene; the other works through radical effacement, so that there never was a human, there never was a life, and no murder has, therefore, ever taken place. In the first instance, something that has already emerged into the realm of appearance needs to be disputed as recognizably human; in the second instance, the public realm of appearance is itself constituted on the basis of the exclusion of that image. The task at hand is to establish modes of public seeing and hearing that might well respond to the cry of the human within the sphere of appearance, a sphere in which the trace of the cry has become hyperbolically inflated to rationalize a gluttonous nationalism, or fully obliterated, where both alternatives turn out to be the same. We might consider this as one of the philosophical and representational implications of war, because politics—and power—work in part through regulating what can appear, what can be heard.

Of course, these schemas of intelligibility are tacitly and forcefully mandated by those corporations that monopolize control over the mainstream media with strong interests in maintaining U.S. military power. The war coverage has brought into relief the need for a broad de-monopolozing of media interests, legislation for which has been, predictably, highly contested on Capitol Hill. We think of these interests as controlling rights of ownership, but they are also, simultaneously, deciding what will and will not be publicly recognizable as reality. They do not show violence, but there is a violence in the frame in what is shown. That latter violence is the mechanism through which certain lives and deaths either remain unrepresentable or become represented in ways that affect their capture (once again) by the war effort. The first is an effacement through occlusion; the second is an effacement through representation itself.

What is the relation between the violence by which these ungrievable lives were lost and the prohibition on their public grievability? Is the prohibition on grieving the continuation of the violence itself? And does the prohibition on grieving demand a tight control on the reproduction of images and words? How does the prohibition on grieving emerge as a circumscription of representability, so that our national melancholia becomes tightly fitted into the frame for what can be said, what can be shown? Is this not the site where we can read, if we still read, the way that melancholia becomes inscribed as the limits of what can be thought? The derealization of loss—the insensitivity to human suffering and death—becomes the mechanism through which dehumanization is accomplished. This derealization takes place neither inside nor outside the image, but through the very framing by which the image is contained.

In the initial campaign of the war against Iraq, the U.S. government advertised its military feats as an overwhelming visual phenomenon. That the U.S. government and military called this a "shock and awe" strategy suggests that they were producing a visual spectacle that numbs the senses and, like the sublime itself, puts out of play the very capacity to think. This production takes place not only for the Iraqi population on the ground, whose senses are supposed to be done in by this spectacle, but also for the consumers of war who rely on CNN or Fox, the network that regularly interspersed its war coverage on television with the claim that it is the "most trustworthy" news source on the war. The "shock and awe" strategy seeks not only to produce an aesthetic dimension to war, but to exploit and instrumentalize the visual aesthetics as part of a war strategy itself. CNN has provided much of these visual aesthetics. And although the *New York Times* belatedly came out against the war, it also adorned its front pages on a daily basis with romantic images of military ordnance against the setting sun in Iraq or "bombs bursting in air" above the streets and homes of Baghdad (which are not surprisingly occluded from view). Of course, it was the spectacular destruction of the World Trade Center that first made a claim upon the "shock and awe" effect, and the U.S. recently displayed for all the world to see that it can and will be equally destructive. The media becomes entranced by the sublimity of destruction, and voices of dissent and opposition must find a way to intervene upon this desensitizing dream machine in which the massive destruction of lives and homes, sources of water, electricity, and heat, are produced as a delirious sign of a resuscitated U.S. military power.

Indeed, the graphic photos of U.S. soldiers dead and decapitated in Iraq, and then the photos of children maimed and killed by U.S. bombs, were both refused by the mainstream media, supplanted with footage that always took the aerial view, an aerial view whose perspective is established and maintained by state power. And yet, the moment the bodies executed by the Hussein regime were uncovered, they made it to the front page of the *New York Times,* since those bodies must be grieved. The outrage over their deaths motivates the war effort, as it moves on to its managerial phase, which differs very little from what is commonly called "an occupation."

Tragically, it seems that the U.S. seeks to preempt violence against itself by waging violence first, but the violence it fears is the violence it engenders. I do not mean to suggest by this that the U.S. is responsible in some causal way for the attacks on its citizens. And I do not exonerate Palestinian suicide bombers, regardless of the terrible conditions that animate their murderous acts. There is, however, some distance to be traveled between living in terrible conditions, suffering serious, even unbearable injuries, and resolving on murderous acts. President Bush traveled that distance quickly, calling for "an end to grief" after a mere ten days of flamboyant mourning. Suffering can yield an experience of humility, of vulnerability, of impressionability and dependence, and these can become resources, if we do not "resolve" them too quickly; they can move us beyond and against the vocation of the paranoid victim who regenerates infinitely the justifications for war. It is as much a matter of wrestling ethically with one's own murderous impulses, impulses that seek to quell an overwhelming fear, as it is a matter of apprehending the suffering of others and taking stock of the suffering one has inflicted.

In the Vietnam War, it was the pictures of the children burning and dying from napalm that brought the U.S. public to a sense of shock, outrage, remorse, and grief. These were precisely pictures we were not supposed to see, and they disrupted the visual field and the entire sense of public identity that was built upon that field. The images furnished a reality, but they also showed a reality that disrupted the hegemonic field of representation itself. Despite their graphic effectivity, the images pointed somewhere else, beyond themselves, to a life and to a precariousness that they could not show. It was from that apprehension of the precariousness of those lives we destroyed that many U.S. citizens came to develop an important and vital consensus against the war. But if we continue to discount the words that deliver that message to us, and if the media will not run those pictures, and if those lives remain unnamable and ungrievable, if they do not appear in their precariousness and their destruction, we will not be moved. We will not return to a sense of ethical outrage that is, distinctively, for an Other, in the name of an Other. We cannot, under contemporary conditions of representation, hear the agonized cry or be compelled or commanded by the face. We have been turned away from the face, sometimes through the very image of the face, one that is meant to convey the inhuman, the already dead, that which is not precariousness and cannot, therefore, be killed; this is the face that we are nevertheless asked to kill, as if ridding the world of this face would return us to the human rather than consummate our own inhumanity. One would need to hear the face as it speaks in something other than language to know the precariousness of life that is at stake. But what media will let us know and feel that frailty, know and feel at the limits of representation as it is currently cultivated and maintained? If the humanities has a future as cultural criticism, and cultural criticism has a task at the present moment, it is no doubt to return us to the human where we do not expect to find it, in its frailty and at the limits of its capacity to make sense. We would have to interrogate the emergence and vanishing of the human at the limits of what we can know, what we can hear, what we can see, what we can sense. This might prompt us, affectively, to reinvigorate the intellectual projects of critique, of questioning, of coming to understand the difficulties and demands of cultural translation and dissent, and to create a sense of the public in which oppositional voices are not feared, degraded or dismissed, but valued for the instigation to a sensate democracy they occasionally perform.

NOTES

1. Emmanuel Levinas and Richard Kearney, "Dialogue with Emmanuel Levinas," in *Face to Face with Levinas* (Albany: SUNY Press, 1986), 23–4. Levinas develops this conception first in *Totality and Infinity: An Essay on Exteriority*, trans. Alphonso Lingis (Pittsburgh: Duquesne University Press, 1969), 187–203.

2. Emmanuel Levinas, *Ethics and Infinity*, trans. Richard A. Cohen (Pittsburgh: Duquesne University Press, 1985), 87.

3. Emmanuel Levinas, "Peace and Proximity," in *Basic Philosophical Writings*, ed. Adriaan T. Peperzak, Simon Critchley, and Robert Bernasconi (Bloomington: Indiana University Press, 1996), 167.

4. Levinas, "Peace and Proximity," 167.

5. *Ibid.*

6. *Ibid.*

7. The theological background of this can be found in Exodus. God makes clear to Moses that no one can see God's face, that is, that the divine face is not for seeing and not available to representation: "Thou canst not see my face: for there shall no man see me, and live" (33:20, *King James*); later, God makes plain that the back can and will substitute for the face: "And I will take away mine hand, and thou shalt see my back parts; but my face shall not be seen" (33:23). Later, when Moses is carrying God's words in the form of the commandments, it is written, "And when Aaron and all the children of Israel saw Moses, behold, the skin of his face shone; and they were afraid to come nigh him" (34:30). But Moses' face, carrying the divine word, is also not to be represented. When Moses returns to his human place, he can show his face: "And till Moses had done speaking with them, he put a veil on his face. But when Moses went in before the Lord to speak with him, he came out, and spake unto the children of Israel that which he was commanded. And the children of Israel saw the face of Moses, that the skin of Moses' face shone: and Moses put the veil on his face again, until he went in to speak with him." I thank Barbara Johnson for calling these passages to my attention.

8. Levinas writes, "But that face facing me, in its expression—in its mortality—summons me, demands me, requires me: as if the invisible death faced by the face of the other … were 'my business.' As if, unknown by the other whom already, in the nakedness of his face, it concerns, it 'regarded me' before its confrontation with me, before being the death that stares me, myself, in the face. The death of the other man puts me on the spot, calls me into question, as if I, by my possible indifference, became the accomplice of that death, invisible to the other who is exposed to it; as if even before being condemned to it myself, I had to answer for that death of the other, and not leave the other alone to his deathly solitude," in Emmanuel Levinas, *Alterity and Transcendence*, trans. Michael B. Smith (New York: Columbia University Press, 1999), 24–5.

9. Levinas, "Peace and Proximity," 167.

10. Levinas, *Ethics and Infinity*, 9.

11. Levinas, *Ethics and Infinity*, 87.

12. Levinas distinguishes sometimes between the "countenance" understood as the face within perceptual experience, and the "face" whose coordinates are understood to transcend the perceptual field. He also speaks on occasion about "plastic" representations of the face

that efface the face. For the face to operate as a face, it must vocalize or be understood as the workings of a voice.

13. See Lila Abu-Lughod, "Do Muslim Women Really Need Saving? Anthropological Reflections on Cultural Relativism and Others," *American Anthropologist*, 104: 3 (2008), 783–90.

14. For an extended discussion of the relation between the media image and human suffering, see Susan Sontag's provocative *Regarding the Pain of Others* (New York: Farrar, Straus, and Giroux, 2002).

15. For a discussion of "failure" as basic to a psychoanalytic conception of the psyche, see Jacqueline Rose, *Sexuality in the Field of Vision* (London: Verso, 1986), 91–3.

16. Levinas writes, "one can say that the face is not 'seen.' It is what cannot become a content, which your thought would embrace; it is uncontainable, it leads you beyond" (*Ethics and Infinity*, 86–7).

Is Autonomy Unethical?

Trauma and the Politics of Responsibility

MARI RUTI

> Autonomy does not consist of putting walls around oneself
> … but instead, of forming essential relationships with oth-
> ers.
>
> —Susan Brison, *Aftermath* (2002)

Judith Butler Meets Susan Brison

Dartmouth philosopher Susan Brison tells us in *Aftermath* that in the summer of 1990, she went for a morning walk on a country road in Southern France. She was attacked from behind, dragged into a nearby ravine, raped, beaten, and strangled unconscious four times. Her assailant tried to kill her to keep her from reporting the rape, responding to her attempts to assure him she would not report it by an insistent *"il le faut"*—"it must be done." Brison regained consciousness after the fourth attack, she pretended to be dead, and her assailant left her in the ravine. She climbed back onto the road, flagged down a farmer on a tractor, and was taken to the hospital where she was treated for serious injuries. Her assailant was apprehended quickly—he lived in the neighborhood—and was eventually sentenced to twelve years in prison for rape and attempted murder. Brison reports that, unlike many rape survivors, she was treated relatively well by the French legal system, presumably in part because she was a white middle-class married woman, and in part because the attack was so grievous that it left no doubt about what had happened. The bulk of her book outlines the aftermath of the attack: her lengthy, and in many ways only partially successful, battle against severe symptoms of post-traumatic stress disorder. Her memoir does not end on a triumphant note, for she writes, in its final pages:

54

I wasn't surprised that my recovery wasn't linear—no one led me to expect that—but by the fact that whatever trajectory my life was on didn't seem to *be* one of recovery. There was (and is) no discernible pattern. I'd like to be able to tell a story of trauma and recovery in a more "conventional" sense.... [But] recovery no longer seems to consist of picking up the pieces of a shattered self (or fractured narrative). It's facing the fact that there never was a coherent self (or story) there to begin with. No wonder I can't seem to manage to put myself together again. I'd have to put myself, as the old gag goes, "together again for the first time."[1]

Brison's overall vision of subjectivity and self-narrativization thus agrees with the one that Judith Butler has advocated in the context of the ethics of precarity that she has developed during the last decade: because there is no coherent self, there is no way to give a coherent account of oneself. Yet Brison repeatedly stresses what Butler would find difficult to integrate into her approach, namely that being able to recover a sense of autonomy is an essential part of surviving trauma. This autonomy will always be incomplete, will always encounter various obstacles, but it is also life-preserving. If trauma results in a loss of control, in utter helplessness, then, as Brison maintains, the seemingly impossible "task faced by the trauma survivor is to regain a sense of control over her or his life."[2] More specifically, Brison confirms what countless other survivors have reported, namely that their repeated efforts to tell their stories are, among other things, an attempt to establish a measure of agency over lives that have been torn apart. Because there is a performative element to self-narrativization—so that in saying something about the trauma one acts on the memory of that trauma—narrativization helps the survivor externalize the trauma; rather than being a passive victim of another's violence, she becomes the (tentatively) active subject of her story. Brison in fact tells us that her recovery would not have been possible without the presence of others willing to respond to her story: "Each time someone failed to respond I felt as though I were alone again in the ravine, dying, screaming."[3] There is no illusion, in Brison's text, that the narrativization of trauma will lead to complete self-mastery. But she recognizes that trauma survivors often urgently need to rebuild a sense of self. Comparable calls for self-determination can be found in texts, such as Frantz Fanon's *The Wretched of the Earth*,[4] that address the need of a traumatized collectivity to reestablish its viability in the face of oppression. Given that this is the case, my question in this essay is whether Butler is correct in positing that ethics is (or should be) a matter of contesting "sovereign notions of the subject"[5]—notions that, as Adriana Cavarero argues, are based on "individualistic doctrines, which are too preoccupied with praising the rights of the *I*."[6]

I understand the reasons for Butler's attack on "the ontology of individualism" characteristic of the humanist subject, particularly of the self-contained Enlightenment subject,[7] for the critique of the violent exploits of this subject—including its imperialist aspirations—has always been central to posthumanist theory. And in recent years, this critique has found a new target: the narcissistic neoliberal subject for whom the fantasy of impermeability and self-sufficiency is foundational. However, the impulse to crush this subject has arguably grown to be so habitual in contemporary progressive theory—including Butler's work—that it has become difficult to remember that not all attempts to gain autonomy are synonymous with arrogant individualism; that trauma survivors, for instance, often pursue autonomy not because of an aggressive desire to dominate the world but because of a desperate need to render the self moderately functioning. More generally speaking, because posthumanist theory is on a mission to discredit the overly confident humanist subject, it cannot always adequately address the struggles of less robust subjects; even when it recognizes the psychic realities of vulnerability—as Butler's ethics of precarity certainly does—it tends to talk as if all efforts to surmount this vulnerability were intrinsically deplorable, with the consequence that it may unwittingly end up further disempowering the very subjects who most need to overcome their disempowerment. That is, the message of much of posthumanist theory seems to be the following: you are not as powerful as you think you are; precariousness is the underpinning of your existence and this is how things should stay; any effort you might make to become more autonomous is essentially unethical (because the worst you could ever do would be to begin to resemble the agentic subject of Enlightenment humanism).

This is not to say that I do not appreciate many components of Butler's ethics of precarity, including its attempt to replace Kantian rationalism by a combination of Levinasian phenomenology and psychoanalysis. Both of these sources reveal the Enlightenment subject to be a hoax by focusing on the subject's social, relational ontology. If Levinas sought, as he put it, to break "the obstinacy of being"[8] by showing that we owe our very existence to the other, and that we are therefore irrevocably responsible for this other, psychoanalysis reveals the ways in which our primary infantile relationships linger into adulthood, repeatedly interrupting any sense of coherence we might attain. In other words, psychoanalysis reminds us that the other dwells within the self—through the unconscious, through the repetition compulsion, and even through our bodily drives—in ways that render us constitutionally incomplete, disoriented, out-of-joint, and riven by alterity. Most importantly for Butler's purposes, our early exposure to the other—what she describes, following Jean Laplanche, as our primordial impingement by the other—is involuntary and always potentially traumatizing. Even when we are not treated badly, we are treated unilaterally, which means that we are completely at the mercy of others. And when we *are* treated badly, our masochism is inevitable in the sense that we are forced to cathect to those who harm us;

our very survival depends on such wounded attachments, with the result that being injured—and injurable—becomes the status quo of our lives.

Butler thus replaces the metaphysical model of subjectivity as autonomous and self-generating with a psychoanalytic model of relational ontology. This relational ontology, in turn, becomes the foundation for her ethics of precarity— an ethics that postulates that our recognition that vulnerability is a shared human condition functions (or, ideally, should function) as a resource for our resolve to protect others against all attempts to exploit their helplessness. That is, there is something about vulnerability—particularly about bodily vulnera- bility—that offers a potentially universal platform for opposing violence in its various forms. Like any good poststructuralist, Butler feels conflicted about this universality, taking care to specify that precariousness, while being a general condition of human life, is always experienced in singular ways, so that it is impossible to draw an easy analogy between one experience of suffering and another. Nevertheless, the fact that all of us are defenseless in the face of suffering allows us, on a very basic level, to connect to the suffering of others.

Furthermore, Butler prompts us to become aware of the biopolitical and necropolitical power structures that distribute precariousness unevenly, so that some individuals and populations are much more precarious than others. I find her arguments about grievability—about the unequal ways in which some people are deemed worthy of being mourned while others are not— quite compelling and I discuss them at length elsewhere.[9] There is absolutely no question that Butler's ethics aims at a more just world—a world where economic, racial, and other social inequalities would be leveled so that every- one's vulnerability would count equally and everyone would be equally pro- tected. However, I would like to propose that Butler's categorical flight from the humanist subject leads to two theoretical dead ends that, ironically enough, neutralize her capacity to speak to the complexities of acute trauma- tization. First—as I have already started to suggest—she fails to validate the legitimate need for autonomy that many trauma survivors express. Second, because she starts from the assumption that the very possibility of autonomy is ethically questionable, she finds it difficult to condemn those who inflict trauma on others, as Susan Brison's assailant did. That is, Butler deems the notion of self-responsibility—which is what autonomy on some level implies—so unpalatable that she constructs an ethical model completely devoid of normative content, with the result that she loses the capacity to distinguish between right and wrong, just and unjust, actions. Instead, she adopts Levinas's somewhat problematic notion that we are irrevocably responsible for the other regardless of how this other behaves. I will proceed by discussing the Levinasian outlook first, before circling back to the con- siderations about traumatization and autonomy that constitute the central preoccupation of this essay.

When Forgiveness Is Not Enough

Levinas argues that our responsibility for the other is unconditional and inescapable, that the other as "face" is inviolable and that, unfortunately for us, even the executioner, even the Nazi guard, has a face. We may feel tempted to attack such a face, but ethics demands that we resist this temptation. So far so good: I do not have a problem with the idea that I should not counter murder with murder, particularly as Levinas emphasizes that it is the task of justice—as opposed to ethics—to arbitrate between different faces. But things become more troublesome when Butler combines Levinas with psychoanalytic insights about the intrinsically opaque nature of subjectivity to promote an ethics of leniency whereby I am exhorted to forgive those who wound me. According to this ethics, I need to recognize that others are driven by unconscious motivations that remain beyond their reach, which means that they do not always know what they are doing. Nor are they capable of giving a full account of their actions, which means that my request for such an account constitutes a form of ethical violence. On the flip side, I can expect similar leniency from others. As Butler proposes, "I will need to be forgiven for what I cannot have fully known, and I will be under a similar obligation to offer forgiveness to others, who are also constituted in partial opacity to themselves."[10] In this way, Butler turns my inner opacity—which is, among other things, an indicator of the extent to which I am *not* an autonomous being—into a semiautomatic grounds for forgiveness. To be sure, she admits that this opacity should not be seen as a license to do whatever I want to do. But, in principle, it deserves the patience, forbearance, and forgiveness of others. Even more pointedly, Butler proposes that because my prehistory—the part of my infantile formation that I cannot, as an adult, reconstruct—keeps interrupting any story I tell of myself, it constitutes "my failure to be fully accountable for my actions, my final 'irresponsibility,' one for which I may be forgiven only because I could not do otherwise."[11] As a result, she concludes, "If we speak and try to give an account from this place [of opacity], we will not be irresponsible, or, if we are, we will surely be forgiven."[12]

Might this not be a little too convenient for us? Butler reads the psychoanalytic insight about our inner opacity to mean that we cannot be held fully responsible for our actions but will, instead, "surely" be forgiven. I would say that this is a fairly self-serving, even dangerous, way to interpret the consequences of the fact that we are often motivated by unconscious currents that we do not entirely understand. I would indeed be tempted to reverse Butler's formulation to argue that I am fully responsible for my actions even when I cannot comprehend how the ghosts of my formative experiences goad me to these actions. Freud's point about making the unconscious conscious, after all, was not that I should resign myself to riding the pulse of the repetition compulsion for the rest of my life; rather, his point was that by developing an active relationship to my unconscious, I might be able to foster the capacity to intervene in this compulsion whenever it threatens to hurt either me or others. By this I obviously do not mean that I expect to master my unconscious. If nothing else, I remain a good Lacanian. But I believe that psychoanalysis teaches me that I am responsible for my actions even—and perhaps *particularly*—when they are unconsciously motivated. In this sense, my opacity does not absolve me of responsibility but rather asks me to become more vigilant in relation to my unconscious patterns. That I have a prehistory that I cannot control does not mean that I have no say over my actions in the present. Nor does my lack of self-transparency mean that I cannot attain a degree of self-understanding. This is why I cannot see my opacity as a get-out-of-jail card; rather, I see it as an invitation to a radical form of self-responsibility.[13]

"My unconscious made me do it" may be a tempting excuse, but it places a potentially unbearable burden on those who have been harmed by my actions. Likewise, though I appreciate Butler's inclination to remain generous with the inner opacities of others, I am not as quick to absolve them of their wrongdoings as Butler is. If anything, I think that there is something questionable about Butler's call for patience, forbearance, and forgiveness in a biopolitical context where some people—say, women—are already expected to offer such patience, forbearance, and forgiveness more than others. I am not at all certain that uncritical charity with respect to others is either ethically prudent or psychoanalytically sound. Indeed, nothing is easier than abusing this charity. From the neoliberal subject who cannot commit to anything, and who therefore expects others to tolerate his ambivalences indefinitely, to the rapist who claims that his victim "provoked" him, as Brison's rapist tried to do, the world is full of people who are used to getting away with more than they should. The refusal to condemn them in the name of a more capacious ethics merely gives them permission to continue their hurtful behavior; indeed, this refusal directly contradicts Butler's own view that we should oppose any and all attempts to exploit human vulnerability. Moreover, looking hack, one might ask whether feminism, the Civil Rights movement, anticolonial struggles, and so on, would have been possible if those involved had decided to be forgiving rather than angry. Butler argues that "it may be that only through an experience of the other under conditions of suspended judgment do we finally become capable of an ethical reflection on the humanity of the other, even when that other has sought to annihilate humanity."[14] Does this mean that if I condemn a person who has "sought to annihilate humanity," as Brison's assailant did, I fail at the task of being ethical?

The Levinasian-Butlerian ethical model shifts the ethical burden from the victimizer to the victim. Because this ethics places no normative limits on the behavior of the victimizer—because it starts from the premise that we are responsible for the other regardless of how brutally he or she behaves—it translates the infant's primordial masochism into a moral virtue. As Butler writes in *Precarious Life*, "our responsibility is heightened once we have been subjected to the violence of others."[15] Consider also the following statement from *Parting Ways*: "The responsibility that I must take for the Other proceeds directly from being persecuted and outraged by that Other. Thus there is violence in the relation from the start: I am claimed by the other *against my will*, and my responsibility for the Other emerges from this subjection."[16] This assertion is not as crazy as it may seem when taken out of context; for what Butler is getting at is the Levinasian connection between my relational ontology and my ethical responsibility. The basic idea is that because the other "interrupts" the coherence of my being, impeding my self-closure, I am, in a sense, always "persecuted" and "outraged" by the other; at the same time, because the other is always already an ingredient of my self, I cannot denounce my responsibility for this other. In this model, responsibility is the reverse of being impinged upon by the other in ways that sometimes feel persecuting and outrageous. As Butler reminds us, according to Levinas, "precisely the Other who persecutes me has a face."[17] Consequently, "I cannot disavow my relation to the Other, regardless of what the Other does, regardless of what I might will." Responsibility, in this sense, is "not a matter of cultivating a will, but of make use of an unwilled susceptibility as a resource for becoming responsive to the Other": "Whatever the Other has done, the Other still makes an ethical demand upon me, has a 'face' to which I am obliged to respond."[18] Simply put, if the individualistic ethical theories that Butler resists praise the "rights of the *I*," Butler's relational ethics, like its Levinasian counterpart, values the other's well-being over the subject's self-preservation. In Butler's words, "One of the problems with insisting on self-preservation as a basis of ethics is that it becomes a pure ethics of the self, if not a form of moral narcissism."[19]

I understand why Butler's relational alternative represents an effective decentering of the Enlightenment subject. But does it not swing too far to the other extreme? Is there not, particularly from a feminist perspective, something quite uncomfortable about the idea that I am responsible for others who violate me "against my will?" Indeed, how would Butler account for Brison's admission that, after her ordeal, it was essential for her to know that she was going to be able to defend herself if attacked again, which is why she undertook self-defense training? Brison writes:

> I also learned, after martial arts training, that I was capable, morally as well as physically, of killing in self-defense—an option that made the possibility of another life-threatening attack one I could live with. Some rape survivors have remarked on the sense of moral loss they experienced when they realized that they could kill their

assailants (and even wanted to!) but I think that this thought can be seen as a salu-
tary character change in those whom society does not encourage to value their own
lives enough.[20]

I wonder what Butler would do with this passage. While I doubt that
even Butler would tell Brison to cultivate patience, forbearance, and forgiveness in relation to her assailant, it is also the case that her Levinasian approach
implies that there is something inherently unethical about Brison's stance.
Butler writes: "Given over from the start to the world of others, [the body]
bears their imprint, is formed within the crucible of social life; only later,
and with some uncertainty, do I lay claim to my body as my own, if, in fact,
I ever do. Indeed, if I deny that prior to the formation of my 'will,' my body
related me to others whom I did not choose to have in proximity to myself,
if I build a notion of 'autonomy' on the basis of the denial of this sphere of
a primary and unwilled physical proximity with others, then am I denying
the social conditions of my embodiment in the name of autonomy?"[21] Physical
vulnerability here is what "saves" me from the demon of autonomy. Does this
mean that my attempts to protect myself physically render me unethical? It
seems to me that if I am always responsible for the other regardless of what
the other has done, and if this responsibility demands that I resist the temptation to injure even those who persecute and outrage me, then obviously I
should not be relishing my realization that I could—and even might *want*
to—kill my assailant (or any future assailant). If Butler raises the self's rev-
erence for the other to an ethical virtue, Brison sees the virtue in being able
to recognize one's own self as worth fighting for, particularly if that self is
one that has been socially denigrated. From a Levinasian perspective, the
quest for self-preservation is the antithesis of ethics; but from an alternative
ethical perspective—in this case, a more straightforwardly feminist one—it
is one of the pillars of an ethical world.

Beyond Bad Autonomy Vs. Good Relationality

More generally speaking, the problem with Butlerian ethics is that it
consistently sets up a rigid dichotomy between bad autonomy and good relationality; indeed, one could say that this is an instance where a vehemently
anti-essentialist thinker, paradoxically enough, falls into the kind poststructuralist "essentialism" where some possibilities—such as the idea that autonomy might sometimes be an important component of human life—become
unthinkable. Butler often talks as if the fact that we are not fully autonomous
creatures means that we have no capacity for autonomy whatsoever. Yet in
the same way that having an unconscious does not erase the conscious mind
but merely complicates its functioning, our lack of seamless autonomy does

not render us completely devoid of it. Nor is autonomy always the antithesis of relationality, as Butler implies. Indeed, Butler portrays autonomy—any attempt at recentering the self—not merely as repugnant but as intrinsically *evil*. As she asserts, there is "no recentering of the subject without unleashing unacceptable sadism and cruelty": "To remain decentered, interestingly, means to remain implicated in the death of the other and so at a distance from the unbridled cruelty … in which the self seeks to separate from its constitutive sociality and annihilate the other."[22] I agree that self-assertion can take place at the expense of others. And I agree that the fantasy of sovereignty can promote contempt not only for others but also for alternative, more relational modalities of being. But I am not convinced that the subject who seeks to recenter itself is automatically sadistic and cruel, driven to annihilate the other.

What I particularly like about Brison's narrative of her (always incomplete) recovery is that, rather than establishing a firm binary between bad autonomy and good relationality, she—like Jessica Benjamin[23]—sees autonomy and relationality as equally necessary and in no way mutually exclusive. Autonomy, Brison maintains, is not a matter of putting up walls around oneself—of claiming complete self-reliance—but can rather serve as the foundation for respectful relationships with others. Conversely, relationality may be a way to cultivate autonomy. Indeed, Brison uses much of her narrative to highlight the relational nature of autonomy, the fact that we often arrive at autonomy *through* relationality. For instance, she explains that One of the most devastating effects of trauma is that it shatters the survivor's trust in others so that relationality may—for the time being at least—seem impossible: if even *some* men rape and murder (or try to murder) women, then what does this say about men in general? How can I ever be sure that the man I interact with is not going to attempt the same? The effect of this type of questioning, in Brison's words, is that "one can no longer *be oneself* even to oneself, since the self exists fundamentally in relation to others."[24] Brison further notes that "the main reason all of us, especially women, have to fear violent intrusions by others is that they severely impair our ability to be connected to humanity in ways we value."[25] The implication of this is that the infringement of autonomy that violence represents wounds us in part because it destroys our capacity for relationality. The antidote to trauma, then, cannot be a retreat into the shell of a self-contained subjectivity but consists of rebuilding one's capacity for relationality. Yet this rebuilding only becomes possible once the survivor feels that she is able to protect the boundaries of her self against intrusions by others—that is, once she has recuperated a degree of autonomy. In this manner, the autonomous self and the relational self, Brison posits, are "shown to be interdependent, even constitutive of one another."[26]

Butler's enthusiasm for relationality as a substitute for autonomy, rather than as its complement, causes her to cut off a considerable part of human experience, including the fact that we *do* usually have a sense of ourselves as quasi-bounded individuals who possess a degree of agency, and who are consequently not indiscriminately subjected to the will and actions of others. An experience such as Brison's is traumatic in part precisely because it pierces the personal boundaries that typically protect us against being impinged upon by others. Moreover, Butler's model overlooks the fact that the individuals who facilitated our formative coming-into-being are not necessarily the same as those we interact with as adults. We may have started our lives in a state of interpersonal vulnerability that made it impossible for us to dissociate ourselves from those who chose to wound us, but what keeps us from doing so now? Surely there is a distinction between the idea that we are inhabited by an ontological otherness that we cannot denounce—that we only have a self to the extent that we partake in structures of sociality—and the idea that we cannot sever our connection to *specific* others who injure us. Although it is true that our infantile experiences will always exert an influence over our lives, it is inaccurate to assert that, as adult subjects, our relationship to the world of others is always (or primarily) one of being persecuted and outraged. Butler consistently downplays the difference between the constitutive vulnerability of the child and the psychic realities of adult subjectivity, failing to consider the possibility that our infantile defenselessness does not necessarily translate into life-long helplessness. We undoubtedly carry the imprint of our formative vulnerability to our graves. But surely this is not the whole story, or even the main story; surely we are also deeply enabled by others, which is precisely why traumatic incidents, such as Brison's, fall outside the "normal" flow of life.

The Need for Normative Limits

It is Butler's resistance to the idea that autonomy is an important feature of human life—a resistance which amounts to an antipathy toward anything that even vaguely reminds us of the humanist subject—that in part explains her hostility to a priori principles of right and wrong. This hostility is of course endemic in posthumanist theory because this theory views ethics primarily as a matter of questioning hegemonic normative paradigms. From the Frankfurt School to Lacan, Foucault, Barthes, Derrida, and Butler, among others, there has been an attempt to unearth the violence intrinsic to our dominant ethical models: the fact that their claim to objectivity rests on a number of constitutive exclusions (say, the exclusion of women, or the exclusion of racialized others). One could indeed say that this is what critical theory—my own field—consists of: it reveals the oppressive underbelly of the norms that we have been taught to take for granted. I have always been—and continue to be—a huge supporter of this type of theorizing. But I have also come to see that sometimes the vehement critique of norms obscures the fact that we still need them. Butler often remarks that moral norms of behavior are not self-evident. This is true. But, then again, sometimes they *are* self-evident. It seems to me that dragging a woman into a ravine, raping her, and beating and strangling her unconscious is not a morally ambiguous act. And it does not bother me that my condemnation of this act arises from a priori principles I have inherited from my culture. I say this because I want to emphasize that there is no reason to think that a priori norms transcend our social world. Critical theorists, such as Butler, tend to be hostile to a priori norms in part because they associate such norms with the Enlightenment, which means that they view them as inherently metaphysical. But, as feminist philosopher Amy Allen has argued persuasively, a priori principles are always historically specific in the sense that they arise in particular social contexts. This, however, does not mean that they are invariably worthless; that is, while the loss of metaphysical foundations for our normative systems undermines their claim to universality, it does not automatically invalidate them. As Allen claims, rejecting "our historical a priori" would mean "surrendering intelligibility."[27] As a result, as is the case with autonomy, the attempt to pretend that normative limits mean nothing gets us nowhere—except, perhaps, into a swamp of theoretical incoherence.

This swamp is where the Butlerian approach lands when it leaps from the recognition of my relational ontology to the conclusion that I am responsible for each and every other I encounter regardless of any normative considerations; this swamp is where this approach lands when it translates the fact that I was once a helpless child mishandled by my caretakers to the idea that I am ethically accountable for the man who tries to kill me after he has forced me to suck his dirty dick. Butler flees from ethical condemnation because it supposedly props up the condemning subject's righteousness by disavowing commonality with the one who is being condemned. As she argues, "condemnation is very often an act that not only 'gives up on' the one condemned but seeks to inflict a violence upon the condemned in the name of 'ethics.'"[28] Butler here—awkwardly enough—judges the violence of judgment to be more violent than the violence of the act that is being judged. I concede that there are situations where the normative moral order inflicts violence by its judgments—and even misjudges—but it seems like an overstatement to suggest that, in condemning those who commit acts of violence, I "lose the chance to be ethically educated or 'addressed' by a consideration of who they are and what their personhood says about the range of human possibility."[29] Butler maintains that condemnation "takes aim at the life of the condemned," among other things because "punishment works to further destroy the conditions for autonomy, eroding if not eviscerating the capacity of the subject addressed for both self-reflection and social recognition, two practices that are, I would argue, essential to any substantive account of ethical life. It also, of course, turns the moralist into a murderer."[30] It is difficult to escape the irony of the fact that this is one of the few places where Butler seems to appreciate autonomy and the capacity for self-reflection. The one who condemns becomes a murderer because she destroys the autonomy of the perpetrator whereas the perpetrator—even the murderer—becomes a victim by virtue of being condemned. Pushed to an extreme, Butler's vision could be argued to imply that those who murder cannot quite help themselves but those who condemn them are culpable of (soul)-murder; pushed to an extreme, it suggests that Brison's assailant—who tried to plead temporary insanity[31]—is less guilty than Brison herself, is for daring to entertain the thought of being able to kill any future assailant.

The lack of normative limits—of a priori ethical principles—in Butlerian theory leads to places that are hard to defend: I am supposed to actively sustain those who hurt me, and this is the case regardless of whether they are sexists, racists, neo–Nazis, or homophobic religious fundamentalists. The lengths to which Butler is willing to go to defend the Levinasian notion that even the executioner has a face is revealed in *Parting Ways*, where she discusses Hannah Arendt's condemnation of Eichmann at the end of her book *Eichmann in Jerusalem*.[32] In her book, Arendt is critical of the ways in which Israel uses the Eichmann trial for its political ends, yet she also holds Eichmann responsible for his crimes, stating in closing that he deserves to die for these crimes. Butler proposes that at the moment that Arendt judges Eichmann, "some disposition of language binds them both together; she is part of a human plurality with him—indeed, with the likes of him. And yet the effect of her address to him is to exclude him from that very domain of plurality."[33] The implication is that Arendt, in judging Eichmann, fails to live up to her own ideal of plurality. In a strictly abstract sense this may be true. But the charge also illustrates the problematic nature of an ethics that operates wholly without norms, where literally nothing a person does renders him worthy of ethical censure. Yes, we need to revere plurality. But we also need some way to decide what types of actions are acceptable. Eichmann emphatically did not respect plurality. I am consequently not sure it was Arendt's responsibility to extend to him the courtesy of respecting his. Butler has so much trouble with notions of sovereignty, autonomy, and agency—notions that imply the capacity for ethical accountability—that she comes close to defending Eichmann against Arendt's insensitivity; though she is not saying that Eichmann is not guilty, she implies that Arendt is *also* guilty for not including him in the plurality of humanity. This is why I find myself in a rare agreement with Slavoj Žižek and colleagues, who observes that Butler's ethics is "an ethics of finitude, of making a virtue out of our very weakness, in other words, of elevating into the highest ethical Value the respect for our very inability to act with full responsibility."[34]

Interestingly, Butler's resistance to a priori principles dissipates in the context of her critique of Israeli state violence against Palestinians, for she argues that Palestinians have the right to have basic rights, such as the right not to be dispossessed of land, due to their membership in a global human community. Regarding Palestine's claim "to the lands that rightfully are its own," Butler writes: "One could formulate the right in light of international law or on the basis of moral and political arguments that may or may not be trained within a specific version of the nation-state."[35] I agree with this stance: I also think that Palestinians should have basic human rights regardless of whether or not they belong to a nation-state. But there is nothing about Butler's Levinasian ethical vision that supports her sudden turn to the kind of liberal rights-based cosmopolitanism that can be traced, through Arendt, all the way back to Kant. If Butler stayed faithful to her Levinasian approach, she would not be calling for equal rights for Palestinians but rather saying that self-preservation should not be a priority for them, that, indeed, there might be something profoundly unethical about their quest for sovereignty and self-determination. Butler makes a valiant effort to show that her cosmopolitanism is not: the same as that of Kant by arguing that it is precarity rather than the integrity of the autonomous self that is the foundation for equal rights. But this does not change the fact that, in this instance, she falls back on the very system of Enlightenment morality that she has spent much of her career criticizing, so that all of a sudden equal rights are all the rage.[36] It would of course be possible to argue that the Enlightenment does not own the ideal of equal rights, that it is possible to think about equal rights beyond their humanistic context, as Derrida does when he claims that "what remains irreducible to any deconstruction" is "an idea of justice—which we distinguish from law or right and even from human rights—and an idea of democracy—which we distinguish from its current concept and from its determined predicates today."[37] But Derrida's elusive definition of justice and democracy is not, what Butler is working with when she, in a Kantian vein, calls for international laws that recognize the rights of individuals not on the basis of their attachment to nation-states but rather on the basis of their humanity.

The Politics of Memory

It seems to me that Butler cannot have it both ways. If she is going to recoil from any mention of the Enlightenment, as she consistently does, then she cannot use its values whenever these happen to suit her political purposes. Furthermore, because Butler's disdain for the Enlightenment subject causes her to strip the posthumanist subject of all autonomy, her theory does not offer much insight into what it might mean to try to rebuild the autonomy of those who have been forcefully deprived of it. Here Brison's commentary on the ways in which self-narrativization can buttress the trauma survivor's sense of self is more helpful. Brison does not pretend that narrativization erases the experience of trauma, or even that it offers a fully satisfactory (let alone accurate) account of it, but merely stresses what I already alluded to above, namely that self-narratives translate devastating traumatic memories into narrative memories that are actively constructed and therefore conducive to a degree of agency. As Brison explains, narrativization "defuses traumatic memory, giving shape and a temporal order to the events recalled, establishing more control over their recalling, and helping the survivor to remake a self."[38] If traumatic memories are repeated involuntarily, narrativization allows the survivor to gain some much needed distance from them. "It does this not by reestablishing the illusions of coherence of the past, control over the present, and predictability of the future," Brison specifies, "but by making it possible to carry on without these illusions."[39]

Brison acknowledges the possibility that excessive narrativization might retraumatize the survivor. And she also admits that listeners might be traumatized by hearing stories of violence, so that, for instance, women who have not been assaulted might grow excessively fearful from having heard countless rape narratives. Recalling her own experience, Brison states, "Given the stories of rape I'd grown up with and the ones I'd heard and read about again and again in adulthood, one might say I remembered the rape even before it happened, as a kind of postmemory … informing the way I lived in my body and moved about in the world."[40] Yet she also notes that we are arguably even more traumatized by silence, for silence often transmits trauma enigmatically, making it all the more difficult for us to process its impact; after all, as Freud already understood, it is hard to process—work through—what we cannot name. Equally problematically, silence isolates us from others, depoliticizing traumas, such as rape, that are intensely political.

Brison reports that hearing other women's rape narratives in her survivors' support group was what allowed her to get angry at her assailant. Like many rape survivors, Brison was initially unable to feel anger toward her rapist. But listening to the stories of other women–women who had also been brutalized and who had, like she, thought they would die—made her so angry at *their* assailants that she was eventually able to see that she, also, had the right to feel rage at her own. In this sense, the memories of other women were essential for her own recovery. Yet the pressure on rape survivors to forget about their experiences is strong, not just because of the stigma attached to rape, but because benevolent onlookers assume that dwelling on what has happened is counterproductive. Brison recalls that her French lawyer said to her: "When the trial is over, you must forget that this ever happened."[41] When she protested that she probably would not be able to, he insisted, "But, *Madame*, you must make an effort."[42] Likewise, after Brison published an article on sexual violence three years after the assault, a well-meaning colleague said to her: "Now you can put this behind you."[43] Brison remarks that not only can she (obviously) not put the assault behind herself but that doing so would turn it into "an isolated event, of concern only to me."[44] That is, forgetting would depoliticize the event, translating-it into a "mere" individual trauma: a matter of bad luck rather than a symptom of systematic heteropatriarchal violence against women. Against this backdrop, Brison concludes that countering the injunction "to forget is the political necessity to bear witness to the injustice of sexual violence."[45]

We are familiar with the notion that remembering traumatic experiences is a political act, particularly in the context of collective traumas, such as slavery, the Holocaust, and more recent genocides. Though Nietzsche[46] may be right in suggesting that an excess of memory can sometimes be paralyzing, impeding the emergence of new modalities of life, of new passions, possibilities, and preoccupations,[47] there is also a great deal to be said for the idea that the commemoration of collective traumas—through public acts of grieving, official apologies and attempts at restoration, museums, monuments, and various artistic interventions, and so on—is both ethically necessary and socially curative. After all, the impulse to let sociopolitical atrocities fall into oblivion, or even to deliberately hide them, can be strong, particularly among those who are responsible for them. Furthermore, acts of remembrance are a means of honoring those who have suffered, of transmitting traumatic memory from one generation to the next, of building community and solidarity, and of making political statements about history, power, and oppression. In such contexts, forgetting would be ethically compromising, even indecent.

Brison emphasizes that, from the perspective of the survivor, the sharing of memories is important because it reintegrates the survivor into a community, thereby allowing her to "be reconnected with humanity."[48] This is a powerful reminder that Butler's tendency to see the other as inherently persecuting can be misleading, limiting our capacity to see the other as a potential source of support. Furthermore, Butler's view of the other as persecuting is directly related to her resistance to normative limits: if the other is intrinsically persecuting, if there is no other who inhabits the world in nonpersecuting ways, then I cannot condemn the other for being that way. That is, admitting that others are not invariably persecuting would force Butler to acknowledge that there are times when *some* others deserve our condemnation. This would, in turn, require the further admission that human beings have agency, and this is Butler's biggest stumbling block, the one thing she does not seem to be willing to grant because this would, in her opinion, lead her back to the sovereign Enlightenment subject, or at the very least to this subject's contemporary avatar: the narcissistic neoliberal subject. Yet it may well be that Butler's flight from a priori norms does not actually allow her to escape the latter, for the rejection of such norms could be argued to be a symptom of the very neoliberal capitalism that she denounces. After all, the narcissistic neoliberal subject, who is used to an endless array of existential possibilities, does not like limitations on its freedom, including its freedom to buy everything that a decent department store makes available. As a consequence, one could say that a priori norms "decenter"—interrupt—this subject to the same extent as the Levinasian-Butlerian other does by introducing within its being "alien" elements that it experiences as constraining. In this sense, a priori norms may war *against* the neoliberal capitalist ethos of unmitigated choice. This is one reason I believe that they are not a completely unreasonable alternative to the "anything goes" relativism that nibbles at the edges of Butlerian ethics and that, paradoxically enough, carries its own violence.

At a key point in *Giving an Account of Oneself*, Butler asks: "According to the kind of theory I have been pursuing, what will responsibility look like? Haven't we, by insisting on something non-narrativizable, limited the degree to which we might hold ourselves or others accountable for their actions? [...] Have we perhaps unwittingly destroyed the possibility of agency with all this talk about being given over, being structured, being addressed?"[49] My response to this is, "Yes, we have." Or, more precisely, *you*—Judith Butler—have. *I* am still doing my best to hold onto some agency. This does not mean that I am about to dust off the skeleton of the Enlightenment subject. I understand the problems—the ethical violence—that this subject represents. But I also think that, for many of us, the lived realities of subjectivity tend to be quite far from the hubris of this subject. Butler sometimes sounds as if she were conducting a witch hunt against enormous egos. But where exactly are these king-sized egos? My sense is that many of us are trying quite hard to scrape together a modicum of ego strength, a modicum of autonomy, a modicum of self-determination. And those of us—like Susan Brison—who have been severely traumatized are working overtime at this for the simple reason that our egos, autonomy, and self-determination have been violently stomped on. I do not think that an ethics of masochism would help them—would help any of us—lead more manageable lives. And it certainly does not do anything for our capacity to take responsibility for the pain that we may, often inadvertently, inflict on other.

NOTES

1. Susan J. Brison, *Aftermath: Violence and the Remaking of a Self* (Princeton: Princeton University Press, 2002), 111, 116.
2. Brison, 73.
3. *Ibid.*, 16.
4. Frantz Fanon, *The Wretched of the Earth*, trans. Constance Farrington (London: Penguin, 1961).
5. Judith Butler, *Parting Ways: Jewishness and the Critique of Zionism* (New York: Columbia University Press, 2012), 9.
6. Quoted in Judith Butler, *Giving an Account of Oneself* (New York: Fordham University Press, 2005), 32.
7. Judith Butler, *Frames of War: When Is Life Grievable?* (New York: Verso, 2010), 33.
8. Emmanuel Levinas, *Entre Nous: On Thinking-of-the-Other*, trans. Michael B. Smith and Barbara Harshav (New York: Columbia University Press, 1998), 202.
9. I discuss the matter in my latest book, *Between Levinas and Lacan: Self, Other, Ethics* (New York: Bloomsbury Press, 2015).
10. Butler, *Giving an Account*, 42.
11. *Ibid.*, 78–79.
12. *Ibid.*, 136.
13. I develop this argument in greater detail in my 2013 book *The Call of Character*.
14. Butler, *Giving an Account*, 45.
15. Judith Butler, *Precarious Life: The Powers of Mourning and Violence* (New York: Verso, 2004), 16.
16. Butler, *Parting Ways*, 59; emphasis added.
17. Butler, *Giving an Account*, 90.
18. *Ibid.*, 91.
19. *Ibid.*, 103.
20. Brison, *Aftermath*, 61.
21. Butler, *Precarious Life*, 26.
22. Butler, *Giving an Account*, 77.
23. Jessica Benjamin, *Like Subjects, Love Objects: Essays on Recognition and Sexual Difference* (New Haven: Yale University Press, 1995). Jessica Benjamin, *The Shadow of the Other: Intersubjectivity and Gender in Psychoanalysis* (New York: Routledge, 1998).
24. Brison, *Aftermath*, 40.
25. *Ibid.*, 61.
26. *Ibid.*
27. Amy Allen, *The Politics of Ourselves: Power, Autonomy, and Gender in Contemporary Critical Theory* (New York: Columbia University Press, 2008), 35.
28. Butler, *Giving an Account*, 46.
29. *Ibid.*, 45.
30. *Ibid.*, 49.
31. The possibility of a psychotic break of course cannot be dismissed, but this was was not Brison's impression of what happened, nor did the jury buy the "temporary insanity" plea.
32. Hannah Arendt, *Eichmann in Jerusalem: A Report on the Banality of Evil* (New York: Penguin, 1994).
33. Butler, *Parting Ways*, 171.
34. Slavoj Žižek, Eric L. Santner, and Kenneth Reinhard, "Neighbors and Other Monsters: A Plea for Ethical Violence," in *The Neighbor: Three Inquiries in Political Theology* (Chicago: University of Chicago Press, 2005), 137.
35. Butler, *Parting Ways*, 205.
36. *Ibid.*, 205–16.
37. Jacques Derrida, *Specters of Marx*, trans. Peggy Kamuf (New York: Routledge, 2006), 74.
38. Brison, *Aftermath*, 71.

39. *Ibid.*, 104.
40. *Ibid.*, 86.
41. *Ibid.*
42. *Ibid.*
43. Brison, *Aftermath*, 35.
44. *Ibid.*, 86.
45. *Ibid.*, 97.
46. Friedrich Nietzsche, *Unfashionable Observations*, trans. Richard T. Gray (Stanford: Stanford University Press, 1995).
47. See also Zupančič's analysis of Nietzsche in chapter 1 of *The Shortest Shadow*. Alenka Zupančič, *The Shortest Shadow: Nietzsche's Philosophy of the Two* (Cambridge, MA: MIT Press, 2003).
48. Brison, *Aftermath*, 71.
49. Butler, *Giving an Account*, 83, 99.

Feminist Reflections on Vulnerability

Disrespect, Obligation, Action

EWA PLONOWSKA ZIAREK

Political and Ethical Vulnerability: What's the Difference?

At least since the 1970s, vulnerability has emerged as a significant area of research in international social sciences. Combining sociology, studies of climate change, politics, and cultural geography, these interdisciplinary studies of vulnerability are concerned with the exposure of populations to natural, economic, and political disasters.[1] In the area of national defense, vulnerability means a failure of security, the exposure to or the risk of an attack by hostile forces or, recently, terrorism.[2] From natural disasters to political catastrophes, from economic/political disempowerment to the weakness of military defense, the patterns and the causes of vulnerability have to be measured, prevented, or at least managed in order to protect populations. Indeed, this is the goal of global vulnerability studies, whether located in academia or in political, national, or international organizations.[3] Since such studies aim to control and protect populations and natural environment across the globe, vulnerability thus conceived represents the expansion of biopolitics on the global scale. The protection of vulnerable people (the emblem of which are often racialized women and children) and nature always occurs in the name of security, which, according to Hardt and Negri, represents a constructive aspect of biopower and the new means of its legitimation.[4] Since the mobilization of the military or police power in the name of security requires a constant threat, the vulnerability of populations to internal or external dangers, from terrorism and the influx of illegal immigrants to drug wars, provides the means of such legitimation.

At the other end of the spectrum and no doubt connected to the security of populations as its "dialectical other," vulnerability occupies the self-help terrain. From books to talk shows, vulnerability signifies a risk that has to be managed by individuals themselves or is reclaimed as a new virtue to be cultivated.[5] As a moral virtue, vulnerability loses its negative connotations and becomes associated instead with empathy and the ability to connect with others—that is, with the capacities traditionally associated with middle-class white femininity. Thus the security of populations has its counterpart in individual morality, understood as either self-management or the cultivation of new virtues.

The central question I want to explore here is whether there can be a different discourse of vulnerability outside the hold of biopolitics, security, and self-management. Can vulnerability signify a different intersection between politics and ethics apart from risk management on a global or individual scale? Can it be mobilized by feminist politics and ethics? On the level of politics, vulnerability, I would like to propose, has two contradictory meanings, which are nonetheless connected. In feminist and anti-racist struggles, vulnerability is intertwined first of all with subjection to racist and sexist violence, with bodily injury and extreme destitution. In other words, it signifies the damaging and indeed disastrous effects of domination and power. Yet vulnerability also has a positive meaning: it can be reclaimed as a condition of intersubjective freedom, action, and political engagement. Consequently, what is opposed to violence and disaster is not personal or national security or risk management. On the contrary, the commitment to security perpetuates biopower, and thus compromises the conditions on which the practice of freedom itself depends. Thus, what I propose as an alternative to risk management is the struggle for more expansive notions of freedom and justice.

The main claim in this essay is that these two political meanings of vulnerability—the subjection to violation and the struggle for freedom—are interconnected with the third, ethical signification of vulnerability. By ethics, I do not mean privatized morality of "virtue," but, rather, I mean a specific understanding of ethics proposed by Emmanuel Levinas. According to Levinas's influential theory of responsibility, ethics shifts the concern from the subject's vulnerability to the plight of the other person. Such an ethics calls for responsibility for the other's exposure to violence and calls for vigilance against aggression that the other's fragility might provoke. Not opposed to political struggles for freedom, responsibility foregrounds what I will call an ethical vector of freedom. I will argue in this essay that, in order to avoid the charge of privatization, liberalism, or biopolitics, all three notions of vulnerability—the effects of domination, struggle for freedom, and ethical obligation—have to be taken into account by feminist analysis. As a political and an ethical issue, vulnerability calls not for increased security or more efficient risk management but, on the contrary, for the invention of more capacious political and ethical discourses and for engagement in political praxis.

Facing Violence: Vulnerability and Ethics

In her work on precariousness and vulnerability, Judith Butler draws on Levinas's ethical signification of the face of the other person. Butler turns to Levinas in order to elaborate a Jewish ethics of non-violence in her courageous political response to the Palestinian-Israeli conflict. As she argues, Levinas offers, "within a tradition of Jewish philosophy, an account of the relationship between violence and ethics that has some important implications for thinking through what an ethics of Jewish nonviolence might be."[6] For Butler, non-violent ethics is intertwined with "an apprehension of the precariousness of life, one that begins with the precarious life of the Other."[7] In Butler's elaboration, a Jewish ethics of non-violence calls for a political critique of violence and vigilance against aggression.

At the core of Levinas's ethics of non-violence is an ethical encounter with the face of the other who calls the subject to responsibility.[8] As I have suggested elsewhere, such an encounter has the status of an "anarchic," disruptive, and unforeseeable event, which befalls the subject prior to any decision or understanding on her part.[9] Irreducible to intentionality, obligation "traverses consciousness contrariwise inscribing itself there as something foreign, as disequilibrium, as delirium, undoing thematization, eluding *principle*, origin, and will. [...] This movement is [...] an-archic."[10] Ethical vulnerability in the case of obligation means an exposure to something foreign, rather than a commitment the subject assumes freely for herself. Manifesting itself as a disequilibrium, or even "delirium," such responsibility reveals the fact that ethical signification of alterity is not a relative term constituted within the differential network of power/knowledge but rather an excess, or transcendence, of differential relations. Consequently, the ethical "relation" to the Other is not a relation in the usual sense of the word; that is, it is neither a relation between already constituted identities nor a relation that constitutes these identities. On the contrary, the ethical encounter calls these identities into question. An ethical relation is therefore an event that manifests itself as a rupture rather than constitution, as a disturbance of both subjective identifications and discursive power relations. Such an unanticipated exposure, which disrupts our identity, makes us vulnerable to the core and at the same time responsible for the vulnerability of others.

What is striking in Levinas's analysis of the ethical signification of the face of the other person is not only the anarchical call of responsibility, but also the temptation to violence that it provokes. Butler is one of the first critics to point out that an ethics of non-violence worthy of its name has to take into account this temptation to harm the other, this aggression which arises out of the other's vulnerability. As Butler argues, "aggression is *not* eradicated in an ethics of nonviolence; aggression forms the incessant matter for ethical struggles."[11] The predominance of violence in contemporary Western societies, ranging from domestic violence, homophobic violence, racist violence, rape, and violence against immigrants to the "war on terror," makes the Levinasian conjunction between obligation, vulnerability, and violence an urgent ethical intervention. This co-implication between ethical vulnerability and violence has been missed by Levinas's previous interpreters, including Derrida's famous critique in "Violence and Metaphysics," who assume that the ethics of peace is opposed to all violence.[12]

To explain this paradoxical relation between responsibility, violence, and vulnerability, let us turn to Levinas's discussion of murder. Levinas argues that the double signification of the face, its sensible appearance in the world and its ethical expression of infinite obligation, makes it vulnerable to murderous violence, which changes the very notion of power. The appropriation of otherness through labor, representation, and even through the killing of animals both negates and preserves otherness in the system of human needs. By introducing the ethical dimension of infinity, only the face can provoke and prohibit murder, which aims at the total gratuitous annihilation of another person. Such a total obliteration of otherness exceeds any need or desire. Since only the face can provoke murder, it introduces and paralyzes the power of total destruction:

> [The face] modifies the very nature of power, which henceforth can no longer take, but can kill. [...] Murder alone lays claim to total negation. Negation by labor and usage, like negation by representation, effect a grasp or a comprehension, rest on or aim at affirmation; they can. To kill is not to dominate but to annihilate; it is to renounce comprehension absolutely. Murder exercises a power over what escapes power. It is still a power, for the face expresses itself in the sensible, but already impotency, because the face rends the sensible [...] I can wish to kill only an existent absolutely independent, which exceeds my powers infinitely, and therefore does not oppose them but paralyzes the very power of power.[13]

The ethical vulnerability of the face creates the vertigo between the provocation and the prohibition of murder. This vertigo does not mean that ethics can prevent violence; on the contrary, all too often the opposite is the case. Rather, the ethical impossibility means that murder always misses the face *qua* face, because the dead no longer have faces. As Jill Robbins points out, murder is "doomed to failure" because it aims at infinity and language but destroys the sensible appearance: "In this way, murder always misses its mark. No doubt it effects an annihilation of the other in his being. But it thereby misses the genuine alterity of the other, namely, that which in him goes beyond the sensible."[14] Murder turns a speaking face, as Levinas puts it, into a "mortuary mask."[15] Reduced to an inanimate object, such a mask no longer speaks; it no longer provokes or prohibits. It is in this sense that the ethical expression of the face provokes and paralyzes the power of total destruction.

There are urgent historical and philosophical reasons why Levinas confronts the possibility and the ethical prohibition of murder. The complicity of philosophy in the history of violence and war, culminating in the Holocaust and genocidal politics, motivates Levinas's turn to ethics as first philosophy. Philosophically, we can also hear in this analysis of murder the undertones of Levinas's polemics with Hegel's struggle to death in the Master/Slave dialectic. Levinas aims to show that both murder and its ethical impossibility exceed the struggle for recognition. Murder does not desire the Other's recognition but aims at the total destruction of infinity; while resistance to murder gives rise not to a struggle with the opponent but to the ethical expression: "thou shall not kill."

However, these political and philosophical critiques of violence do not quite answer the question of why the signification of the face provokes the temptation of murder in the first place. It is perhaps easier to understand why the ethical signification of the face prohibits murder. Although murder is the extreme manifestation of power over the other, it is nonetheless difficult to explain why it belongs to the *primordial* signification of the face, why language itself is born in this "vertigo," between the temptation and the impossibility of total annihilation? Why is "[t]he primordial signifyingness of the existent, its presentation in person or its expression [...] produced concretely as a temptation to total negation, and as the infinite resistance to murder"?[16] Is it the vulnerability of the other that provokes the desire to kill, or—vice-versa—is it the exposure to murder that constitutes the "quintessence" of vulnerability? Why is it the case, as Blanchot puts it, that before the other we are limited to "the speech/murder alternative"?[17] Is such an alternative explicable by the insurmountable tension between the finite sensible appearance and the infinite otherness of the face? Is it not equally plausible, as Irigaray argues, that prior to the murderous rejection or the ethical welcome of the other, infinite alterity provokes wonder, an affect that does not have an opposite and thus precedes the rejection/welcome, negation/generosity dualities?[18] If, following Irigaray, we accept that wonder precedes violence, then the temptation to murder no longer has a primordial character and the origin of such a temptation has to be accounted for.

At times Levinas suggests that provocation to violence occurs when the other is misperceived as an obstacle to my freedom, but in such a case the temptation to murder would belong to the motivations of the subject and not to the primordial ethical vulnerability of the face. Indeed, Butler herself seeks to explain the temptation to murder in terms of the anxiety that the otherness provokes in the subject: "Levinas considers the fear and anxiety that aggression seeks to quell, but argues that ethics is precisely a struggle to keep fear and anxiety from turning into murderous action."[19] Certainly, psychoanalysis from Freud to Lacan and Kristeva can provide different explanations of the subject's propensity to violence, ranging from the primordial aggression of the death drive, to the alienation of the imaginary ego in the mirror stage in which the other provides a specular image for the nascent self and alienates the ego in that image. The ontological status of the death drive, the ego's alienation in the mirror stage, or the sadistic severity of the super-ego are just a few psychoanalytic explanations of subjective aggression and its transformation either into violence or the sublimated negativity of language, critique, or art.

For Levinas, however, the ethical signification of the face exceeds both the ontological explanation and the subjective propensity to violence; the other's infinity is neither the imaginary image nor the ego's equivalent. The face, or what Levinas calls in his later work the trace of the other, exceeds ontology, including the ontological status of the death drive. It also calls into question the subject's capacity to signify and to represent, as if such capacities are not called for in the ethical relation. Rather, such capacities are secondary, arising from the response, from being called by the other to respond. Displaced from the initiative of the subject, violence and aggression are horrific forms that the response can take. Rather than offering reassurance, Levinas's analysis of vulnerability discloses, therefore, the vertigo between the possibility of total annihilation and obligation, between aggression and the ethics of non-violence.

Femininity and Ethical Disrespect

The oscillation between ethical obligation and the provocation to murder raises the question of whether some faces are more vulnerable to violence than others. In her reading of Levinas, Butler is very careful to take into account the fact that not every face—for example, the reified media images of Palestinians or Muslims, or the "liberated" faces of Afghan women disrobed from burkas on American media—inspires ethical obligations. How can such reification of the other be transformed into responsibility and justice? How can it lead to critique of the unjust social order? In a more obvious way, this unequal "distribution" of vulnerability and violence is a matter of politics and power. Paradoxically, such susceptibility to violence also depends on the performative force of obligation—that is, on the capacity of the face to call the subject to responsibility.

At first sight, the very claim that the face might be deprived of its ethical signification runs against the grain of Levinas's entire philosophy. Nonetheless, Levinas himself offers us a paradigmatic instance in which the face "inverts" its ethical signification and no longer utters the prohibition of murder. Such inversion characterizes femininity, which is *au delà du visage* (beyond the face). Though it maintains a negative reference to ethics, the face of the female lover in the heterosexual encounter is nonetheless beyond ethics proper. In this ambiguous position of female sexuality within and outside ethics, the phenomenological, cultural, and political levels of analysis are mixed together. Needless to say, this ambiguity of the feminine face has provoked numerous feminist critiques, from Simone de Beauvoir to Luce Irigaray, from Kelly Oliver to Tina Chanter.[20] In addition to the critiques of the exclusion of the feminine and sexuality from ethics, feminist readers, attentive to the ambiguities of Levinas's text, have pointed out that the "feminine" still performs the positive role of hospitality, welcome, and making the world habitable. What has not, however, received sufficient attention is the trope of inversion in Levinas's discussion of feminine vulnerability (*fragilité*).[21]

Let us look, therefore, more carefully at the inversion of the ethical obligation that the feminine performs. Levinas uses two different expressions for such inversion: *l'envers* and *à rebours*.[22] It is the second of these terms that has a more negative connotation since it is associated with decadence, falsity, and perversion, with something that goes against the natural or moral order of things, as the title of Huysmans's famous decadent novel *À Rebours* (*Against Nature*)[23] implies. In this inversion of the feminine face, ethical responsibility is transformed into "disrespect"; vulnerability into "disfigurement"; and the prohibition of murder into "non-signifyingness."[24] As Levinas puts it, the erotic "nudity" of the feminine

> is as it were an inverted signification, a signification that signifies falsely [...] an *expression that ceases to express itself*, that expresses its renunciation of expression and speech, that sinks into the equivocation of silence [...] The beloved is opposed to me not as a will struggling with my own [...] but on the contrary as an irresponsible animality [*animalité irresponsible*[25]] which does not speak true words. The beloved, returned to the stage of infancy without responsibility [...] *has quit her status as a person.*[26]

I want to read this and other similar passages against the grain (*á l'envers*), so to speak, as the diagnosis of the unequal distribution of the ethical, cultural, and political significance of vulnerability.[27]

What the trope of inversion raises here is the relation between vulnerability, silence, and sexual violence. If the feminine is deprived of speech, how can she say no to sexual violence, rape, and assault? How can her face signify, for example, the prohibition of rape? Why is the prohibition of rape not analyzed in tandem with the prohibition of murder? Levinas does not consider these questions because he does not interrogate the relation between ethics and sexual violence. Yet his own analysis of murder not only opens the possibility of such an inquiry, but makes it especially urgent for a feminist analysis of vulnerability.

Another question that Levinas's analysis provokes is whether the inversion of the feminine face is limited to gender and Eros, or whether it can also occur in other cases of "disrespected" or "feminized" faces whose fragility, instead of calling the subject to responsibility and political action, is deprived of the possibility of speech. If we accept the premise that there is no "inherent" connection between the feminine and disrespect—that this connection is cultural and political rather than ethical—then we have to account for a more generalized economy of "disrespect." What I want to propose is that in the context of political domination, vulnerability signifies ethical "disrespect" rather than responsibility. And this political inversion of obligation into disrespect means that ethics does not have the absolute primacy over politics, that ethics does not transcend power relations. The general economy of disrespect for subjugated others is characterized by two salient features. First, disrespect is intertwined with the silencing of the other—his or her speech is deprived of its performative force. In contrast to the prohibition of murder, disrespect does not paralyze power: we no longer experience the "vertigo" of the temptation and the impossibility of violence. On the contrary, disrespect appears to be eminently possible. And this possibility has disastrous political consequences. What, in the last resort, separates ethical disrespect from political contempt or aggression?

The second implication of disrespect is the kinship of the feminized face with animality. Despite the fact that it refers only to persons, disrespect transforms the very status of the human into the animal. Because of this kinship, both femininity and animality are excluded from ethics. In recent years, there has been a rigorous critique of the exclusion of the animal from ethics on the part of John Llewelyn,[28] Kelly Oliver,[29] Jacques Derrida,[30] and Georgio Agamben,[31] to name just a few interlocutors of Levinas on this issue. For example, Andrew Benjamin argues that the Levinasian rehabilitation of the other, which pertains only to inter-human relations, reproduces anthropocentrism—and we should say androcentrism—reinforced by the primacy of language.[32] Although numerous feminist critics of Levinas have questioned this negative association of femininity with the animal, what has not been interrogated are the ethical possibilities of the kinship between femininity and animality. Can we invert the Levinasian inversion once again, re-read the female/animal vulnerability against the grain of his text, deprive this kinship of its negative connotations, and approach it as an unexpected resource for a re-thinking of human/animal relations?

Within and Beyond Political Context

The unequal distribution of obligation, vulnerability, and domination across the political spectrum calls for a rigorous political analysis and critique of the political representations of the other. The possibility of such an analysis is already implied (though not fully developed) by Levinas's own emphasis on the double—ethical and historical/political—manifestation of the face. In *Totality and Infinity* such a double manifestation is articulated in terms of the tension between the ethical expression and the sensible appearance of the face, an appearance which, in "The Trace of the Other," becomes intertwined with historical, political, and cultural power relations. Consequently, political analysis of vulnerability depends on how one understands "the cultural context" and the historical world in which the face appears and which it disrupts: "The other is present in a cultural whole and is illuminated by this whole, like a text by its context. [...] His cultural signification is revealed and reveals as it were *horizontally*, on the basis of the historical world to which it belongs. [...] But this mundane signification is found to be disturbed and shaken by another presence, abstract, not integrated into the world."[33] Surely, the historical world to which the face "belongs" is constituted by the contingent and antagonist relations of power/knowledge. Levinas's scholars, however, have initially focused more attention on the way the anarchic signification of alterity disrupts cultural representations: as disequilibrium within the historical world, the trace of the other withdraws from the representation that manifests the face in political life. It is this disruptive ethical signification of alterity that calls the subject to responsibility. The focus on the anarchic disruption of the political is of course entirely warranted since it constitutes the most original contribution of Levinas's ethics. Nonetheless, for a feminist politics of vulnerability, the crucial implication of the disjunction between ethical alterity and the cultural signification of the face entails a rigorous critique of the political construction of the other within historical networks of power.

The politics of vulnerability, the concern with the other's exposure to subjugation and violence, demands an analysis not only of the "mundane"— that is, of political, institutionalized inequality—but also of the exclusion of the other from the historical world. One of the crucial contributions of feminist and postcolonial studies is to introduce the political meaning of otherness, most frequently associated with women, people of color, and colonized, subjugated subjectivities. Associated with subjugation rather than with ethical responsibility, the political signification of alterity is constituted by discursive power relations structuring hierarchies in the political world. In this context, the important task of the politics of vulnerability is to transform the institutional conditions of inequality and to demand equality and justice for those who have been so "othered." Yet, upon a closer analysis, the political category of "the other" is characterized by a crucial ambiguity, which complicates the political task of reclaiming equality for subjugated groups. Designating power hierarchy within the world, political otherness is in one sense a relative term, whose meaning is determined by its differentiation from the subjects who occupy positions of political power. Yet, in another sense, otherness signifies a more radical exclusion, or abjection, from the political world. Orlando Paterson's notion of social death,[34] Spivak's the subaltern,[35] and Agamben's bare life[36] are some of the terms that indicate extreme deracination and political vulnerability.[37] As Butler suggests, the expulsion of the other from the collective life is an effect of two different "forms of normative power: one operates through producing a symbolic identification of the face with the inhuman, foreclosing our apprehension of the human in the scene; the other works through radical effacement, so that there never was a human, there never was a life, and no murder has therefore ever taken place."[38] In such extreme cases, the other ceases to be human, because either its face becomes the hypervisible embodiment of evil,[39] or, on the contrary, it is radically excluded from the worldly domain of visibility.

This exclusion from the world and the exposure to violence, which political otherness designates, complicate Levinas's distinction between the political appearance of the face within the world and its ethical transcendence of the world. When political otherness is synonymous with exclusion, it calls into question the Levinasian notion of "belonging" to the historical world. Beings who are so "othered" are not necessarily illuminated by their historical context; on the contrary, they are rendered invisible, vulnerable, expelled from the realm of political subjects. Consequently, in place of Levinas's opposition between political representation of the other and the ethical face, I would like to propose the tension between the traces of those who are violently excluded from the world and the traces of ethical responsibility. In the last resort, the politics and ethics of vulnerability confront us not only with hierarchical power relations, but also with traces of what cannot be contained within these relations: the trace of the violent erasure of the other from the world versus the trace of the ethical signification that cannot be obliterated from the world. Can the indelible ethical trace prevent the total defacement or the invisibility of the other? Can the anarchical signification of the other as an ethical interlocutor disrupt power relations and obligate political agents to restructure the conditions of belonging to the historical world?

Vulnerability and Action

If vulnerability, understood in the sense of domination, calls for an urgent intervention, what kind of action and agency does it imply? As I have repeatedly argued, any contestation of political exclusion and domination has to be situated within the horizon of ethical responsibility. In other words, action can be motivated not only by one's own injury or by political convictions, but also by ethical responsibility for the other. Understood as a response rather than an initiative of a subject, action expands Levinas's argument that justice, solidarity, and the desire for a better society are inconceivable without the ethical "relation" to the other, who calls the subject to responsibility. Since for Levinas the ethical character of politics originates in responsibility for the other, action itself can be seen as a modality of response. Thus, to challenge domination it is necessary not only to reclaim subjecthood for the oppressed, but also to reclaim their ethical signification, which repositions them not merely as vulnerable, disrespected victims, but also as demanding and accusing interlocutors.

However, to reclaim the ethical signification of alterity, we need to diagnose and contest the systematic and politically motivated distribution of disrespect, which, as we have seen, deprives the other not only of her political status as a person, but also of her ethical significance as the source of obligation. What the category of disrespect shows is that the ethical encounter itself—its primordial and transcendent character—can nonetheless be "inverted" or even obliterated in situations of oppression—for example, in the context of so-called normal erotic heterosexual relations. Disrespect and its correlative—contempt—leave us with the conundrum of vulnerability: if political intervention has to acknowledge the "primacy" of ethical responsibility, such responsibility in turn might depend upon political praxis. This mutual codependency is not a vicious circle, but rather an enabling intersection between ethics and politics.

Yet what notion of political action and agency is presupposed by the interrelation between the ethics and the politics of vulnerability? Is not agency associated with resilience and strength rather than vulnerability or weakness? To indicate an outline of such praxis in a preliminary way, I propose to reinterpret Levinas's ethics in the context of Hannah Arendt's political theory.[40] At the core of Arendt's political work is the contingent, relational, and transformative character of political action. One of the most important preconditions of action is the heterogeneity and plurality of political agents: political engagement depends on the coming together of strangers. Although such plurality can be a target of violence or disciplinary power, it cannot be eradicated without the destruction of what Arendt calls the human condition itself. Despite its limitations (for instance, the separation between the private

and the political), Arendt's notion of praxis challenges not only liberal individualism, but also impersonal laws of history. Neither individualism nor
biopolitics can account for political transformations, because such transformations depend on intersubjective political movements.

Supported by democratic institutions, action presupposes the worldly
space of the "in-between" or the formation of the public. One crucial implication of feminist analysis of political "othering" is that the political spaces
of intersubjective participation are constituted by the multiple exclusions of
subjugated groups from the political domain, and perhaps even from ethics
itself. Nonetheless, as the history of political protests, marches, and struggles
shows us again and again, from the Arab Spring to Occupy Wall Street, marginalized groups can contest or occupy the public space in order to reconstruct it and change political relations. This is the implication of Arendt's
claim that action is fundamentally intertwined not only with the realization
of new political goals but with "world building capacity."[41] As a response to
exclusion from the political, such a "world building" capacity is one of the
crucial issues in feminist struggles with political exclusion. In a very suggestive formulation, Arendt argues that freedom in the positive and transformative sense reveals a political capacity to enact with others the "birth" of a
new world.[42] The political birth of a new world, or what Arendt famously
calls natality, not only implicitly inscribes the feminine inflection of agency
into the political, but also connects it with the most creative aspect of action,
rather than with procreation.

By underscoring plurality and the otherness of political agents, Arendt
provides an enabling intersubjective theory of collective action without pre-
supposing subjective agency, identity, or common interests. This approach
is especially important for feminist critiques of the subject, which, as Butler
points out, are often viewed as incapable of formulating a non-foundational
account of action. Arendt reverses the usual understanding of agency, according to which action realizes intentions of the subject. As she puts it, "nobody
is the author or producer" of action.[43] Thus, it is not agency that "produces"
action, but, on the contrary, it is action that discloses intersubjective agency
for the first time. And what the performative praxis reveals is not identity,
but the uniqueness and plurality of political agents. The first important consequence of this reversal is that agency is irreducible to strength that can be
possessed or identity that can be known—it is neither sovereignty nor knowledge. The second consequence is that agency does not exist in isolation, but
emerges from our relations with others. And finally, intersubjective agency
means that every agent is at the same time an actor and a passive "sufferer,"
that she affects and is being affected by others: "to do and to suffer are like
opposite sides of the same coin."[44] Thus, action acts upon the agent who in
turn responds to others, and such response constitutes a new action.

It is this fundamental shift from the pre-existing identity/agency of the subject to acting with and being affected by others that enables a certain *rapprochement* between the politics and the ethics of vulnerability. In both cases the uniqueness of the subject is derived from the exposure to others. If the ethics of responsibility is based on the face-to-face encounter, action is based on multiple engagements with others, on the creation of alliances among strangers.[45] Furthermore, like Levinas's analysis of ethical obligation, Arendt's approach to action and intersubjective agency underscores the profound vulnerability of democratic politics. Why this fragility? The greatest vulnerability of intersubjective agency is of course that it will be diminished with the dispersal of the group. Since agency is created through praxis, human capacities depend on the relations with strangers coming together "for the purpose of action," and they disappear "when, for whatever reason, [the participants] disperse."[46] Since agency cannot endure apart from human togetherness, it can be dispersed by brutal violence, as we witness it right now in Syria, or dissipated from within when the participants become disappointed or driven apart by internal conflicts. Conflict, therefore, or what I call in my work dissensus, is another manifestation of the instability of action, even though it is also its condition of possibility. Another way the instability of action manifests itself lies in the obscurity of political motivations. Once we depart from the premise of the self-grounding political subject, we have to accept that actors not only do not know others with whom they act, but, as Arendt insists, they do not know themselves—their motivations are like "demons" or "dark oracles," more visible to others than to themselves.

Since action is distinct from economic production, it is vulnerable because it lacks the support and durability of material objects. The effects of action are not commodities—which can be produced, consumed, or stored— but human relations. Thus, since its only "material mediums" are language, interhuman relations, and memory, action might not endure in history, even if the transformation of political relations is encoded in institutions and legislation. Furthermore, action does not have a quantifiable dimension: it is not measurable strength, applicable force, or a predictable law of history. On the contrary, the open-ended and dynamic process of action is characterized by the unpredictability and the uncertainty of outcomes. As we can see in the historical election and re-election of President Obama, despite CNN's "magic wall," statistical analyses, and the obscene influence of money, political engagement is unpredictable: its results are always "too close to call." And once the political process becomes predictable, it is no longer action.

In the traditional language of political philosophy, such fragility is expressed in terms of the contingency of institutions and power relations. Yet, in Arendt's analysis, contingency characterizes not only constituted power, but action itself (that is, the constituting intersubjective power). One may wonder how action is possible under these conditions at all. According to Arendt, what enables action despite the frailty and the unpredictability of human interactions is the alliance based on mutual promises. Promise is the only force that can create a sense of togetherness while respecting the plurality and divergence of the participants. It is promise, rather than sovereignty or a "magically" unified common body,[47] that gathers together diverse participants for the purpose of action. The performative force of promise creates alliances even though we do not know ourselves or the consequences of our actions. Since such alliances are based on the performative power of the address and language, promise is the very antithesis of disrespect and silencing. Since it provides an alternative to the usual binaries of political thought— to the oppositions between sovereignty and powerlessness, mastery and anarchy, knowledge and relativism—promise contests the notion of power based on the domination of oneself and others as well as its opposite—the total dissolution of social bonds. By gathering strangers together for the purpose of action, promise is merely "a guidepost" in "an ocean of uncertainty."[48] Once it is transformed into predictability and security—and Nietzsche has taught us the cost of such transformation[49]—promise becomes self-defeating.

In the history of political thought, the political vocabulary of promise has been incorporated into contract theory. The force of promises, however, is fundamentally different from that of contracts, which are based on the notion of equivalent economic exchange and the calculation of common interests. Well ahead of Foucault, Arendt is adamant that politics is irreducible to the economic model of exchange and production. Consequently, it is important to distinguish between contractual obligations, which are economic in nature and thus calculable, and the ethical responsibility characteristic of the incalculable promise. As Arendt suggests, promise reveals an ethical dimension, which arises from action itself and is not imposed on political engagement by external morals.[50] To distinguish the ethical dimension of politics from contractual exchange, I would argue that promises are intertwined with ethical responsibility in the Levinasian sense of the word. Promises obligate participants to each other: such bonds of obligation are not an expression of subjective initiative (just as agency is not reducible to initiative) but rather a political modality of responsibility for others and for the common world in which we live. For instance, when I find myself obligated to oppose racism, Anti-Semitism, homophobia, or trans-gender violence, this responsibility is not my initiative, but a response to encounters with others and with the history of oppression, which destroys human plurality and uniqueness. Thus, if, as I have argued, ethics does not have the absolute priority over political engagement, activism in turn presupposes ethical responsibility to others.

The main point I want to make is that the political and ethical vulnerability of action enables rather than impairs its transformative possibilities. Insofar as it implies contingency, being with others, and unpredictability, vulnerability—rather than security—is a paradoxical condition of political transformation. Consequently, vulnerability is not a weakness to be eliminated or managed in the name of security because, as Arendt puts it, it is a "price" of mundane freedom. In fact, all the characteristics of vulnerability pertaining to action are also the conditions of intersubjective agency and political change. Forming alliances with others is what creates new capacities of political agents and new forms of political life. In contrast to political theories of contract or sovereignty, which equalize or diminish agency, praxis augments human capacities, and in so doing it creates new possibilities in political life. What is particularly promising in such a theory of praxis is that vulnerability of social relations enables the creation of a new beginning in history. Indeed, the unpredictability and fragility of action is the other side of such a beginning. As Arendt writes, though we are mortal, we "are not born in order to die, but in order to begin."[51] This is the case because action is the only activity that can interrupt natural and historical causality: "action, seen from the viewpoint of the automatic processes which seemed to determine the course of the world, looks like a miracle. In the language of natural science, it is the 'infinite improbability which occurs regularly.'"[52]

Although vulnerability can be an effect of domination, sexual violence, and othering, insofar as it is intertwined with transformative praxis, it also opens the possibility of freedom. To put it a different way, what the analysis of vulnerability shows us is that obligation and freedom are mutually intertwined. Freedom in this context is neither the property nor the capacity of the isolated subject, but is fundamentally relational, contingent, and created by acting with others. Furthermore, political freedom in the contingent historical world is different from liberation, even though liberation is its necessary precondition. As Arendt argues, liberation is primarily negative—it is associated with resistance, that is, with the struggle to end oppression or exclusion from polis—while freedom is positive, implying a creation of new political arrangements and new creative capacities. And since such freedom is created by acting and responding to others, it is not opposed to ethical obligation, but emerges from intersubjective promises and responsibilities.

In my exploration of vulnerability outside the parameters of biopolitics, which is focused on the security of populations, and liberal individualism, which is concerned with self-management, I have explored the possible intersections between Levinas's ethics and feminist politics. These intersections pose new tasks for feminist analysis of vulnerability—namely, how to restore the ethical signification for disrespected, feminized others, and how to contest the political exclusions of subjugated groups from the realm of politics. Ultimately, what I propose in response to these questions is that the intersubjective capacity to create a new world is the indispensable counterpart of any attempt to theorize an ethics or a politics of vulnerability. Both of these inter-subjective modalities of vulnerability—the unpredictable creation of a new political world and the obligation to others—exceed the agency of the indi-vidual or collective subject, without plunging us into political powerlessness. Although at first glance this configuration of vulnerability, obligation, and intersubjective freedom might seem contradictory, it in fact cuts across the binary oppositions structuring most approaches to politics: power/weakness, violence/security, agency/passivity, vulnerability/resilience. It is only by link-ing vulnerability with both ethical obligation and political action that we can move beyond the two dominant discourses of vulnerability—the risk man-agement of populations and the self-management of the liberal subject. The first of these approaches treats population as the passive target of biopower; the second one locates all the initiative in the individual. Although respon-sible praxis takes risk prevention and protection seriously, it replaces the ethos of security with intersubjective engagement.

NOTES

1. One of the indications of how established vulnerability studies has become is a detailed entry devoted to different methodologies of vulnerability on Wikipedia. See in par-ticular the article on "Social Vulnerability," which defines social vulnerability as "the inability of people, organizations, and societies to withstand adverse impacts from multiple stressors to which they are exposed." For sociological accounts of vulnerability, see, for example, Anthony Oliver-Smith, "Theorizing Disasters: Nature, Power and Culture," in *Catastrophe and Culture: The Anthropology of Disaster*, ed. Susan M. Hoffman and Anthony Oliver Smith; Koko Warner, and Thomas Loster, *A Research and Action Agenda for Social Vulnerability*. United Nations University Institute of Environment and Human Security. 24 Jun. 2011; Michael J. Watts and Hans. G. Bohle, "The Space of Vulnerability: The Causal Structure of Hunger and Famine," *Progress in Human Geography* 17, no. 1 (1993): 43–67; and Ben Wisner, et al., *At Risk: Natural Hazards, People's Vulnerability and Disasters*, 2nd ed. (London: Rout-ledge, 2004).

2. See the "National Vulnerability Database" website which "is the U.S. government repository of standards based vulnerability management data" that "enables automation of vulnerability management, security measurement, and compliance." See also the *Social Vul-nerability Index for the United States* website.

3. For examples of academic institutes devoted to vulnerability, see the Hazard Reduc-tion and Recovery Center of Texas A&M University, the Hazards and Vulnerability Research Institute of the University of South Carolina, and the United Nations University's Institute for Environment and Human Security.

4. Michael Hardt and Antonio Negri, *Multitude: War and Democracy in the Age of the Empire* (London: Penguin, 2004), 18–31.

5. For example, Brené Brown, "The Power of Vulnerability," TEDTalks, Jun. 2010.

6. Judith Butler, *Precarious Life: The Powers of Mourning and Violence* (London: Verso, 2006), 140.

7. *Ibid.*, xvii–xviii.

8. For an excellent discussion of Levinas's responsibility in the postcolonial context, see Simone Drichel, "Disgrace," in *Companion to the Works of J.M. Coetzee*, ed. Tim Mehigan (Rochester: Camden House, 2011), 148–71.

9. See my *Ethics of Dissensus* and "Dissensus, Ethics, and the Politics of Democracy."

10. Emmanuel Levinas, "Substitution," in *Emmanuel Levinas: Basic Philosophical Writings*, ed. Adriaan Peperzak, Simon Critchley, and Robert Bernasconi (Bloomington: Indiana University Press, 1996), 81.

11. Butler, *Precarious Life*, xviii.

12. An important exception here is Jill Robbins's analysis of murder in *Totality and Infinity* in *Altered Reading: Levinas and Literature* (Chicago: University of Chicago Press, 1999), 64–69. Jacques Derrida, "Violence and Metaphysics: An Essay on the Thought of Emmanuel Levinas." *Writing and Difference*. Trans. Alan Bass (Chicago: University of Chicago Press, 73–153.

13. Emmanuel Levinas, *Totality and Infinity* (Pittsburgh: Duquesne University Press, 1969), 198.

14. Robbins, *Altered Reading*, 10.

15. Levinas, *Totality and Infinity*, 262.

16. Levinas, *Totality and Infinity*, 262.

17. Maurice Blanchot, *The Infinite Conversation*, trans. Susan Hanson (Minneapolis: University of Minnesota Press, 1993), 62.

18. Luce Irigaray, *An Ethics of Sexual Difference*, trans. Carolyn Burke and Gillian C. Gill (Ithaca: Cornell University Press, 1993), 12–13.

19. Butler, *Precarious Life*, xviii.

20. For the most comprehensive volume collecting for the first time feminist engagements with Levinas, see Tina Chanter, ed, *Feminist Interpretations of Emmanuel Levinas* (University Park: Pennsylvania State University Press, 2001).

21. Emmanuel Levinas, *Totalité et infini: Essai sur l'exteriorite* (The Hague: Martinus Nijhoff, 1984), 233.

22. *Ibid.*, 241.

23. Joris-Karl Huysmans, *À Rebours*. (Paris: G. Charpentier, 1884).

24. Levinas, *Totality and Infinity*, 262.

25. *Ibid..* 241

26. *Ibid.*, 263; emphases added.

27. As Chanter argues, feminist readers often have to read Levinas faithfully and unfaithfully, in order to diagnose the limits of his thought and ask "what is foreclosed" from his analysis ("Introduction" 6).

28. John Llewellyn, "Am I Obsessed by Bobby? (Humanism of the Other Animal)," in *Re-Reading Levinas* (Bloomington: Indiana University Press, 1991), 234–45.

29. Kelly Oliver, *Animal Lessons: How They Teach Us to Be Human* (New York: Columbia University Press, 2009).

30. Jacques Derrida, *The Beast and the Sovereign*, ed. Michel Lisse, Marie-Louise Mallet, and Ginette Michaud, trans. Geoffrey Bennington (Chicago: University of Chicago Press, 2009).

31. Giorgio Agamben, *The Open: Man and Animal*, trans. Kevin Attell (Stanford: Stanford University Press, 2003).

32. Andrew Benjamin, *Of Jews and Animals* (Edinburgh: Edinburgh University Press, 2010), 95.

33. Emmanuel Levinas, "The Trace of the Other," in *Deconstruction in Context: Literature and Philosophy*, trans. Alphonso Lingis, ed. Mark C. Taylor (Chicago: University of Chicago Press, 1986), 351.

34. Orlando Paterson, *Slavery and Social Death: A Comparative Study* (Cambridge: Harvard University Press, 1985).

35. Gayatri Chakravorty Spivak, "Can the Subaltern Speak?" in *Marxism and the Interpretation of Culture*, ed. Cary Nelson and Lawrence Grossberg (Urbana: University of Illinois Press, 1988), 271–313.

36. Giorgio Agamben, *Homo Sacer: Sovereign Power and Bare Life*, trans. Daniel Heller-Roazen (Stanford: Stanford University Press, 1998).

37. See Paterson; Spivak; Agamben, *Homo Sacer*. For my discussion of the vulnerability of bare life, see Ewa Plonowska Ziarek, "Bare Life on Strike: Notes on the Biopolitics of Race and Gender," *South Atlantic Quarterly* 107, no.1 (2008): 89–105.

38. Butler, 147. The extreme vulnerability of bare life, according to Agamben, is its exposure to unlimited violence that does not even count as a crime.

39. As Butler argues, the reification of the other as absolute evil "efface[s] what is most human about the 'face' for Levinas," that is, its precariousness (xviii).

40. Arendt's political philosophy has attracted the renewed attention of feminist scholars. See, for instance, Seyla Benhabib, *The Reluctant Modernism of Hannah Arendt* (Lanham: Rowman and Littlefield, 2003) and Peg Birmingham, *Hannah Arendt and Human Rights: The Predicament of Common Responsibility* (Bloomington: Indiana University Press, 2007).

41. Hannah Arendt, *On Revolution* (London: Penguin, 1990), 175.

42. *Ibid.*, 42.

43. Hannah Arendt, *The Human Condition* (Chicago: University of Chicago Press, 1998), 184.

44. *Ibid.*, 190.

45. Because they are characterized by plurality, such alliances cannot be unified by Levinas's notion of the Third, the other Other, who enables a transition from the dual ethical relation to political justice for all.

46. Arendt, *On Revolution*, 175. Additionally, for Arendt's discussion of political action, see *The Human Condition*, 175–245.

47. Arendt, *The Human Condition*, 245.

48. *Ibid.*

49. Arendt herself refers to Nietzsche's analysis of promise, but criticizes him for aligning promise with the will to power of the isolated subject (*Human Condition*, 245).

50. Arendt, *The Human Condition*, 246.

51. *Ibid.*

52. *Ibid.*

SECTION 2

States of Exception

From "Right of Death and Power over Life"

Michel Foucault

For a long time, one of the characteristic privileges of sovereign power was the right to decide life and death. In a formal sense, it derived no doubt from the ancient *patria potestas* that granted the father of the Roman family the right to "dispose" of the life of his children and his slaves; just as he had given them life, so he could take it away. By the time the right of life and death was framed by the classical theoreticians, it was in a considerably diminished form. It was no longer considered that this power of the sovereign over his subjects could be exercised in an absolute and unconditional way, but only in cases where the sovereign's very existence was in jeopardy: a sort of right of rejoinder. If he were threatened by external enemies who sought to overthrow him or contest his rights, he could then legitimately wage war, and require his subjects to take part in the defense of the state; without "directly proposing their death," he was empowered to "expose their life": in this sense, he wielded an "indirect" power over them of life and death.[1] But if someone dared to rise up against him and transgress his laws, then he could exercise a direct power over the offender's life: as punishment, the latter would be put to death. Viewed in this way, the power of life and death was not an absolute privilege: it was conditioned by the defense of the sovereign, and his own survival. Must we follow Hobbes in seeing it as the transfer to the prince of the natural right possessed by every individual to defend his life even if this meant the death of others? Or should it be regarded as a specific right that was manifested with the formation of that new juridical being, the sovereign?[2] In any case, in its modern form—relative and limited—as in its ancient and absolute form, the right of life and death is a dissymmetrical one. The sovereign exercised his right of life only by exercising his right to kill, or by refraining from killing; he evidenced his power over life only

93

through the death he was capable of requiring. The right which was formulated as the "power of life and death" was in reality the right to *take* life or *let* live. Its symbol, after all, was the sword. Perhaps this juridical form must be referred to a historical type of society in which power was exercised mainly as a means of deduction (*prélèvement*), a subtraction mechanism, a right to appropriate a portion of the wealth, a tax of products, goods and services, labor and blood, levied on the subjects. Power in this instance was essentially a right of seizure: of things, time, bodies, and ultimately life itself; it culminated in the privilege to seize hold of life in order to suppress it.

Since the classical age the West has undergone a very profound transformation of these mechanisms of power. "Deduction" has tended to be no longer the major form of power but merely one element among others, working to incite, reinforce, control, monitor, optimize, and organize the forces under it: a power bent on generating forces, making them grow, and ordering them, rather than one dedicated to impeding them, making them submit, or destroying them. There has been a parallel shift in the right of death, or at least a tendency to align itself with the exigencies of a life-administering power and to define itself accordingly. This death that was based on the right of the sovereign is now manifested as simply the reverse of the right of the social body to ensure, maintain, or develop its life. Yet wars were never as bloody as they have been since the nineteenth century, and all things being equal, never before did regimes visit such holocausts on their own populations. But this formidable power of death—and this is perhaps what accounts for part of its force and the cynicism with which it has so greatly expanded its limits—now presents itself as the counterpart of a power that exerts a positive influence on life, that endeavors to administer, optimize, and multiply it, subjecting it to precise controls and comprehensive regulations. Wars are no longer waged in the name of a sovereign who must be defended; they are waged on behalf of the existence of everyone; entire populations are mobilized for the purpose of wholesale slaughter in the name of life necessity: massacres have become vital. It is as managers of life and survival, of bodies and the race, that so many regimes have been able to wage so many wars, causing so many men to be killed. And through a turn that closes the circle, as the technology of wars has caused them to tend increasingly toward all-out destruction, the decision that initiates them and the one that terminates them are in fact increasingly informed by the naked question of survival. The atomic situation is now at the end point of this process: the power to expose a whole population to death is the underside of the power to guarantee an individual's continued existence. The principle underlying the tactics of battle—that one has to be capable of killing in order to go on living—has become the principle that defines the strategy of states. But the existence in question is no longer the juridical existence of sovereignty; at stake is the biological existence of a population. If genocide is indeed the dream of modern powers, this is not because of a recent return of the ancient right to kill; it is because power is situated and exercised at the level of life, the species, the race, and the large-scale phenomena of population.

On another level, I might have taken up the example of the death penalty. Together with war, it was for a long time the other form of the right of the sword; it constituted the reply of the sovereign to those who attacked his will, his law, or his person. Those who died on the scaffold became fewer and fewer, in contrast to those who died in wars. But it was for the same reasons that the latter became more numerous and the former more and more rare. As soon as power gave itself the function of administering life, its reason for being and the logic of its exercise—and not the awakening of humanitarian feelings—made it more and more difficult to apply the death penalty. How could power exercise its highest prerogatives by putting people to death, when its main role was to ensure, sustain, and multiply life, to put this life in order? For such a power, execution was at the same time a limit, a scandal, and a contradiction. Hence capital punishment could not be maintained except by invoking less the enormity of the crime itself than the monstrosity of the criminal, his incorrigibility, and the safeguard of society. One had the right to kill those who represented a kind of biological danger to others.

One might say that the ancient right to *take* life or *let* live was replaced by a power to *foster* life or *disallow* it to the point of death. This is perhaps what explains that disqualification of death which marks the recent wane of the rituals that accompanied it. That death is so carefully evaded is linked less to a new anxiety which makes death unbearable for our societies than to the face that the procedures of power have not ceased to turn away from death. In the passage from this world to the other, death was the manner in which a terrestrial sovereignty; the pageantry that surrounded it was in the category of political ceremony. Now it is over life, throughout its unfolding, that power establishes its dominion; death is power's limit, the moment that escapes it; death becomes the most secret aspect of existence, the most "private." It is not surprising that suicide—once a crime, since it was a way to usurp the power of death which the sovereign alone, whether the one here below or the Lord above, had the right to exercise—became, in the course of the nineteenth century, one of the first conducts to enter into the sphere of sociological analysis; it testified to the individual and private right to die, at the borders and in the interstices of power that was exercised over life. This determination to die, strange and yet so persistent and constant in its manifestations, and consequently so difficult to explain as being due to particular circumstances or individual accidents, was one of the first astonishments of a society in which political power had assigned itself the task of administering life.

In concrete terms, starting in the seventeenth century, this power over life evolved in two basic forms; these forms were not antithetical, however; they constituted rather two poles of development linked together by a whole intermediary cluster of relations. One of these poles—the first to be formed, it seems—centered on the body as a machine: its disciplining, the optimization of its capabilities, the extortion of its forces, the parallel increase of its usefulness and its docility, its integration into systems of efficient and economic controls, all this was ensured by the procedures of power that characterized the *disciplines*: an *anatomo-politics of the human body*. The second, formed somewhat later, focused on the species body, the body imbued with the mechanics of life and serving as the basis of the biological processes: propagation, births and mortality, the level of health, life expectancy and longevity, with all the conditions that can cause these to vary. Their supervision was effected through an entire series of interventions and *regulatory controls: a biopolitics of the population*. The disciplines of the body and the regulations of the population constituted the two poles around which the organization of power over life was deployed. The setting up, in the course of the classical age, of this great polar technology—anatomic and biological, individualizing and specifying, directed toward the performances of the body, with attention to the processes of life—characterized a power whose highest function was perhaps no longer to kill, but to invest life through and through.

The old power of death that symbolized sovereign power was now carefully supplanted by the administration of bodies and the calculated management of life. During the classical period, there was a rapid development of various disciplines—universities, secondary schools, barracks, workshops; there was also the emergence, in the field of political practices and economic observation, of the problems of birthrate, longevity, public health, housing, and migration. Hence there was an explosion of numerous and diverse techniques for achieving the subjugation of bodies and the control of populations, marking the beginning of an era of "biopower." The two directions taken by its development still appeared to be clearly separate in the eighteenth century. With regard to discipline, this development was embodied in institutions such as the army and the schools, and in reflections on tactics, apprenticeship, education, and the nature of societies, ranging from the strictly military analyses of Marshal de Saxe to the political reveries of Guibert or Servan. As for population controls, one notes the emergence of demography, the evaluation of the relationship between resources and inhabitants, the constructing of tables analyzing wealth and its circulation: the work of Quesnay, Moheau, and Süssmilch. The philosophy of the "Ideologists," as a theory of ideas, signs, and the individual genesis of sensations, but also a theory of the social composition of interests—Ideology being a doctrine of apprenticeship, but also a doctrine of contracts and the regulated formation of the social body—no doubt constituted the abstract discourse in which one sought to coordinate these two techniques of power in order to construct a general theory of it. In point of fact, however, they were not to be joined at the level of a speculative discourse, but in the form of concrete arrangements (*agencements concrets*) that would go to make up the great technology of power in the nineteenth century: the deployment of sexuality would be one of them, and one of the most important.

This bio-power was without question an indispensable element in the development of capitalism; the latter would not have been possible without the controlled insertion of bodies into the machinery of production and the adjustment of the phenomena of population to economic processes. But this was not all it required; it also needed the growth of both these factors, their reinforcement as well as their availability and docility; it had to have methods of power capable of optimizing forces, aptitudes, and life in general without at the same time making them more difficult to govern. If the development of the great instruments of the state, as *institutions* of power, ensured the maintenance of production relations, the rudiments of anatomo- and bio-politics, created in the eighteenth century as *techniques* of power present at every level of the social body and utilized by very diverse institutions (the family and the army, schools and the police, individual medicine and the administration of collective bodies), operated in the sphere of economic processes, their development, and the forces working to sustain them. They also acted as factors of segregation and social hierarchization, exerting their influence on the respective forces of both these movements, guaranteeing relations of domination and effects of hegemony. The adjustment of the accumulation of men to that of capital, the joining of the growth of human groups to the expansion of productive forces and the differential allocation of profit, were made possible in part by the exercise of bio-power in its many forms and modes of application. The investment of the body, its valorization, and the distributive management of its forces were at the time indispensable.

One knows how many times the question has been raised concerning the role of an ascetic morality in the first formation of capitalism; but what occurred in the eighteenth century in some Western countries, an event bound up with the development of capitalism, was a different phenomenon having perhaps a wider impact than the new morality; this was nothing less than the entry of life into history, that is, the entry of phenomena peculiar to the life of the human species into the order of knowledge and power, into the sphere of political techniques. It is not a question of claiming that this was the moment when the first contact between life and history was brought about. On the contrary, the pressure exerted by the biological on the historical had remained very strong for thousands of years; epidemics and famine were the two great dramatic forms of this relationship that was always dominated by the menace of death. But through a circular process, the economic—and primarily agricultural—development of the eighteenth century, and an increase in productivity and resources even more rapid than the demographic growth it encouraged, allowed a measure of relief from these profound threats: despite some renewed outbreaks, the period of great ravages from starvation and plague had come to a close before the French Revolution; death was ceasing to torment life so directly. But at the same time, the development of the different fields of knowledge concerned with life in general, the improvement of agricultural techniques, and the observations and measures relative to man's life and survival contributed to this relaxation: a relative control over life averted some of the imminent risks of death. In the space for movement thus conquered, and broadening and organizing that space, methods of power and knowledge assumed responsibility for the life processes and undertook to control and modify them. Western man was gradually learning what it meant to be a living species in a living world, to have a body, conditions of existence, probabilities of life, an individual and collective welfare, forces that could be modified, and a space in which they could be distributed in an optimal manner. For the first time in history, no doubt, biological existence was reflected in political existence; the fact of living was no longer an accessible substrate that only emerged from time to time, amid the randomness of death and its fatality; part of it passed into knowledge's field of control and power's sphere of intervention. Power would no longer be dealing simply with legal subjects over whom the ultimate dominion was death, but with living beings, and the mastery it would be able to exercise over them would have to be applied at the level of life itself; it was the taking charge of life, more than the threat of death, that gave power its access even to the body. If one can apply the term *bio-history* to the pressures through which the movements of life and the processes of history interfere with one another, one would have to speak of *bio-power* to designate what brought life and its mechanisms into the realm of explicit calculations and made knowledge-power an agent of transformation of human life. It is not that life has been totally integrated into techniques that govern and administer it; it constantly escapes them. Outside the Western world, famine exists, on a greater scale than ever; and the biological risks confronting the species are perhaps greater, and certainly more serious, than before the birth of microbiology. But what might be called a society's "threshold of modernity" has been reached when the life of the species is wagered on its own political strategies. For millennia, man remained what he was for Aristotle: a living animal with the additional capacity for a political existence; modern man is an animal whose politics places his existence as a living being in question.

This transformation had considerable consequences. It would serve no purpose here to dwell on the rupture that occurred then in the pattern of scientific discourse and on the manner in which the twofold problematic of life and man disrupted and redistributed the order of the classical episteme. If the question of man was raised—insofar as he was a specific living being, and specifically related to other living beings—the reason for this is to be sought in the new mode of relation between history and life: in this dual position of life that placed it at the same time outside history, in its biological environment, and inside human historicity, penetrated by the latter's techniques of knowledge and power. There is no need either to lay further stress on the proliferation of political technologies that ensued, investing the body, health, modes of subsistence and habitation, living conditions, the whole space of existence.

Another consequence of this development of bio-power was the growing importance assumed by the action of the norm, at the expense of the juridical system of the law. Law cannot help but be armed, and its arm, *par excellence*, is death; to those who transgress it, it replies, at least as a last resort, with that absolute menace. The law always refers to the sword. But a power whose task it is to take charge of life needs continuous regulatory and corrective mechanisms. It is no longer a matter of bringing death into play in the field of sovereignty, but of distributing the living in the domain of value and utility. Such a power has to qualify, measure, appraise, and hierarchize, rather than display itself in its murderous splendor; it does not have to draw the line that separates the enemies of the sovereign from his obedient subjects; it effects distributions around the norm. I do not mean to say that the law fades into the background or that the institutions of justice tend to disappear, but rather that the law operates more and more as a norm, and that the judicial institution is increasingly incorporated into a continuum of apparatuses (medical, administrative, and so on) whose functions are for the most part regulatory. A normalizing society is the historical outcome of a technology of power centered on life. We have entered a phase of juridical regression in comparison with the pre-seventeenth-century societies we are acquainted with; we should not be deceived by all the Constitutions framed throughout the world since the French Revolution, the Codes written and revised, a whole continual and clamorous legislative activity: these were the forms that made an essentially normalizing power acceptable.

Moreover, against this power that was still new in the nineteenth century, the forces that resisted relied for support on the very thing it invested, that is, on life and man as a living being. Since the last century, the great struggles that have challenged the general system of power were not guided by the belief in a return to former rights, or by the age-old dream of a cycle of time or a Golden Age. One no longer aspired toward the coming of the emperor of the poor, or the kingdom of the latter days, or even the restoration of our imagined ancestral rights; what was demanded and what served as an objective was life, understood as the basic needs, man's concrete essence, the realization of his potential, a plenitude of the possible. Whether or not it was Utopia that was wanted is of little importance; what we have seen has been a very real process of struggle; life as a political object was in a sense taken at face value and turned back against the system that was bent on controlling it. It was life more than the law that became the issue of political struggles, even if the latter were formulated through affirmations concerning rights. The "right" to life, to one's body, to health, to happiness, to the satisfaction of needs, and beyond all the oppressions or "alienations," the "right" to rediscover what one is and all that one can be, this "right"—which the classical juridical system was utterly incapable of comprehending—was the political response to all these new procedures of power which did not derive, either, from the traditional right of sovereignty.

[...]

NOTES

1. Samuel von Pufendorf, *Le Droit de la nature* (French trans., 1734), 445.

2. "Just as the composite body can have properties not found in any of the simple bodies of which the mixture consists, so a moral body, by virtue of the very union of persons of which it is composed, can have certain rights which none of the individuals could expressly claim and whose exercise is the proper function of leaders alone." *Ibid.*, 452.

Introduction to *Homo Sacer*

GIORGIO AGAMBEN

The Greeks had no single term to express what we mean by the word "life." They used two terms that, although traceable to a common etymological root, are semantically and morphologically distinct: *zoē*, which expressed the simple fact of living common to all living beings (animals, men, or gods), and *bios*, which indicated the form or way of living proper to an individual or a group. When Plato mentions three kinds of life in the *Philebus*, and when Aristotle distinguishes the contemplative life of the philosopher (*bios theōrētikos*) from the life of pleasure (*bios apolaustikos*) and the political life (*bios politikos*) in the *Nichomachean Ethics*, neither philosopher would ever have used the term *zoē* (which in Greek, significantly enough, lacks a plural). This follows from the simple fact that what was at issue for both thinkers was not at all simple natural life but rather a qualified life, a particular way of life. Concerning God, Aristotle can certainly speak of a *zoē aristē kai aidios*, a more noble and eternal life,[1] but only insofar as he means to underline the significant truth that even God is a living being (similarly, Aristotle uses the term *zoē* in the same context—and in a way that is just as meaningful—to define the act of thinking). But to speak of a *zoē politikē* of the citizens of Athens would have made no sense. Not that the classical world had no familiarity with the idea that natural life, simple *zoē* as such, could be a good in itself. In a passage of the *Politics*, after noting that the end of the city is life according to the good, Aristotle expresses his awareness of that idea with the most perfect lucidity:

> This [life according to the good] is the greatest end both in common for all men and for each man separately. But men also come together and maintain the political community in view of simple living, because there is probably some kind of good in the mere fact of living itself [*kata to zēn auto monon*]. If there is no great difficulty as to the way of life [*kata ton bion*], clearly most men will tolerate much suffering and hold on to life [*zoē*] as if it were a kind of serenity [*euēmeria*, beautiful day] and a natural sweetness.[2]

101

In the classical world, however, simple natural life is excluded from the *polis* in the strict sense, and remains confined—as merely reproductive life— to the sphere of the *oikos*, "home."[3] At the beginning of the *Politics*, Aristotle takes the greatest care to distinguish the *oikonomos* (the head of an estate) and the *despotes* (the head of the family), both of whom are concerned with the reproduction and the subsistence of life, from the politician, and he scorns those who think the difference between the two is one of quantity and not of kind. And when Aristotle defined the end of the perfect community in a passage that was to become canonical for the political tradition of the West,[4] he did so precisely by opposing the simple fact of living (*to zēn*) to politically qualified life (*to eu zēn*): *ginomenē oun tou zēn heneken, ousa de tou eu zēn,* "born with regard to life, but existing essentially with regard to the good life" (in the Latin translation of William of Moerbeke, which both Aquinas and Marsilius of Padua had before them: *facta quidem igitur vivendi gratia, exis- tens autem gratia bene vivendi*).

It is true that in a famous passage of the same work, Aristotle defines man as a *politikon zōon*.[5] But here (aside from the fact that in Attic Greek the verb *bionai* is practically never used in the present tense), "political" is not an attribute of the living being as such, but rather a specific difference that determines the genus *zōon*. (Only a little later, after all, human politics is dis- tinguished from that of other living beings in that it is founded, through a supplement of politicity [*policita*] tied to language, on a community not sim- ply of the pleasant and the painful but of the good and the evil and of the just and the unjust.)

Michel Foucault refers to this very definition when, at the end of the first volume of *The History of Sexuality*, he summarizes the process by which, at the threshold of the modern era, natural life begins to be included in the mechanisms and calculations of State power, and politics turns into *biopolitics*. "For millennia," he writes, "man remained what he was for Aristotle: a living animal with the additional capacity for political existence; modern man is an animal whose politics calls his existence as a living being into question."[6]

According to Foucault, a society's "threshold of biological modernity" is situated at the point at which the species and the individual as a simple living body become what is at stake in a society's political strategies. After 1977, the courses at the Collège de France start to focus on the passage from the "territorial State" to the "State of population" and on the resulting increase in importance of the nation's health and biological life as a problem of sov- ereign power, which is then gradually transformed into a "government of men."[7] "What follows is a kind of bestialization of man achieved through the most sophisticated political techniques. For the first time in history, the pos- sibilities of the social sciences are made known, and at once it becomes pos- sible both to protect life and to authorize a holocaust." In particular, the development and triumph of capitalism would not have been possible, from this perspective, without the disciplinary control achieved by the new bio-power, which, through a series of appropriate technologies, so to speak created the "docile bodies" that it needed.

Almost twenty years before *The History of Sexuality,* Hannah Arendt had already analyzed the process that brings *homo laborans*—and, with it, biological life as such—gradually to occupy the very center of the political scene of modernity. In *The Human Condition,* Arendt attributes the transformation and decadence of the political realm in modern societies to this very primacy of natural life over political action. That Foucault was able to begin his study of biopolitics with no reference to Arendt's work (which remains, even today, practically without continuation) bears witness to the difficulties and resistances that thinking had to encounter in this area. And it is most likely these very difficulties that account for the curious fact that Arendt establishes no connection between her research in *The Human Condition* and the penetrating analyses she had previously devoted to totalitarian power (in which a biopolitical perspective is altogether lacking), and that Foucault, in just as striking a fashion, never dwelt on the exemplary places of modern biopolitics: the concentration camp and the structure of the great totalitarian states of the twentieth century.

Foucault's death kept him from showing how he would have developed the concept and study of biopolitics. In any case, however, the entry of *zoē* into the sphere of *the polis*—the politicization of bare life as such—constitutes the decisive event of modernity and signals a radical transformation of the political-philosophical categories of classical thought. It is even likely that if politics today seems to be passing through a lasting eclipse, this is because politics has failed to reckon with this foundational event of modernity. The "enigmas"[8] that our century has proposed to historical reason and that remain with us (Nazism is only the most disquieting among them) will be solved only on the terrain—biopolitics—on which they were formed. Only within a biopolitical horizon will it be possible to decide whether the categories whose opposition founded modern politics (right/left, private/public, absolutism/democracy, etc.)—and which have been steadily dissolving, to the point of entering today into a real zone of indistinction—will have to be abandoned or will, instead, eventually regain the meaning they lost in that very horizon. And only a reflection that, taking up Foucault's and Benjamin's suggestion, thematically interrogates the link between bare life and politics, a link that secretly governs the modern ideologies seemingly most distant from one another, will be able to bring the political out of its concealment and, at the same time, return thought to its practical calling.

One of the most persistent features of Foucault's work is its decisive abandonment of the traditional approach to the problem of power, which is based on juridico-institutional models (the definition of sovereignty, the theory of the State), in favor of an unprejudiced analysis of the concrete ways in which power penetrates subjects' very bodies and forms of life. As shown by a seminar held in 1982 at the University of Vermont, in his final years Foucault seemed to orient this analysis according to two distinct directives for research: on the one hand, the study of the *political techniques* (such as the science of the police) with which the State assumes and integrates the care of the natural life of individuals into its very center; on the other hand, the examination of the *technologies of the self* by which processes of subjectivization bring the individual to bind himself to his own identity and consciousness and, at the same time, to an external power. Clearly these two lines (which carry on two tendencies present in Foucault's work from the very beginning) intersect in many points and refer back to a common center. In one of his last writings, Foucault argues that the modem Western state has integrated techniques of subjective individualization with procedures of objective totalization to an unprecedented degree, and he speaks of a real "political 'double bind,' constituted by individualization and the simultaneous totalization of structures of modern power."[9]

Yet the point at which these two faces of power converge remains strangely unclear in Foucault's work, so much so that it has even been claimed that Foucault would have consistently refused to elaborate a unitary theory of power. If Foucault contests the traditional approach to the problem of power, which is exclusively based on juridical models ("What legitimates power?") or on institutional models ("What is the State?"), and if he calls for a "liberation from the theoretical privilege of sovereignty" in order to construct an analytic of power that would, not take law as its model and code, then where, in the body of power, is the zone of indistinction (or, at least, the point of intersection) at which techniques of individualization and totalizing procedures converge? And, more generally, is there a unitary center in which the political "double bind" finds its *raison d'être*? That there is a subjective aspect in the genesis of power was already implicit in the concept of *servitude volontaire* in Etienne de La Boétie. But what is the point at which the voluntary servitude of individuals comes into contact with objective power? Can one be content, in such a delicate area, with psychological explanations such as the suggestive notion of a parallelism between external and internal neuroses? Confronted with phenomena such as the power of the society of the spectacle that is everywhere transforming the political realm today, is it legitimate or even possible to hold subjective technologies and political techniques apart?

Although the existence of such a line of thinking seems to be logically implicit in Foucault's work, it remains a blind spot to the eye of the researcher, or rather something like a vanishing point that the different perspectival lines of Foucault's inquiry (and, more generally, of the entire Western reflection on power) converge toward without reaching.

The present inquiry concerns precisely this hidden point of intersection between the juridico-institutional and the biopolitical models of power. What this work has had to record among its likely conclusions is precisely that the two analyses cannot be separated, and that the inclusion of bare life in the political realm constitutes the original—if concealed—nucleus of sovereign power. *It can even be said that the production of a biopolitical body is the original activity of sovereign power.* In this sense, biopolitics is at least as old as the sovereign exception. Placing biological life at the center of its calculations, the modern State therefore does nothing other than bring to light the secret tie uniting power and bare life, thereby reaffirming the bond (derived from a tenacious correspondence between the modern and the archaic which one encounters in the most diverse spheres) between modern power and the most immemorial of the *arcana imperii.*

If this is true, it will be necessary to reconsider the sense of the Aristotelian definition of the *polis* as the opposition between life (*zēn*) and good life (*eu zēn*). The opposition is, in fact, at the same time an implication of the first in the second, of bare life in politically qualified life. What remains to be interrogated in the Aristotelian definition is not merely—as has been assumed until now—the sense, the modes, and the possible articulations of the "good life" as the *telos* of the political. We must instead ask why Western politics first constitutes itself through an exclusion (which is simultaneously an inclusion) of bare life. What is the relation between politics and life, if life presents itself as what is included by means of an exclusion?

The structure of the exception delineated in the first part of this book appears from this perspective to be consubstantial with Western politics. In Foucault's statement according to which man was, for Aristotle, a "living animal with the additional capacity for political existence," it is therefore precisely the meaning of this "additional capacity" that must be understood as problematic. The peculiar phrase "born with regard to life, but existing essentially with regard to the good life" can be read not only as an implication of being born (*ginomenē*) in being (*ousa*) but also as an inclusive exclusion (an *exceptio*) of zoē in the *polis*, almost as if politics were the place in which life had to transform itself into good life and in which what had to be politicized were always already bare life. In Western politics, bare life has the peculiar privilege of being that whose exclusion founds the city of men.

It is not by chance, then, that a passage of the *Politics* situates the proper place of the *polis* in the transition from voice to language. The link between bare life and politics is the same link that the metaphysical definition of man as "the living being who has language" seeks in the relation between *phonē* and *logos*:

Among living beings, only man has language. The voice is the sign of pain and pleasure, and this is why it belongs to other living beings (since their nature has developed to the point of having the sensations of pain and pleasure and of signifying the two). But language is for manifesting the fitting and the unfitting and the just and the unjust. To have the sensation of the good and the bad and of the just and the unjust is what is proper to men as opposed to other living beings, and the community of these things makes dwelling and the city.[10]

The question "In what way does the living being have language?" corresponds exactly to the question "In what way does bare life dwell in the *polis*?" The living being has *logos* by taking away and conserving its own voice in it, even as it dwells in the *polis* by letting its own bare life be excluded, as an exception, within it. Politics therefore appears as the truly fundamental structure of Western metaphysics insofar as it occupies the threshold on which the relation between the living being and the *logos* is realized. In the "politicization" of bare life—the metaphysical *task par excellence*—the humanity of living man is decided. In assuming this task, modernity does nothing other than declare its own faithfulness to the essential structure of the metaphysical tradition. The fundamental categorial pair of Western politics is not that of friend/enemy but that of bare life/political existence, *zoē/bios*, exclusion/inclusion. There is politics because man is the living being who, in language, separates and opposes himself to his own bare life and, at the same time, maintains himself in relation to that bare life in an inclusive exclusion.

The protagonist of this book is bare life, that is, the life of *homo sacer* (sacred man), who *may be killed and yet not sacrificed*, and whose essential function in modern politics we intend to assert. An obscure figure of archaic Roman law, in which human life is included in the juridical order [*ordinamento*][11] solely in the form of its exclusion (that is, of its capacity to be killed), has thus offered the key by which not only the sacred tests of sovereignty but also the very codes of political power will unveil their mysteries. At the same time, however, this ancient meaning of the term *sacer* presents us with the enigma of a figure of the sacred that, before or beyond the religious, constitutes the first paradigm of the political realm of the West. The Foucauldian thesis will then have to be corrected or, at least, completed, in the sense that what characterizes modern politics is not so much the inclusion of *zoē* in the *polis*—which is, in itself, absolutely ancient—nor simply the fact that life as such becomes a principal object of the projections and calculations of State power. Instead the decisive fact is that, together with the process by which the exception everywhere becomes the rule, the realm of bare life—which is originally situated at the margins of the political order—gradually begins to coincide with the political realm, and exclusion and inclusion, outside and inside, *bios* and *zoē*, right and fact, enter into a zone of irreducible indistinction. At once excluding bare life from and capturing it within the political order, the state of exception actually constituted, in its very separateness, the hidden foundation on which the entire political system rested. When its borders begin to be blurred, the bare life that dwelt there frees itself in the city and becomes both subject and object of the conflicts of the political order, the one place for both the organization of State power and emancipation from it. Everything happens as if, along with the disciplinary process by which State power makes man as a living being into its own specific object, another process is set in motion that in large measure corresponds to the birth of modern democracy, in which man as a living being presents himself no longer as an *object* but as the *subject* of political power. These processes—which in many ways oppose and (at least apparently) bitterly conflict with each other—nevertheless converge insofar as both concern the bare life of the citizen, the new biopolitical body of humanity.

If anything characterizes modern democracy as opposed to classical democracy, then, it is that modern democracy presents itself from the beginning as a vindication and liberation of *zoē*, and that it is constantly trying to transform its own bare life into a way of life and to find, so to speak, the *bios* of *zoē*. Hence, too, modern democracy's specific aporia: it wants to put the freedom and happiness of men into play in the very place—"bare life"—that marked their subjection. Behind the long, strife-ridden process that leads to the recognition of rights and formal liberties stands once again the body of the sacred man with his double sovereign, his life that cannot be sacrificed yet may, nevertheless, be killed. To become conscious of this aporia is not to belittle the conquests and accomplishments of democracy. It is, rather, to try to understand once and for all why democracy, at the very moment in which it seemed to have finally triumphed over its adversaries and reached its greatest height, proved itself incapable of saving *zoē*, to whose happiness it had dedicated all its efforts, from unprecedented ruin. Modern democracy's decadence and gradual convergence with totalitarian states in post-democratic spectacular societies [...] may well be rooted in this aporia, which marks the beginning of modern democracy and forces it into complicity with its most implacable enemy. Today politics knows no value (and, consequently, no non-value) other than life, and until the contradictions that this fact implies are dissolved, Nazism and fascism—which transformed the decision on bare life into the supreme political principle—will remain stubbornly with us. According to the testimony of Robert Antelme, in fact, what the camps taught those who lived there was precisely that "calling into question the quality of man provokes an almost biological assertion of belonging to the human race."[12]

The idea of an inner solidarity between democracy and totalitarianism (which here we must, with every caution, advance) is obviously not (like Leo Strauss's thesis concerning the secret convergence of the final goals of liberalism and communism) a historiographical claim, which would authorize the liquidation and leveling of the enormous differences that characterize their history and their rivalry. Yet this idea must nevertheless be strongly maintained on a historico-philosophical level, since it alone will allow us to orient ourselves in relation to the new realities and unforeseen convergences of the end of the millennium. This idea alone will make it possible to clear the way for the new politics, which remains largely to be invented.

In contrasting the "beautiful day" (*euemeria*) of simple life with the "great difficulty" of political *bios* in the passage cited above, Aristotle may well have given the most beautiful formulation to the aporia that lies at the foundation of Western politics. The 24 centuries that have since gone by have brought only provisional and ineffective solutions. In carrying out the metaphysical task that has led it more and more to assume the form of a biopolitics, Western politics has not succeeded in constructing the link between *zoē* and *bios*, between voice and language, that would have healed the fracture. Bare life remains included in politics in the form of the exception, that is, as something that is included solely through an exclusion. How is it possible to "politicize" the "natural sweetness" of *zoē*? And first of all, does *zoē* really need to be politicized, or is politics not already contained in *zoē* as its most precious center? The biopolitics of both modern totalitarianism and the society of mass hedonism and consumerism certainly constitute answers to these questions. Nevertheless, until a completely new politics—that is, a politics no longer founded on the *exceptio* of bare life—is at hand, every theory and every praxis will remain imprisoned and immobile, and the "beautiful day" of life will be given citizenship only either through blood and death or in the perfect senselessness to which the society of the spectacle condemns it.

Carl Schmitt's definition of sovereignty ("Sovereign is he who decides on the state of exception") became a commonplace even before there was any understanding that what was at issue in it was nothing less than the limit concept of the doctrine of law and the State, in which sovereignty borders (since every limit concept is always the limit between two concepts) on the sphere of life and becomes indistinguishable from it. As long as the form of the State constituted the fundamental horizon of all communal life and the political, religious, juridical, and economic doctrines that sustained this form were still strong, this "most extreme sphere" could not truly come to light. The problem of sovereignty was reduced to the question of who within the political order was invested with certain powers, and the very threshold of the political order itself was never called into question. Today, now that the great State structures have entered into a process of dissolution and the emergency has, as Walter Benjamin foresaw, become the rule, the time is ripe to place the problem of the originary structure and limits of the form of the State in a new perspective. The weakness of anarchist and Marxian critiques of the State was precisely to have not caught sight of this structure and thus to have quickly left the *arcanum imperii* aside, as if it had no substance outside of the simulacra and the ideologies invoked to justify it. But one ends up identifying with an enemy whose structure one does not understand, and the theory of the State (and in particular of the state of exception, which is to say, of the dictatorship of the proletariat as the transitional phase leading to the stateless society) is the reef on which the revolutions of our century have been shipwrecked.

This book, which was originally conceived as a response to the bloody mystification of a new planetary order, therefore had to reckon with problems—first of all that of the sacredness of life—which the author had not, in the beginning, foreseen. In the course of the undertaking, however, it became clear that one cannot, in such an area, accept as a guarantee any of the notions that the social sciences (from jurisprudence to anthropology) thought they had defined or presupposed as evident, and that many of these notions demanded—in the urgency of catastrophe—to be revised without reserve.

NOTES

1. Aristotle, *Metaphysics*, 1072b, 28.
2. Aristotle, *The Politics*, 1278b, 23–31.
3. *Ibid.*, 26–35.
4. *Ibid.*, 30.
5. *Ibid.*, 4.
6. Michel Foucault, 1926–1984. *The History of Sexuality* (New York:Pantheon Books, 1978), 188.
7. Michel Foucault, et al. *Dits et écrits: 1954–1988.* (Paris: Gallimard, 1994) 3: 719.
8. François Furet, ed. *L[apost]Allemagne nazie et le génocide juif* (Paris: Seuil, 1988), 7.
9. Foucault, *Dits et écrits*, 4: 229–32.
10. Aristotle, *The Politics*, 1253a, 10–18.
11. "Order" renders the Italian *ordinamento*, which carries the sense not only of order but of political and juridical rule, regulation, and system. The word *ordinamento* is also the Italian translation of Carl Schmitt's *Ordnung*. Where the author refers to *ordinamento* as *Ordnung*, the English word used is the one chosen by Schmitt's translators, "ordering."—Trans.
12. Robert Antelme, *L'espèce humaine* (Paris: Gallimard, 1994), 2.

Liberal Multiculturalism and the Ethics of Hospitality in the Age of Globalization

Meyda Yegenoglu

The increasing political presence of refugees and immigrants in post–Cold War Europe has generated considerable debate about the nature of multicultural society. The demand for the recognition of cultural, racial, and ethnic differences has come to occupy a central place in the forms of post-national politics emergent today. Yet, a closer examination of the juridico-political regulations developed in response to these demands reveals a troubling tendency: cultural/racial difference is translated into an understanding of cultural diversity that treats minorities, to use David Bennett's term, as "add-ons"[1] to the existing nation form. Thus, the question becomes whether such an "additive model"[2] is capable of inducing a radical transformation in the concept of the sovereign position of the national self. This essay addresses the limitations of this procedural multiculturalist valorization and argues that the liberal imperative to tolerate and respect cultural difference is far from displacing the sovereignty of the host society in question. In discussing these limitations, I will situate liberal multiculturalism in the context of today's capitalist globalization.

When we examine the policies and programs through which the culturally different is valorized today, it becomes clear that liberalism has become the regulative principle in many metropolitan countries. Yet it is far from clear whether such a liberal valorization and the granting of legal rights to non-normative citizens, the ethnically and racially "different," will prove to be a counter-hegemonic political force. Is the legal codification of respect for identities in their particularity adequate for reinventing a democratic political space? If such politicization does not flourish in particularist liberal multiculturalism, then we need to be vigilant about what is being left intact. In fact, we need to take our vigilance one step further and question the ways in which such codification regulates the destabilizing force of the political and entails its repudiation, suspension, limitation, or foreclosure.

We are witnessing an increasing proliferation of literature trying to understand the new economic, political, and cultural arrangements that are inaugurated by global capital. The accelerating rate of the international division of labor, the extended capacity of multinational production; the development and concentration of global financial, banking services, and culture industries; the rapid development in telecommunications; and the growth of a global mass culture have led many to talk about a process by which the world is now becoming a single and unified space. Globalization, according to the advocates of this position, marks the beginning of a process whereby difference is dissolved within the logic of sameness and cultural homogenization. Consequently, we are reminded of the hazards and shortcomings of limiting our inquiries with nations and nation-states, for the sovereignty of nation-states has been declared to be undermined in the age of cultural, economic, social homogeneity, and integration.

On the other side of the debate, there are those who emphasize the impossibility of envisioning a unified global culture. For example, in "Disjuncture and Difference in the Global Cultural Economy,"[3] Arjun Appadurai suggests that, when forces are brought from various metropoles into different societies, they tend to become indigenized in some way. To understand the complexity of the process of globalization, he suggests that we examine the fundamental disjunctures between economy, politics, and culture. For Appadurai the global cultural flows occur in and through the disjunctures between five "scapes": ethnoscapes, mediascapes, technoscapes, finanscapes, and ideoscapes. Such disjunctures and flows point not only to the fluid and irregular nature of international capital, but also constitute the building blocks of the replacement of Benedict Anderson's "imagined community" with "imagined worlds."

Those who, like Appadurai, are critical of the global homogenization argument suggest that the globalized world is a contested and contradictory space. These critics point to the increasing proliferation of ethnic and racial struggle to argue that the homogenizing pressure of globalization paradoxically produces cultural heterogeneity. It is the encounter of the local with the global that is deemed to force the recognition of alternative histories, traditions, and cultures that have hitherto remained silent under the ruins of the project of modernity and colonialism. For example, Ulf Hannerz, in "Cosmopolitans and Locals in World Culture,"[4] points out that cultural differences now exist *not between cultures but within cultures* and suggests that world culture implies a reorganization of diversity rather than a replication of uniformity. It is no longer possible to talk about the homogenization of systems of meaning; between the different regions of the globe there are now flows of meanings, people, and goods. The globe can be imagined as a homogenized unity only when localities are discarded and when power relations among its constituting parts are ignored.

Thus, globalization increasingly reveals the limits of Western modernity: various ethnic and racial minorities, their traditions, memories, myths, and symbols are now woven together in the increasingly dense web of metropolitan culture. In an attempt to understand how particularity and difference are articulated in this global culture, Stuart Hall, in "The Local and the Global,"[5] questions attributing a singular and unitary logic to capital. The notion of the global which is capable of getting hold of and neutralizing everybody and everything and thereby contains all marginality in an uncontradictory and uncontested space does not accurately capture the specificity of this decentralized and de-centered form of globalization. Hall suggests that with the accelerating rate of migration, older unitary cultural formations are now breaking down. The emergent form of globalization simultaneously valorizes the local and the global. Hall does not deny the homogenizing form of this new cultural representation, but he argues that it is a peculiar form of homogenization—one that simultaneously absorbs and recognizes difference. This form of global homogenization does not obliterate difference but rather works in and through difference. While capital is spreading globally, it works through specificity. Although the growing global culture is now located in the West and speaks English, it is increasingly invaded by other languages and accents. It is therefore forced to negotiate and incorporate a difference that it formerly tried to conquer. In a paradoxical turn, as minorities reclaim representation for themselves, marginality has been turned into a powerful space. The identities that have hitherto been excluded now signal the emergence of new subjects, new ethnicities, and new communities, and they have acquired the means to speak for themselves. Although Hall acknowledges that resorting to such localities by retreating into exclusivist and defensive enclaves might become dangerous and can lead to forms of fundamentalism, he nevertheless thinks that ethnicity is the necessary position of enunciation from which the formerly excluded marginality speaks and grounds itself.

As is clear from this brief review of current critical discourse, one of the characterizing features of the debate on globalization is the opposition between homogenization and heterogenization or between universalization and particularization. Moreover, the particular or different is presumed to be endowed with some resistive and liberative capacity in the face of the universalizing tendency of global capital. I would suggest that this is a misleading opposition as it identifies globalization with universalization and consequently locates the counter-hegemonic political struggle against the global force of capital in the affirmation of particular identities. In "A Leftist Plea for Eurocentrism," Slavoj Žižek rightly points out that it is deeply misleading to posit the rising globalization in opposition to particular identities since the true opposition is between globalization and universalism. For him, the new world is global but not universal; it is an order, which, rather than negating the particular, allocates each and every particular a place. Therefore, what is threatened by globalization is not particularity but universality itself. Universalism, for Žižek, is the "properly political domain" as it implies "universalizing one's particular fate as representative of global injustice."[6] If we want to go beyond the rather simplistic praising of the particular, one of the tasks that awaits us is to develop a conceptual framework that will allow us to rethink globalization and the apparent counter-tendency of valorization of particular identities as a double gesture of capital. What needs to be questioned is whether the particular that is valorized in multiculturalist politics constitutes a destabilizing political force in the wake of global abstraction of transnational capitalism which now operates completely divorced from its specific origins in Europe, as Dirlik argues in "The Global in the Local," and whose immanent logic remains indifferent to the boundaries of the nation-state, as Žižek suggests in "Multiculturalism, or, the Cultural Logic of Multinational Capitalism."

The decentering of capitalism, its deterritorialization and abstraction, implies the difficulty of pointing to any nation or region as the center of global capitalism. This has led many to emphasize the qualitatively different nature of global capitalism from its earlier forms. For Dirlik, this qualitative difference of global capitalism can be discerned in the authentic global abstraction capitalism has achieved, in the decentering and production of networks of urban formations without a clearly definable center—a network which is then relinked via transnational corporations.[7] Likewise, in "Ambiguous Universality," Etienne Balibar delineates the transformations created in the geographical and geopolitical pattern of the world and points to the multiplication of centers, which form a network rather than a "core" area.[8] Similarly, Žižek suggests that the final moment of capitalism entails the cutting of the umbilical cord of global companies with their mother-nation. It is thus no longer possible to pin down a colonizing agency as in the case of traditional imperialist colonialism. The paradox of this form of colonization resides in the fact that it takes place without a colonizing nation-state, as the colonizing agents now become the global companies themselves.[9] Dirlik finds the concern with the local in the wake of global capitalism ironic for the following reason: while disorganizing earlier forms and reconfiguring global relations, global capitalism enhances an awareness of the local so as to be able to render the local manipulatable in its hands, pointing to it as the site of resistance to capitalism.[10] Therefore the privileging of the local without the recognition of this context and the concomitant ideological criticism of global capitalism voiced from the presumably resistive site of the local falls prey to the ideological legitimization of the structures which are indeed the very production of global capitalism. For Dirlik, the limitations of such criticism stem from the fact that global capitalism leaves no local that is not already worked over, continually disorganized, reconstituted, or assimilated as part of its universalizing and homogenizing operations.[11]

What do we make of the growing liberal multiculturalist dictum to respect and tolerate the racially, culturally, and ethnically different in the wake of the tendency of capital for global abstraction? Can these two trends be regarded as contradictory? In other words, does multiculturalist tolerance for difference, which not only acknowledges the value of each and every group's cultural characteristics but also tries to amend the wrong each one of them is subjected to through various juridical and legal procedures, signal the emergence of a counter-political force against the global hegemony of capital?

Slavoj Žižek, in his reading of the three different meanings of universality distinguished by Balibar, sees multiculturalist tolerance, respect and protection of human rights, democracy, and so forth as the hegemonic fiction of the real universality of today's globalization.[12] The concrete universality of global order is supplanted by allowing each particular lifestyle to flourish in its particularity. For Žižek, the modern era, whose predominant form of concrete universality is the nation-state, worked by seizing the individual directly, restraining his or her freedom as the citizen of a nation-state. Against the de-nationalization of the ethnic into the national of the modern period, the intensification of global market forces entails the ethnicization of the national and renewed reconstitution of ethnic roots. Respect and tolerance for the ethnically different is a reaction to the universal dimension of the world market and hence occurs against its background and on its very terrain.[13] Multiculturalism, in Žižek's formulation, is the form of the appearance of universality in its exact mirror opposite and is therefore the ideal form of the ideology of global capitalism. In *A Critique of Postcolonial Reason*, Gayatri Spivak also points to the bond between liberal multiculturalism and global capitalism. She suggests that "liberal multiculturalism is determined by the demands of contemporary transnational capitalisms"[14] which secure the means of gaining the consent of developing nations in the financialization of the globe.

Perhaps the originality of Žižek's argument does not lie in the link he establishes between multiculturalism and the interests of global capitalism. Spivak, Jameson, Dirlik, and Hall, in their different ways, have developed similar arguments. But there is more to Žižek's formulation. Focusing his attention particularly on the implications of the notions of respect and tolerance, he suggests that multiculturalism entails a *Eurocentric distance* when it respects and tolerates the local and particular cultures.[15] In this sense, multiculturalism is based on a disavowed and inverted self-referential form of racism as it empties its own position of all positive content. The racism of multiculturalism does not reside in its being against the values of other cultures. Quite the contrary: it respects and tolerates other cultures, but in respecting and tolerating the different, it maintains a distance which enables it to retain a privileged position of empty universality. It is this emptied universal position which enables one to appreciate (or depreciate) other local cultures. Thus, multiculturalist respect for the particularity of the other is indeed a form of asserting one's own superiority and sovereignty. As David Lloyd cogently describes in "Race under Representation," the alleged neutrality and universality is at the same time a process that secures a sovereign status for the subject:

> The position occupied by the dominant individual is that of the Subject without properties. The Subject with "unlimited properties" is precisely the undetermined subject.... Its universality is attained by virtue of literal indifference: this Subject becomes representative in consequence of being able to take anyone's place, of occupying any place, of a pure exchangeability. Universal where all others are particular, partial, this Subject is the perfect, disinterested judge formed for and by the public sphere.[16]

In *Colonial Fantasies: Towards a Feminist Reading of Orientalism*, I have suggested that it is the centering of the self, which, by setting itself off from the particular, allows its universalizing gesture.[17] But, as Žižek suggests, the critical task here is not to expose the truth of multiculturalism, which is presumed to be the concealment of particular roots behind the mask of universality. Rather, the problematic of multiculturalism, premised on the hybrid co-existence of diverse cultural forms, "is the form of appearance of its opposite, of the massive presence of capitalism as *universal*[18] Therefore, for Žižek[19] Precisely for this reason, the fight for cultural[20] The task, therefore, is to understand the mechanisms by which this regulation, suffocation, and foreclosure are managed. If the institutionalized multiculturalist pluralism that characterizes the post-national global order implies a foreclosure of politics proper and is far from offering a potential for democratic politicization, then where do we locate the possibility of a politics that interrupts this foreclosure? To discuss this, allow me to make a detour through Jacques Derrida's argument concerning *conditional* and *unconditional hospitality*.

Hospitality as Law

In *Adieu to Emmanuel Levinas*, Derrida reads Kant's writings on cosmopolitan law and draws our attention to his essay "Toward Perpetual Peace:

A Philosophical Project," particularly the "Third Definitive Article for a Perpetual Peace" which pertains to the "right of hospitality": "The Law of World Citizenship Shall be Limited to Conditions of Universal Hospitality." Derrida notes that this article is limited by a number of conditions. From the very beginning we are confronted with the question of *conditional* hospitality. The question of hospitality in Kant's writings pulls us into the domain of law, citizenship and the relation the state has with its subjects. Universal hospitality here is only juridical and political. Cosmopolitan law is about international agreement and refers to the condition of justice and law that is to be decided by nations. Hospitality is treated as a question of *rights*, justice and obligation that is to be *regulated by law*.[21] Resting on a juridical and political definition, the Kantian formulation is based not on granting the right of residence but only the right of temporary sojourn. As a juridical regulation, it concerns the rights of citizens of states that are to be regulated and deliberated by a cosmopolitical constitution. As such, it suspends and conditions the immediate, infinite, and unconditional welcoming of the other.[22]

Derrida directs our attention to the fact that conditional hospitality is offered at the owner's place, home, nation, state, or city—that is, at a place where one is defined as the master and where unconditional hospitality or unconditional trespassing of the door is not possible. The host, the non-guest, the one who accepts, the one who offers hospitality, the one who welcomes, is the owner of a home and therefore is the master of the home.[23]

As I mentioned above, Derrida directs our attention to the fact that in Kant's essay, hospitality is framed as a question of law, an obligation, a duty, and a right: it refers to the welcoming of an alien/stranger other as a non-enemy. The formulation of hospitality as a question of law weaves it with contradiction because the welcoming of the other within the limits of law is possible on the condition that the host, the owner of the home, the one who accepts, remains the master of the home and thereby retains his/her authority in that place. The *law of hospitality* is the *law of oikonomia*, the law of one's home. Offered as the law of place, hospitality lays down the limits of a place and retains the authority over that place, thus limiting the gift that is offered, retaining the self as *self* in one's own home as the condition of hospitality. In making this the condition of hospitality, it affirms the law of the same. Hospitality is a giving gesture. But with the hospitality as law, what this gesture in fact does is to subject the stranger/foreigner to the law of the host's home. In this way, the foreigner is allowed to enter the host's space under conditions the host has determined. Hence conditional welcoming entails a way of insinuating a place from which one invites the other and hence lays down the conditions for "appropriating for oneself a place to *welcome* the other, or, worse, *welcoming* the other in order to appropriate for oneself a place and then speak the language of hospitality."[24] Therefore the *law of hospitality* is characterized by a limitation. The host affirms the position of a master in his/her own home; in the space and things he/she provides to the stranger/guest, the host assures his/her sovereignty and says: this space belongs to me; we are in my home. Welcome to me. Feel at home but on the condition that you obey the rules of hospitality.[25] This gesture affirms one's sovereignty and one's being at one's own home. For this reason, *hospitality as law* limits itself with a threshold.[26]

Drawing on Derrida's deconstructive reading of the contradictions inherent in conditional hospitality, we can suggest that multiculturalist tolerance of minorities within the host nation-state is not for nothing. Welcoming the other in the form of codified multiculturalist tolerance implies a conditional welcoming, as the hospitality offered remains limited within law and jurisdiction. But, more importantly, this kind of tolerance does not result in a fundamental modification of the host subject's mode of inhabiting the territory that is deemed to be solely within his/her possession. Far from laying the grounds for an interruption of sovereign identity of the self, multiculturalist respect and tolerance implies the conditional welcoming of the guest within the prescribed limits of the law and, hence, implies a reassertion of mastery over the national space as it enables the subject to appropriate a place for itself—an empty and universal and therefore sovereign place—from which the other is welcomed. Thus, the place from which multiculturalist tolerance welcomes the particularity of the other, fortified by codifications such as affirmative action and other legal measures, is what precisely enables the disavowed and inverted self-referentiality of racist hospitality which by emptying the host's position from any positive content asserts its superiority and sovereignty.

The inherent paradox of multiculturalism's conditional and lawful welcoming of the other as guest can be productively understood as conforming to "the structure of exception" that Giorgio Agamben discusses in *Homo Sacer: Sovereign Power and Bare Life*. In discussing this, I want to refer to the German case where the paradox of the inclusion of minorities within the limits of law can be illustrated. All of the laws that regulate the conditions of arrival, presence, and departure of "guest-workers" in Germany reveal that the overriding concern is that of recruitment of a short-term labor force. For this reason, residence permits are conferred only as work permits. Laws explicitly anticipate that the workers will leave Germany when the needs of capital are fulfilled. The fact that the workers' presence is regarded as temporary makes clear that the new regulations are seen as an exception: a parenthesis to be opened and eventually closed. The logic underlying these laws is that the acceptance/welcoming of foreign labor is a conditional one, as the workers' presence, which is expected to be temporary, is deemed to be an exception to the general rule. Tellingly, the term "migrant" is not typically used to name this group. As guests, these workers are accepted as an exception to the general rule of membership in the German polity. Their welcoming is not regulated within the framework of the general rule of law. In accordance with the persistent and widespread sentiment that declares that "Germany is not a land of immigration," the conditional welcoming or the temporary hosting of foreign labor appears at first glance to be set outside the purview of general law. Hence, these regulations are nothing but the name of an interim, an exception.

Following Agamben, we can ask whether as an exception, the conditional welcoming of workers indicates that they are left outside the sovereign law of the host society? It is clear that this temporary foreign labor force has been included in the German territory without being turned into proper members of the polity. Their membership is undecidable from the perspective of the German self and law since their inclusion exceeds membership, testifying to the impasse of a system based on law, which is incapable of making their inclusion coincide with membership. As guests having temporary abode, they are not properly inside. But does this indicate that they are outside the purview of sovereign and general law? One way to approach this dynamic between outside and inside is to see them as a *limit figure* which brings into crisis the clear distinction between what is inside and what is outside. Surely this not an altogether invalid way of grasping the dynamic between the guest and the host that is structured through the law, but it is a limited one insofar as the paradox of exception is concerned.

Exception, Agamben notes, "embodies a kind of membership without inclusion."[27] What defines the German sovereign claim of ownership of the land can be understood with Agamben's following remarks: "what defines the character of the sovereign claim is precisely that it applies to the exception in no longer applying to it, that it includes what is outside itself.... What cannot be included in any way is included in the form of the exception."[28] It seems that we can talk about a *paradoxical inclusion* of guest-workers, which is indeed an "inclusive exclusion."[29] For Agamben, the regulation that is exercised by the law is achieved not by a command or prescription, but by the creation of "the sphere of its own reference in real life and *make that reference regular.*"[30] The sovereign claim of the general law is constituted by having a grip over the exception and by articulating it into its domain through an *inclusive exclusion.* It is through the exception, through the inclusive exclusion of the exception, that the law is able to generate and cultivate itself. The apparent exclusion of the exception is in fact an indication of its paradoxical inclusion in the juridical order.

For Agamben, when we see exception as fundamental to the structure of the constitution of sovereignty, then sovereignty can be grasped neither as an exclusively political nor as a juridical category; it is not "a power external to law (Schmitt)" or to the supreme rule of juridical order (Hans Kelsen): it is the originary structure in which law refers to life and includes it in itself by suspending it."[31] Following Jean-Luc Nancy's suggestion, he gives the name *ban* to "this potentiality … of the law to maintain itself in its own privation, to apply in no longer applying."[32] The law, in excluding or banning, does not place the exception to its exteriority, but abandons or threatens it on a threshold where the distinction between outside and inside, life and law, becomes blurred. It becomes difficult to say in a definite manner whether the one who is banned is outside or inside the juridical order. The paradox of sovereignty is that it leaves nothing outside the law as it has a hold on life even when it abandons what it interdicts.

In offering hospitality that is conditional, the German national self appropriates a place for himself/herself so as to be able to say welcome. This entails not only maintaining the status of the German national self as master, but more importantly it institutes a welcoming in order to nourish the sovereignty of the German subject that was already in place. To understand the dynamic that is operating here, we can establish a link between Derrida's understanding of "conditional hospitality" and what Agamben calls "inclusive exclusion." Though pushed outside, the provisional acceptance of the guest-workers enables the regeneration and nourishment of the German national self, which needs to reconstitute its sovereignty each time anew. Such a sovereign self maintains and nurtures itself not by pushing particular others to its exteriority or outside the purview of general law. On the contrary, it is their inclusive exclusion, which the conditional welcoming enables, that is indispensable for a reassertion of a sovereign German national self. The empty and universal position of the sovereign claim enabled by the general rule of law is capable of instituting conditional hospitality as an *exception* and this enables the means to codify respect and tolerance for the different and confer upon them rights in the form of law. It is precisely at this point that we need to be vigilant and to problematize this codification by asking what is being negated and foreclosed here. Does this codification entail the opening of the space of politics or does it effectively signal the circumscription of what Žižek calls "politics proper" or what Antonio Negri[33] calls "constituent power"?

Politics

In his discussion of the three forms of universality, Balibar gives the proposition concerning human rights as the example of *ideal universality*.[34] Reversing the traditional relationship between subjection and citizenship, ideal universality justifies the universal extension of political (civic) rights by explaining that equality and liberty are inseparable, which Balibar calls "equaliberty." As such, it introduces the notion of *unconditional* into the realm of politics: "equaliberty is an all-or-nothing" notion and hence cannot be relativized. It is either recognized or ignored as a principle or as a demand. Balibar links this characteristic of equaliberty to what Hannah Arendt calls "the right to have rights," which is distinct from having this or that specific right that is guaranteed by law. Nor is it a moral notion. It is a political notion and delineates a process, which starts with resistance and ends with the actual exercise of constituent power.[35] For this reason, for Balibar, the "right to have rights" can also be called the "right to have politics." As an unconditional force, the demand for equaliberty sets in motion a permanent insurrection that can never be gentrified or "fully integrated into the harmonious whole of the concrete universality."[36] But does this mean that constituent power, as the irreducible excess (to use Žižek's formulation), is allowed to exercise its full destabilizing potential of the political? Certainly not. The question thus becomes: what are the means through which this insurrectionary demand is domesticated, suffocated, limited, regulated, neutralized, or congealed?

To answer this question—to understand the dynamic by which the "right to have rights" or the "right to have politics" of minorities and foreigners is regulated and hence limited through institutionalized multiculturalism and through the granting of a set of rights guaranteed by law—it is useful to turn to (and to revise) Antonio Negri's conception of constituent and constitutive power as articulated in *Insurgencies: Constituent Power and the Modern State*. I have already suggested, following Žižek, that it is through liberal multiculturalist institutional and juridical regulations that the post-national global order renders its global universalizing tendency indiscernible and thereby forecloses the possibility for a right to have politics or democratic politics. But does the current global management of the conditional and legal hosting of immigrants mean that *any* change in the law or *any* attempt to modify the law will by definition play into the hands of the forces of globalization? Can the legal conditions of hospitality or laws on immigration be improved? The analysis that Negri offers regarding the relation between constitutive and constituent power seems to imply that any attempt to improve or change the law is a vain effort; that it's futile to attempt to replace existing laws with better ones, for any politics that remains within the purview of law is doomed to fail as it implies suffocation of democratic politics through constitutional arrangements. After a brief discussion of the analysis Negri offers and its limitations, I will discuss Derrida's deconstructive reading of the relation between *law* and *justice* on the one hand and *conditional* and *unconditional* hospitality on the other hand and suggest that the latter offers a radically different opening of politics.[37]

For Negri, to speak of *constituent power* is to speak of democracy for it is constituent power that regulates democracy. It is not only all-powerful, but also has an expansive and unlimited quality. It emerges from the vortex of the void and is characterized by the openness of its needs and the absence of determinations and finalities. Its strength lies in the fact that it never ends up in power, nor its multitude results in a totality. As an open multiplicity, it is always based upon a set of singularities. Its all-powerful and expansive tendency, its strength, which opens a horizon, never results in a vertical or totalitarian dimension. The active elements of constituent power are resistance, desire, and an *ethical impulse.* It does not seek institutionality but aims at constructing an *ethical being.* It is for these reasons that Negri emphasizes the strong link between constituent power and democracy. Democracy is the political form of constituent power. The concept of democracy in Negri's formulation is not treated as a subspecies or a subcategory of liberalism but refers to a form of governability that enables the freeing of constituent power, because it entails a totality without a closure and the exclusion of any sign of external definition. It is a project of the multitude and is a creative force. This multitude is not an ungraspable multiplicity but is the strength of singularities and differences. As a singular multidirectionality it refers to an irreducible concept of the political and to an ethics that recognizes singularities. Like democracy, constituent power resists being constitutionalized.

The *opposite* of democracy and constituent power is not totalitarianism but *sovereignty* itself and *constitutional* power. The establishment of constitutional power presents a closure to the always-open nature of constituent power. When constituent power is articulated in juridical definitions, it is limited, closed, reduced to juridical categories, and is restrained in administrative routines. The State's constitutionality and its various other regulatory activities bring a form of control, well-defined limits, and procedures to the all-expansive force of the constituent power. Once it is situated in the concept of the nation and absorbed by the mechanism of representation, constituent power is perverted, desiccated, congealed in a static system. Representation is one of the fundamental juridical-constitutional instruments in exercising control and in segmenting constituent power. Its dilution in representative mechanisms manifests itself in political space but is disguised in the activity of the Supreme Court and other organs of the State. These mechanisms restore traditional sovereignty and close the possibility of democratic innovation. The taming and suffocation of constituent power by constitutionalist arrangements entails the mediation of inequalities and hence the neutralization of its strength. The fixing and institutionalization of constituent power implies its *de facto* termination and negation. And in this way, the sovereignty inverts the ostensible foundation of democratic polity and reconstructs itself as the foundation.

Although Negri's analysis of the ways in which constitutive power tames and suffocates constituent power is a useful one to think how laws of conditional hospitality limit the unconditional welcoming of foreigners, it nevertheless suffers from certain limitations. Negri does not use the concept of constituent power as a theoretical or philosophical device that enables him to better understand how constitutive arrangements limit a more expansive politics. Rather, he treats constituent power as something that can actually be established as such by its affirmation or as a self-affirming power. Moreover, Negri posits the relation between constitutive and constituent power as an opposition or a dialectical contradiction; he poses the relation between constitutive and constituent power as an either/or question. The heterogeneity between the two is reduced to an antinomy. As such, his analysis risks leaving intact the very structure it aims to criticize; it risks repeating the same desire for a sovereign position, shifted now to the side of the hegemonized second term.

In an attempt to rethink another philosophical and theoretical framework that might help us to envision the possibility of reinventing a political space that is neither locked within the limits and congealments of conditional hospitality nor one that pretends to go beyond the law by simply reversing it, I want to discuss Derrida's reading of the relation between conditional and conditional hospitality and law and justice.

Ethics of Hospitality and the Possibility of Democratic Politics

How does Derrida think the relationship between conditional and unconditional hospitality? Are they mutually exclusive of each other and hence standing in a relation of opposition? Does unconditional hospitality simply imply that nation-states make it their official policy and open their borders and unconditionally welcome anyone who wants to come? Does it have the status of a regulative idea and hence constitute the name of a correct politics? Or does it have the status of a deconstructive tool devised to read the limits of conditional hospitality?

While Kant is concerned with hospitality as law and thereby with the conditions and limitations of hospitality, Levinas engages with it as a question of ethics or as the question of *ethicity itself*. In his reading of Levinas's formulation of the ethics of hospitality, Derrida orients our attention to the fact that in the lawful admittance of the other as guest there is a level that exceeds and hence cannot be captured by those analyses that take the nation-state and the juridical regulation as the model to work on. Or rather, his question is whether the ethics of hospitality, in Levinas's thought, is conducive for "a law and a politics beyond the familial dwelling, within a society, nation, State, or Nation-State."[38] It is this level that Derrida's reading of Levinas's ethics of hospitality brings to the fore.

Pointing to a hiatus between the law and ethics of hospitality, Derrida underlines how the ethics of hospitality cannot be treated as a decree nor can it be imposed by a command. The hiatus between the law and ethics of hospitality also pertains to the fact that it is unthematizable, implying that a particular law or politics of hospitality cannot be deduced from Levinas's discourse of the ethics of hospitality, for it is irreducible to a theme, thematization, or some kind of formalization. Ethics *as such* is an attentive intention, a welcome and tending toward the other, an *unconditional "yes" to the other. Hospitality as ethicity* is infinite (*it is either infinite, unconditional or not at all*) and cannot be limited in the sense that Kant talks about it; it cannot be regulated by a particular political or juridical practice of a nation and therefore cannot be circumscribed.

Derrida notes that the ethics of hospitality, the welcome made to the other, entails the subordination or putting in question of the freedom of the subject and an *interruption of the self as other*. But this interruption is not something that can be enforced by a decree or law. It is an interruption produced in the intentional attention to the other. The subordination of the freedom of the subject does not imply depriving the subject of its birth. Rather it implies the *subjection of the subjectum* and enables the birth of the subject along with freedom: the coming of the subject to itself as it welcomes the other. Responsibility for the other, the being-host of the subject, puts the subject into question; it puts the subject's being in question. Therefore, for Derrida, "the host is a hostage insofar as he is a subject put into question, obsessed (and thus besieged), persecuted in the very place where he takes place, where as emigrant, exile, stranger, a guest from the very beginning, he finds himself elected to or taken up by a residence before himself electing or taking one up."[39]

Unconditional hospitality entails a reversal, since the owner of the home can perform hospitality on the condition that she is invited to her own home by the one whom she invites, by being welcomed, accepted by the one whom she welcomes or accepts, and shown hospitality in her own home by the guest. Unconditional hospitality or hospitality as ethics implies the interruption of a full possession of a place called home and when its inhabitant becomes a guest received in her home—that is, when the owner becomes a tenant in her place. The inexorable law of hospitality therefore involves a situation in which

> the *hote* who receives (the host), the one who welcomes the invited or received *hote* (the guest), the welcoming *hote* who considers himself the owner of the place, is in truth a *hote* received in his own home. He receives the hospitality that he offers *in* his own home; he receives it *from* his own home—which, in the end, does not belong to

> him. The *hote* as host is a guest. The dwelling opens itself to itself, to its "essence"
> without essence, as a "land of asylum or refuge." The one who welcomes is first wel-
> comed in his own home. The one who invites is invited by the one whom he invites.
> The one who receives is received, receiving hospitality in what he takes to be his own
> home, or indeed his own land....[40]

Hospitality in this sense precedes property, since home, in this unconditional welcoming, is not owned, or is owned only in a very singular sense. That is, only insofar it is already hospitable to its owner, when the master of the house is already a received *hote* or a guest in her own home. When home is no longer a property but a place that welcomes its owner, the question of hospitality cannot be reduced to a multiculturalist tolerance, for there is no longer a question of limiting, restricting, or regulating tolerance for the other. As Derrida puts it:

> That a people, as a people, "should accept those who come and settle among them—
> even though they are foreigners," would be the proof [*gage*] of a popular and public
> commitment [*engagement*], a political *res publica* that cannot be reduced to a sort of
> "tolerance," unless this tolerance requires the affirmation of a "love" without mea-
> sure.[41]

In the hospitality without conditions, the host should, in principle, receive even before knowing anything about the guest. A pure welcome consists not only in not knowing anything or acting as if one knows nothing, but also in avoiding any questions about the Other's identity, their desire, their rules, their language, their capacity for work, for integration, for adaptation... . From the moment that I formulate all of these questions, and posit these conditions ... the ideal situation of non-knowledge—*non-savoir*—is broken—*rompue*.[42]

Above I have delineated the characterizing features of what unconditional hospitality is. To be able to understand its relation to conditional hospitality, I want to briefly review how Derrida understands the relation between law and justice in "Force of Law: The 'Mystical Foundation of Authority,'"[43] as it has a parallel structure with conditional and unconditional hospitality. This will enable us to better comprehend the nature of the relation between conditional and unconditional hospitality and thus better understand how unconditional hospitality is not simply the name of a political program.

For Derrida, there lies an *aporia* within the drive for justice because it has to respect universality on the one hand and absolute singularity on the other. One faces difficulty in justice precisely because of the necessity to speak in terms of the universal principles when one is deciding about particular cases. Since law includes these two conditions simultaneously, the singularity has to be translated into universality. The *aporia* resides in the principle of universality which cannot directly speak to the particular case: in the fact that it is not possible to be just for everyone and for every single case. This is what Derrida means in saying that "justice is impossible." However, justice is the principle in the name of which law is deconstructed; that is, it is possible to change and improve the law, the legal system. Law can be criticized and therefore is deconstructible, but justice is not deconstructible. Thus, despite the absolute radical heterogeneity between the two, the relation between them is not one of opposition. Law is not opposed to justice, nor is justice opposed to law. Derrida makes clear that justice and law are indissociable because *it is in the name of justice that one deconstructs the law.* The relation between them will remain endlessly open and irreducible. To tend to justice, one has to deconstruct and improve the law, but it is never just—and it is there, in the space between law and justice, that one negotiates between the universal and the particular.

Like justice, unconditional hospitality is also impossible. But this impossibility does not mean that one does not aspire to pure hospitality. Its impossibility lies in the very structure of unconditional hospitality itself. In principle, it is offered to an unlimited number of Others and to an unlimited extent, without asking any questions. The Other's welcoming is not to be contingent upon the Other's identity or the questions asked. The very notion of pure or unconditional hospitality assumes that one must offer to any stranger the right of entry to a territory, home, or nation of which one is legitimately in possession.

With the concept of unconditional hospitality, Derrida is not trying to offer a political program about how a pure hospitality might be implemented; rather, he is trying to expose the presuppositions of conditional hospitality and the series of concepts that it is based upon—such as one's proper residence, proper identity, and proper cultural identity. For Derrida, there is an essential link between society or culture and hospitality. In every society there is space allocated for those who are invited, and this enables the welcoming of the strangers who arrive. In other words, conditional hospitality is what enables one's being at home. There is no culture, no home, no nation, or family without a door. It is the opening of this door that functions as a means of welcoming strangers. When the stranger, the Other, is welcomed on the condition that he adjust to the *chez soi*, the hospitality that is offered is a conditional one, one of *visitation*: the stranger is welcome only as long as he respects the order and rules of the home, the nation or culture, and learns to speak the language. In contrast (but not in opposition) to conditional hospitality is unconditional or pure hospitality: the pure welcoming of the unexpected guest or anyone who arrives or visits, the hospitality of *invitation*. Conditional hospitality of *invitation* is distinguished from the unconditional hospitality of *visitation* by the fact that in the former, the master remains the master, the host remains the host at home, and the guest remains an invited guest. As an invited guest, one is expected not to alter the rule and order of the home. Derrida imagines the hospitality of visitation in order to distinguish it from the hospitality of invitation where the stranger is not an invited guest, but one who arrives unexpectedly, where the host opens the house without asking any questions.

Derrida reminds us that the relation between the two forms of hospitality has the same structure between law and justice (and let's remember that according to Derrida justice is impossible); they are heterogeneous but at the same time absolutely indissociable. These two forms of hospitality refer to the legal and just forms of hospitality. Like justice, unconditional hospitality is impossible as one cannot deduce a rule from it. In other words, it is impossible to make it a rule that nations, families, cultures, or governments should open their house unconditionally to everyone and hence to turn it into an official policy. Although it is impossible, Derrida nevertheless designates with the term unconditional what hospitality should be in principle. Thus, the concept of conditional hospitality enables Derrida to conceive of unconditional hospitality. As he puts it:

> to think of this conditional hospitality one has to have in mind what would be a pure hospitality to the messianic Other, the unexpected one who just lands in my country and to whom I simply say: come and eat and sleep and I won't even ask your name.[44]

If we have a concept of conditional hospitality, it's because we have also the idea of a pure hospitality, of unconditional hospitality.[45] If unconditional or pure hospitality is impossible, then what is the possibility of the politics of hospitality? Like the relation between law and justice, where it is in the name of justice that one deconstructs the law, it is in the name of unconditional hospitality that conditional hospitality can be deconstructed. To tend to unconditional hospitality one has to deconstruct and improve the laws on hospitality (such as immigration laws), but these laws will never guarantee unconditional hospitality as such. The relation between them will remain open and irreducible. As Derrida notes, the law is perfectible and there is progress to be performed on the law that will improve the conditions of hospitality. The condition of the laws on immigration has to be improved without claiming that unconditional law should become an official policy. The very desire for unconditional hospitality is what regulates the improvement of the laws of hospitality.

Conclusion

So how, then, can we rethink the forces of capitalist globalization and institutionalized multiculturalism, which I suggested are working hand in hand, in light of the Derridian notion of unconditional hospitality? This essay has not meant to imply that the operation of the forces of globalization are limited by the laws that regulate the welcoming of immigrants or through institutionalizing multiculturalist respect and tolerance. Globalization works on many fronts, and we need to be vigilant: about the complicated links between globalization and the workings of nation-states in the so-called Third World; about the novel ways in which the rural is now accessed by global capital; about the interventions of the World Trade Organization, the International Monetary Fund, and the World Bank, which impose as international law the laws of the national economies of the Global North; about the reinstitution of the repressive powers of the nation-states in the Third World so as to enable the smooth operation of global capital.[46] My analysis here engages with the question of globalization in terms of its ideological and political presuppositions. The reason for my discussion of how liberal multiculturalism functions as the ideal form of global capitalism and how it is conditioned by its demands is twofold: first, to examine the hegemonic ideological form of global capitalism as it relates to the ethnically and culturally Other; and, second, to challenge the idea that the valorization of particular identities can be seen as a destabilizing counter-hegemonic political force in the wake of the global abstraction of transnational capitalism. I have suggested that Derrida's concept of conditional hospitality is a useful philosophical and theoretical apparatus for deconstructing the ideology embedded in liberal multiculturalism.

But let me be clear: I do not mean to suggest that conditional hospitality should be dismantled, that the welcoming of immigrants based on legal regulations should be done away with, or that unconditional hospitality should be substituted as the official policy of the host nations. I do not recommend the concept of unconditional hospitality as a technical application of a rule or norm. Unconditional hospitality is not to be regarded as the name of a counter-political program against the global management of the ethnically and culturally different. Nor is it a command that can be conformed to or deviated from, as it cannot be treated as a rule or an injunction that can organize the nature of the relation with immigrants. Unconditional hospitality is neither a means of determining judgment nor a rule of action. It is, rather, the condition of the possibility of the perfection and improvement of conditional hospitality. Speaking of unconditional hospitality, Derrida notes:

> It's impossible as a rule, I cannot regularly organize unconditional hospitality, and that's why, as a rule, I have a bad conscience. I cannot have a good conscience because I know that I lock my door, and that a number of people would like to share my house, my apartment, my nation, my money, my land, and so on and so forth. I say not as a rule, but sometimes, exceptionally, it may happen. I cannot regulate, control, or determine these moments, but it may happen, just as an act of forgiveness, some forgiveness may happen, pure forgiveness may happen. I cannot make a

determinate, a determining judgement and say: "this is pure forgiveness," or "this is pure hospitality," as an act of knowledge, there is no adequate act of determining judgment. That's why the realm of action, of practical reason, is absolutely heterogeneous to theory and theoretical judgments here, but it may happen without even my knowing it, my being conscious of it, or my having rules for its establishment. Unconditional hospitality can't be an establishment, but it may happen as a miracle ... in an instant, not lasting more than an instant, it may happen. This is the ... possible happening of something impossible which makes us think what hospitality, or forgiveness, or gift might be.[47]

This "possible happening of something impossible" can be seen as the condition of a democratic possibility. To use Derrida's formulation in *The Other Heading: Reflections on Today's Europe,* this condition of democratic possibility is something "to be thought and *to come* [*à venir*]: not something that is certain to happen tomorrow, not the democracy (national or international, state or trans-state) of the *future,* but a democracy that must have the structure of a promise—*and thus the memory of that which carries the future, the to-come, here and now."*[48] It is the introduction of the notion of unconditionality into politics—or to put it in Balibar's term, the politics of equaliberty, which is an all-or-nothing notion—that can open the possibility of a democratic politics. As we saw earlier, Balibar argues that as an unconditional force, the demand for equaliberty or the right to have rights cannot be relativized. The unconditional nature of equaliberty, like the unconditionality of hospitality, is distinct from this or that specific right guaranteed by law. However, neither equaliberty nor unconditional hospitality in themselves are possible. But their impossibility should not be taken as the closure of the possibility of democracy; on the contrary, it is the principle of unconditionality which is the driving force behind the condition of possibility of a democratic opening and, with it, a revision in law.

At this point, it might be useful to situate the demand for equaliberty and the ethics of hospitality in the context of contemporary global capitalism, as my aim is not to theorize them as pure, atemporal, and context-independent forces ultimately separated from forces of economy and politics.

From the point of view of politics proper, globalization can be characterized as a contradictory process: on the one hand, the very processes of globalization produce the demand for equaliberty. The globalization of production and other market forces necessarily create the conditions for the welcoming of immigrants as well as the granting of certain rights. These very same groups, as a consequence of the production of new political and ideological needs, make claims that may be against the interests of global capitalism. On the other hand, however, globalization is a law-governed process, and institutionalizing forces, such as the International Monetary Fund and the World Bank, absorb the demand for equaliberty through the mechanism of the law. Thus, the ideal of the right to have rights or the demand for equaliberty is necessarily compromised as it becomes articulated within global capitalism. And it is in this regard that Negri's analysis becomes useful for understanding the constriction of politics proper through constitutional means. Such institutionalization coincides with the direction global capitalism has taken. Demands for equaliberty are always compromised, diluted, and contained by their expression within lawful and institutionalized processes.

In the face of this compromise, where can we situate the possibility of a democratic politics? In the face of this containment of the politics for equaliberty in global capitalism, must we forfeit the desire for unconditional hospitality? In a word: no. But the task is to rethink the very force of the demand for equaliberty not in terms of its full realization—as this would imply a total transcendence of global capitalism, which at the very least will not come any time soon—but precisely in terms of its inevitable containment or dilution by global forces. For unconditional hospitality or the demand for equaliberty is not exhausted by or reduced to the current historical context of the granting of conditional and legal rights. Neither is its full realization contingent upon the transcendence of the capitalist world system. Instead, unconditional hospitality has to be understood as immanent to the present—"the possible happening of something impossible"—demanding, in the present, the immediate transformation of the present conditions of hospitality.

NOTES

1. David Bennett, Introduction, *Multicultural States: Rethinking Difference and Identity*, ed. David Bennett (London: Routledge, 1998), 5.

2. *Ibid.*

3. Arjun Appadurai, "Disjuncture and Difference in the Global Cultural Economy," in *Global Culture: Nationalism, Globalization and Modernity*, ed. Mike Featherstone (London: Sage, 1990), 295–310.

4. Ulf Hannerz, "Cosmopolitans and Locals in World Culture," in *Global Culture: Nationalism, Globalization and Modernity*, ed. Mike Featherstone (London: Sage, 1990), 237–251.

5. Stuart Hall, "The Local and the Global: Globalization and Ethnicity," in *Culture, Globalization and the World System: Contemporary Conditions for the Representation of Identity*, ed. Anthony D. King (Binghamton, NY: Macmillan, 1991), 19–39.

6. Slavoj Žižek, "A Leftist Plea for 'Eurocentrism,'" *Critical Inquiry* 24, no. 4 (Summer 1998): 1007.

7. Arif Dirlik, "The Global in the Local," in *Global/Local: Cultural Production and the Transnational Imaginary*, ed. Rob Wilson and Wimal Dissanayake (Durham: Duke University Press, 1996), 30.

8. Étienne Balibar, "Ambiguous Universality," *differences* 7, no. 1 (1995): 52.

9. Slavoj Žižek, "Multiculturalism, Or, the Cultural Logic of Multinational Capitalism." *New Left Review* 225, no. 1 (Sept./Oct. 1997): 43–52.

10. Dirlik, "The Global," 35.

11. *Ibid.*, 37.

12. Žižek, "Multiculturalism," 41.

13. *Ibid.*, 42.

14. Gayatri Chakravorty Spivak. *A Critique of Postcolonial Reason: Toward a History of the Vanishing Present* (Cambridge: Harvard University Press, 1999), 397.

15. Žižek, "Multiculturalism," 44.

16. David Lloyd, "Race under Representation," *Oxford Literary Review* 13, no. 1–2 (1991): 70.

17. Meyda Yegenoglu, *Colonial Fantasies: Towards a Feminist Reading of Orientalism* (Cambridge: Cambridge University Press, 1998), 103.

18. Žižek, "Multiculturalism," 45.

19. *Ibid.*, 46.

20. For Žižek the term "politics proper" "always involves a kind of short circuit between the universal and the particular; it involves a paradox of a singular that appears as a stand-in for the universal.... This *singulier universel* is a group that ... not only demands to be heard on equal footing with the ruling oligarchy or aristocracy ... but, even more, presents itself as the immediate embodiment of society as such, in its universality, against the particular power interests of aristocracy and oligarchy" ("A Leftist Plea," 988–89).

21. Derrida notes that the German word for hospitality is about the stranger's right, upon arrival to the domain of another, to be treated not as an enemy. Hence hospitality is in opposition precisely to opposition itself, that is, to hostility. The guest, who is hosted as the opposite of the one who is treated as an enemy, is a stranger who is treated as an ally.

22. Jacques Derrida, *Adieu to Emmanuel Levinas*, ed. Werner Hamacher and David E. Wellbery, trans. Pascale-Anne Brault and Michael Naas (Stanford: Stanford University Press, 1999), 87.

23. Kant adds the word *Wirbarkeit* as synonymous to the word *hospitality*. The word *Wirt(in)*, Derrida writes, refers to host and guest, the host who accepts the guest. Derrida notes that the word *Gastgeber* refers to the owner (proprietor) of a hotel or restaurant. Like *Gastlich*, *Wirtlich* also means the one who hosts or accepts. *Wirt, Wirtschaft* thus refers to the domain of economy, the governing of home.

24. Jacques Derrida, *Hospitality*, Angelaki 5, no. 3 (Dec. 2000), 15–6.

25. *Ibid.*, 14.

26. In this way, hospitality becomes the threshold itself. For hospitality to exist there has to be a door. But when there are doors, that means there is no (unconditional) welcoming, as this implies that someone has the key for the door and thus controls the condition of hospitality.

27. Giorgio Agamben, *Homo Sacer: Sovereign Power and Bare Life*, trans. Daniel Heller-Roazen (Stanford: Stanford University Press, 1998), 24.

28. *Ibid.*

29. *Ibid.*, 21.

30. *Ibid.*, 26.

31. *Ibid.*, 28.

32. *Ibid.*

33. Antonio Negri, *Insurgencies: Constituent Power and the Modern State*, trans. Maurizia Boscagli (Minneapolis: University of Minnesota Press, 1999).

34. Étienne Balibar, [qm]Ambiguous Universality,[qm] *differences* 7, no. 1 (1995): 65.

35. *Ibid.*, 66.

36. *Ibid.*, 65.

37. As it will become clear in the following pages, it is legitimate to discuss the relation between these two as they have the same structure.

38. Derrida, *Adieu*, 20.

39. *Ibid.*

40. *Ibid.*, 41–2.

41. *Ibid.*, 72.

42. Jacques Derrida, "A Discussion," *Theory and Event* 5, no. 1 (2000): 9.

43. Jacques Derrida, "Force of Law: The 'Mystical Foundation of Authority,'" in *Deconstruction and the Possibility of Justice*, ed. Drucilla Cornell et al. (New York: Routledge, 1992), 3–67.

44. Derrida, "A Discussion," 13.

45. *Ibid.*, 15.

46. For a fuller discussion of these issues see Yegenoglu and Mutman, "Mapping the Present: Interview with Gayatri Spivak," *New Formations* 45, no. 1 (Winter 2001–02): 9–23.

47. Derrida, "A Discussion," 15–16.

48. Jacques Derrida, *The Other Heading: Reflections on Today's Europe*, trans. Pascale-Anne Brault and Michael B. Naas (Bloomington: Indiana University Press, 1992), 78.

Decoloniality and Ethics

"Sensibility" and "Otherness" in Emmanuel Levinas

Enrique Dussel

I turned to Levinas when I began to write *Para una ética de la liberación latinoamericana* (*Towards an Ethic of Latin American Liberation*) and it was Levinas who gave me the opportunity to go beyond the Heidegger of *Being and Time*. Without abandoning the approach to liberation that I took in writing that text, I shall continue my argument from the "pulsional" perspective.[1] As the phenomenological critic that he was, Levinas's first approach to understanding otherness was to place himself systematically outside the straightforward gnoseological order.[2] Unlike the study of the subject prior to him, his life was the reference situation for his own thinking of the other. A Lithuanian Jew, whose mother tongues were Russian and Hebrew and who acquired French as a student in Strasbourg and German in Freiburg, he lived the "experience" of five traumatic years in the Nazi French prisoner of war camp at Stammlanger. He was a *victim* of the Jewish holocaust in the heart of modernity. He was a survivor who began his mature work as follows: "To the memory of those who were closest among the six million assassinated by the National Socialists, and of the millions on millions of all confessions and all nations ... *victims* of the same hatred of the other man, of the same anti–Semitism."[3]

As a South American, I asked myself: When Levinas spoke of victims of the same anti–Semitism, what did he imply about all those others who are not Semitic? In 1972, in Louvain, I got a group of students together to talk with Levinas. I asked: "What about the fifteen million Indians slaughtered during the conquest of Latin America, and the thirteen million Africans who were made slaves, aren't they the other you're speaking about?" Levinas stared at me and said: "That's something for you to think about." And so I continued to develop the Liberation Philosophy on which I had already begun to work.

135

At the end of the meeting at which I asked Levinas my pressing question, he said to us: "I see all of you as though you were *hostages*." I didn't grasp what he meant. Shortly after that, while I was reading *Otherwise than Being*, I understood. As a group of young teachers and students, obsessed by our Latin American victims, Levinas saw us as hostages in Europe; that is, Europe took us as hostages for our distant and oppressed peoples. I didn't know if he was insulting us by making this observation, but as I read *Otherwise than Being*, it dawned on me that it had been a vast, undeserved, and encouraging appraisal of us.

It seems to me that Levinas the prisoner in the Stammlanger camp is a clear reference situation that must be kept in mind when reflecting on his idea of otherness. In prison, as a "hostage" for his persecuted people, he was aware of himself as guilty, because he had survived. Obsessed about his brothers, the victims, through his ethical-critical philosophy he bore witness to the evil of Being through which the other is closed out. In the experience of being a hostage, a substitution takes place. The hostage is an innocent, just person who "witnesses" the victim (the other). The victim suffers a traumatic action. The hostage suffers "for" the other. The theme of one who suffers persecution for the other (the multitude *rabim*) is treated dramatically in the four poems of the "Servant of Yahweh" in Isaiah 42:1–53. The servant finds him/herself before a court as *a ransom victim* for the sake of the multitude. Among the people that are to be ransomed, there were two poles: *my people* who are pardoned and are an object of pity and the *multitude*, the undetermined, that which could be the object of the pardon. "My people" is the portion of the saved multitude; the multitude is the symbol of all humanity—present or future—who *could be my people*.[4] We shall see the diachrony in due course going from the "multitude" (a mere contradictory social block) to the "people" (historical subject). The ethical question Levinas analyzed is structured around several Hebrew words for the ideas of redemption, redeem, and ransom. To redeem refers to paying a ransom, buying the freedom of the slave, liberating him, saving the victim. In thinking of otherness, Levinas puzzled out the relation between those who *are* "my people" and those who *could be* "my people." An ethics of responsibility is built between these two groups and between the hostage and the victim.

Sensibility

Levinas explored differences in the experience of desire from the perspective of the hostage and from the perspective of the victim.[5] I will discuss the idea of otherness by detailing the interplay between the meaning of desire and the action of the hostage in his or her concern for the victim. Levinas situated himself in the place of the hostage who he understood to be a (gratified) member of the social system but who nevertheless is willing the receive the impact of an appeal for help from the victim. The hostage is not exactly in the place of the victim. That is, hostages enjoy the rewards of the social system of which they are members but also are able to face victims and heed their appeals for help. Out of his or her own satisfaction (i.e., the absence of need), the hostage responds to the victim.

This re-sponsibility (from *spondere,* to "take something into one's charge" in Latin) towards the other comes before the taking of any decision. Responsibility, according to Hans Jonas,[6] is an *a posteriori* responsibility for the life of the planet. In contrast, with Levinas, we are dealing with an *a priori* responsibility since it places us in a position of having charge of the victim who unexpectedly appears before us. Victims appear before us: someone is begging, someone is injured beside the road, a street kid is cleaning our car, we encounter a victim of repression, we meet a woman who has been brutally beaten, we speak with a student unfairly treated by the teacher. The victim is another whose accusing presence we can no longer "shake off" when it comes to our obligation to "do something" for that person. I can reflect on the encounter afterwards, turn away and forget about it, or do something concrete for him or her. These conscious decisions or acts are *a posteriori.* They come after the experience in which an accusing presence obligates us.

Is it rational to respond to an appeal for help? If we go on the understanding that the emotional, corporeal, and material worlds of pulsions, that is, a "life that is complacent in itself, that lives of its life,"[7] in no way denies reason, we see rather that this life defined the limits of reason. Not everything is rational! Levinas told us, and he was right—at least from the point of view of an Ethics of Liberation, which is liberation of victims and not of the satisfied. Heideggerian ontology, traditional phenomenology, the linguistic logics of sense-meaning, and even of intersubjective validity, are philosophies of the "satisfied"—whose satisfaction is an unacknowledged starting point and is taken unquestioningly as reality. To come face to face with the unsatisfied—the poor, the abused women—is to begin to wonder about this whole dimension which Levinas opened up before us—a dimension that he opened up in ways different from those of Marx, Horkheimer, and Freud, although at bottom he agreed with them.

In the desire for the victim, Levinas identified a shift in the hostage's experience in which happiness and desire separate from one another. For Levinas, desire is an aspiration not conditioned by a previous lack. In a strange way he enters into the discourse on liberation with which I have been dealing when he wrote: The I exists as separated in its enjoyment, that is, as happy; it can sacrifice its pure and simple being to happiness. It *exists* in an eminent sense; it exists above being. But in Desire[8] the being of the I appears still higher since it can sacrifice to Desire its very happiness. It thus finds itself above, or, at the apex, at the apogee of being by enjoying (happiness) and by desiring (truth and justice). To Levinas, desire moves above being and above happiness.

What more can be said of desire? In Levinas, the desire of the hostage for the victim is a creative pulsion,[9] that is, desire creatively causes something to emerge, but it lies beyond mere Dionysian instinct and is totally transcendental with regard to it. He wrote that the other, metaphysically desired, is not "Other" like the bread I eat. The metaphysical desire tends towards *something else entirely*, toward the *absolutely other*. As commonly interpreted, need would be at the basis of desire.[10] But need is not at the basis of metaphysical desire when the term is used by Levinas. Metaphysical desire is like goodness—the Desired does not fulfill it, but deepens it. Metaphysical desire is a desire without satisfaction in that it *understands* [*entend*] the remoteness, the alterity of the other.[11]

Earlier I said that, in Levinas, Desire moves above being and above happiness, that is, Desire is twice removed above Being. Let us assume that, as in the case of Nietzsche, Levinas relied upon a conception of "happiness" as a state to be surpassed. In Nietzsche's case, desire is surpassed by "pleasure" (*Lust*), an idea that Levinas thought was "narcissistic" and inadequate. In Levinas, "Desire" is pleasure that is neither erotic nor narcissistic, but rather transcendental—"for-the-Other" (*pour l'Autre*). In the *Cantique des colonnes*, Valéry speaks of desire without defect (*désir sans défaut*). He is presumably referring to Plato who, in his analysis of pure pleasures, found an aspiration not conditioned by any previous lack. Let us take up this term "desire" again. We confront a subject inclined towards himself or herself. The subject is characterized by the tendency to persist in his or her being, and is one for whom, using the Heideggerian formula, his or her existence is essential to his or her existence itself; this is a subject also characterized by a concern with himself or herself, and who achieves in happiness his or her for-himself or for-herself. If Desire for the Other emanates from a satisfied being, in this sense, that is, from one who is independent and who does not want for himself or herself, then Desire, in the hostage, is founded on the need of someone who no longer has needs.

Or, to put it another way: The I endowed with personal life, for example, the atheist I whose atheism is without wants, surpasses itself in the Desire that comes to it from the presence of the other. This Desire is a desire in a being already happy. For this reason, "desire is the misfortune of the happy" but "misfortune" is intended ironically. The person summoned to responsibility by the other is plucked out of his or her tranquility, peace, and security and is hurled into a risky adventure, beyond the quest for personal happiness. The adventure is a search for justice, for the sake of the Other. Justice for the poor, the widow, and the orphan, is unthinkable for Nietzsche amidst his

Will to Power. In Levinas this compelling, propelling inclination—this pulsion towards justice—was his Will to Alterity. Desire marks a sort of inversion with regard to the classical notion of substance. When the victim (the other) appears before me, I am drawn powerfully toward the other and my spontaneity is challenged by the other's presence. It is in this sense that I am a hostage. Ethics is the name we give to this calling into question of my spontaneity by the presence of the other. Just as "ontology ... reduces the other to the same,"[12] theory traditionally understood enters upon a course that renounces metaphysical Desire, renounces the marvel of exteriority from which that Desire lives. But theory understood as a respect for exteriority has a critical intention that does not reduce the other to the same as does ontology, but rather calls into question the exercise of the same. Metaphysics, transcendence, the welcoming of the other by the same, of the other by me, is concretely produced as the calling into question of the same by the other, that is, as the ethics that accomplishes the critical essence of knowledge. And as critique precedes dogmatism, metaphysics precedes ontology.

So Levinas proposed, on the one hand, a creative or alterative pulsion that returns to the Totality the pulsions of self-preservation or reproduction (the same, the egotistical psychism), and even those same Dionysian, narcissistic pulsions (the egotistical eros or mere constituted cultural need),[13] and at the same time, on the other hand, he proposed a corresponding *"critical reason."* Eros is a window, but an ambiguous one, since in "the primacy of the self," egoism, can be "narcissistic." Levinas did not want to follow the path of narcissism. The sensibility that he proposed, this pulsion of Alterity, is an "exiting" (*Ausgang*) but a very different one from the Kantian, Enlightenment exiting. It does not only involve overcoming a pre-critical intellectual state of self-blamable immaturity,[14] but also includes exiting from the irresponsibility of the insignificance of the other—by having "habitually" rejected his or her appeal. I suppose we might say that egotistical irresponsibility (a very different sensibility from that which Levinas would promote) is the price to be paid for habitually rejecting the other's appeal.

Otherness

I think that if we are going to make Levinas's thought comprehensible, our point of departure should be a double scenario that would be defined by three moments of his life. To show this I will base my analysis upon two of his works: *Difficult Freedom* and *Otherwise Than Being*. Let us see how this phenomenological adventure with the other happened. Using his analytical apparatus, he reached some supremely fine distinctions, but, at the same time, showed the limits of this apparatus, especially where his philosophy of history and politics are concerned. I will outline aspects of his life that highlight what I will refer to as two scenarios representing certain aspects of his views on otherness.

The first moment of Levinas's life, which takes us as far as 1961 (the moment of the first scenario), covers three major stages. The first is a preparatory stage, in Strasbourg and Freiburg, with Heidegger and Husserl, whose influence can be seen in his doctoral thesis.[15] There is no question that the French translation of Husserl's *Cartesian Meditations*, which Levinas published in Paris in 1931, inevitably plunged him into the question of "the Other."[16] His preparation continued throughout the 1930s. In the second stage, we have the Second World War and his confinement in the prisoner of war camp, Stammlanger. In 1946 he turns to the material that appeared in *Time and the Other*,[17] in which repeated attempts are made to overcome the cognitive position, the "intention" of phenomenological knowing, the ontology of "individual being" (of the "self" in the world) in the face of an "I am"[18] only facing the other, in the "face-to-face" (firstly as the erotic feminine). The third stage came between the war and 1961. During this third stage, in the development of his thought, the other breaks with one's selfness, one's aloneness. In 1947 he published *De l'existence à les existents* (translated in 1988 as *Existence and Existents*).[19]

Indeed, the first scenario, visible in Levinas's *Totalité et infini: essai sur l'extériorité*, published in 1961,[20] described as a starting point in "psychism" that precedes understanding in the Heideggerian world. In a moment which is *before* being-in-the-world, the pre-ontological *metaphysical* conditions of possibility are analyzed phenomenologically.[21] These conditions could be summed up as sensibility.[22] Sensibility has to do with a pre-opening up to the world as a vulnerable, traumatizable corporeality, i.e., even before I meet the other I am prepared to open up to him or her. But this living, life-relishing sensibility which eats and dwells (residing in a home with safety and warmth) is constituted *as an ethic* by the face-to-face experience with the Other, so that its ethical sensibility arises from the "responsibility" before the face of the other.

After the Holocaust, responsibility for the other is shaped by the needs inherent in suffering. The other's demand upon me emerges out of that desperate condition of suffering. Out of its condition as a victim, the being that *expresses* itself imposes itself, but does so precisely by appealing to me with its destitution and nudity, without my being able to be deaf to that appeal.

But the fact that the face of the destitute person can "appeal" to me is possible because I am "sensibility" *a priori* vulnerable corporeality. Sensibility is expressed as hospitality. The appearance of the other is not a mere manifestation but rather a revelation; its capture is not comprehension but rather hospitality. In the presence of the Other, reason is not representative, but rather listens sincerely to what is being said. The incomprehensible nature of the presence of the other is not to be described negatively. The formal structure of language announces the ethical inviolability of the other. The fact that the face maintains a relation with me by discourse does not range him in the same; rather the face remains absolute within the relation.

Reason and language arise out of the face-to-face relation with the other prior to representation. That is, "reason lives in language … the first rationality gleams forth in the opposition of the face to face … the first intelligibility, the first signification, is the infinity of the intelligence that presents itself (that is, speaks to me) in the face."[23] But what we lend an ear to from the beginning is the way in which Levinas posed the problem of asymmetry. As he said: "The presence of the face coming *from beyond the world* but committing me to human fraternity, does not overwhelm me as a numinous essence arousing fear and trembling…. The other who dominates me in his transcendence is thus the stranger, the widow, and the orphan, to whom I am obligated."[24] To Levinas at least, the idea of asymmetry did not entail being overwhelmed by one's obligation to the victim. The will of the hostage is neither deficient, arbitrary, egotistical, nor speeding towards suicide. The other of the asymmetrical relation is a victim and therefore comes from above and appears as ethically superior to me due to his or her suffering. It is the asymmetry of the relation with the victim that obligates me. The will of the hostage, no matter what decision is subsequently made, feels the impact, finds itself now "re-sponsible" (as that which first and foremost finds itself taking care of the other). The will is free to assume this responsibility in whatever sense it likes; it is not free to refuse this responsibility itself; it is not free to ignore the meaningful world into which the face of the other has introduced it. In the welcoming of the face the will opens to reason. The asymmetrical relation links the hostage to the victim. The asymmetry constitutes a hostage, who responds in welcome. The absolutely new is the other.[25] Levinas concluded that the terror of reason enclosed within Totality, the reason of modernity, is situated at the antipodes of the brave subject living for the other. Such a being confronts death out of pure courage and the cause for which he dies.[26] Levinas's idea of sensibility grew through his experience with Nazi heroic fanaticism. Likewise in South America, we lived through the heroism and fanaticism of the ideologues of Western Christian Civilization.

And so we come to the second Levinas (1961–1974), with its second scenario. From 1963 onward he showed a clear command of the theme of the other who provokes an ethical movement in consciousness and through Desire disturbs the awareness of a coincidence of the Same.[27] He slowly began to develop new categories for the position of the hostage. In 1974 when *Autrement qu'être ou au-delà de l'essence* was published (translated in 1981 as

Otherwise than Being or Beyond Essence), the new scenario had already been sketched. Following Rosenzweig, Levinas radicalized the situation he was using for his phenomenological analysis in terms of the *exposure* felt by the hostage. In a taxi, before a lecture in Louvain in 1972, I asked: "What does *exposure* mean?" And Levinas, as though he were violently pulling open his shirt with both hands and ripping off the buttons to expose his chest, exclaimed: "It's like when one *exposes* oneself in front of a firing squad!" The new scenario is more dramatic than the first. In the second scenario there is a different perspective. The one who is appealed to is "persecuted" because of the other, i.e., the victim.[28] In the ethical relation, the one who is appealed to, and feels the obligation, is taken as a "hostage" and is "substituted" for the victim.[29] It is the old question of offering up one's own life to "pay the ransom" for the life of a slave. In the new scenario, we have the theme of the "redemption" for the other in the face of the power of the system, a System in which one "bears witness" to one's own "obsession" for the victim. The "third party" is an observer, but is also Power.

Responsibility[30] for the victim is prior to dialogue. It is a persecuting obsession in which an identity individuates itself as unique without recourse to any system of references, in the impossibility of evading the assignment from the other—without experiencing blame. The representation of self grasps the assignment. The absolution of the one who feels obligated and responds is neither an evasion nor an abstraction; it is a concrete fact. For *under* accusation by everyone, the responsibility for everyone goes to the point of substitution. A subject becomes a hostage.[31] Obsessed with responsibilities and accused of what others do and suffer, the uniqueness of the self is the very fact of bearing the suffering and fault of another—persecution turns into expiation.

The point of departure for the hostage is a subjectivity that is sensibility expressed through pain. Pain is nudity more naked than all destitution, sacrificed rather than sacrificing itself, and bound to the adversity of pain. This existence, with sacrifice imposed on it, is without conditions. Subjectivity is vulnerable, exposed to affection, and is a sensibility more passive than any passivity: it is extreme patience. The hostage is exposed, exposed to expressing, and thus to saying, and thus to giving.

Pain marks the start of creation. Levinas said: "How the adversity of pain is ambiguous!" His work on the relation between the hostage and the victim, in the presence of the third party, was not enclosed within a vulnerable sensibility that was the *conatus essendi*.[32] The corporeal subject "exposes" itself before the Totality, the system, the third party, as being intimately tied to the other.[33] The hostage is discovered, without intending or deciding, to be in "proximity" to the other through contact. For Levinas, to be in contact is neither to invest the other and annul his alterity, nor to suppress one's self in the other. In contact, the one touching and the one touched separate, as though the touched moved off and was already other, as though he or she did not have anything in common with the hostage. But now the *ethical* step as such is taken. All that has gone before has been preparatory. The other, i.e., sensitive carnality (like the psychic ego), appears on contact not only as face but as a victim. Here Levinas reached the pinnacle of his contemporary thought:

> The face of a neighbor that I meet in proximity signifies for me an unexceptional responsibility, preceding every free consent, every pact, every contract. It escapes representation; it is the very collapse of phenomenality.... The disclosing of a face is nudity, non-form, abandon of the self, aging, dying, more naked than nudity. It is poverty, skin with wrinkles, which are a trace of itself.[34]

He identified what had not been emphasized in Western thought. In describing the victim's destitution, he moved from statements of fact to normative obligations. For instance, he moved from "This victim cannot live in this system," as a statement of fact, to an articulation of the hostage's experience of obligation to the other. It is the obsession of the other, my neighbor, accusing me of a fault that I have not committed freely[35] that reduces the ego to a self on the hither side[36] of my identity, prior to all self-consciousness, and denudes me absolutely. I recognize in the face by which I am "captured," a "re-sponsibilty," an "obedience," and an "obligation": Obedience precedes any hearing of the command. The other presents himself as an anarchic being that slips into me *like a thief* through the outstretched nets of consciousness. This trauma surprises me completely—this unheard command of obligation. This responsibility that puts us under an ethical obligation on behalf of the other, as victim, was described by Levinas as follows:

> We call prophecy this reverting in which the perception of an order coincides with the signification of this order given to him that obeys it. Prophecy would thus be the very psyche in the soul: the other in the same.... An obedience preceding the hearing of the order the anachronism of inspiration or of prophecy is, for the recuperable time of reminiscence, more paradoxical than the prediction of the future by an oracle.[37]

Conclusion

And so Levinas spelled out the final content of his ethics as such: the one for the other as a re-sponsibility that obligates. And why? Wasn't he, who was to some extent the father of French post-modernism, guilty of a lapse of rationality? Not at all. Levinas clearly showed the importance of the rational, but also untiringly showed its *origin* and *meaning*. Reason—rationality, intentionality, the order of being and the world, language, the said—arises from the context already described and eventually returns to it. The intention in Levinas's work can therefore be defined as follows: In starting with sensibility, which is interpreted not as a knowing but as proximity, proximity appears as the relationship with the other, who cannot be resolved into "images" or be exposed in a theme.

The impossibility to reduce the other to an image or theme may seem unforgivable to a rationalist. But Levinas has a positive yet critical view of rationality. Between the hostage and the victim appears the "Third Party."[38] In my case the Third Party was the Europe that held us hostage, those of us who comprised that small group of teachers and students from South America. The system, the Totality is justice (or injustice).

The ethical relation is born of responsibility for the other. To Levinas, responsibility for the other through communication is the primary adventure of science and philosophy. It is a rationality of peace. Clearly we are now in an unexpected radicality. Re-sponsibility for the other obligates me to search in the prevailing system or Totality for the causes of the victimization of the victim, and this is the critical moment of ethics as such. Levinas generalized this fact, going so far as to say that the world, consciousness—i.e., the whole order of knowing—is really an answer to this "obligating re-sponsibility":

> The way leads from responsibility to problems. A problem is posited by proximity itself, which, as the immediate itself, is without problems. The extraordinary commitment of the other to the third party calls for control, a search for justice, society and the State, comparison and possession, thought and science, commerce and philosophy, and outside of anarchy, the search for a principle. Philosophy is this measure brought to the infinity of the being-for-the-other of proximity, and is like the wisdom of love.[39]

Marx showed that all capital is accumulated value. Levinas wanted to show that everything "about truth,"[40] beginning with Heidegger and the institutions of all the historic systems, was in its ethical origin, an answer to the problem posed by the unjust pain of the victim. So now we have to take the final step. In a diachrony[41] of ethics we have to redefine philosophy itself. As Levinas said:

> Philosophy is the wisdom of love at the service of love … and serves justice by thematizing the difference and reducing the thematized to difference … philosophy justifies and criticizes the laws of being and of the city.[42]

I have said more than enough. The legacy of Levinas will have much to tell us in the near future.

NOTES

1. *Pulsional* conveys a relation characterized by a vital energy and impels and compels in an iterative way. In terms of alterity, it signifies a relation that throbs with a regular, alternating motion between one person and the other that obligates.

2. *Gnoseological* conveys a sense of secret knowledge, unavailable to the crowd or masses, that concerns itself with metaphysics and mystical knowledge. It is knowledge that requires special access. On the theme of the other prior to Levinas, see Pedro Lain Entralgo, *Teoria y realidad del otro* (Madrid: Revista del occidente, 1961); Michael Theunissen, *Der Andere* (Berlin: de Gruyter, 1965); English translation: *The Other* (Cambridge: MIT Press, 1986). See also recent work on Levinas as Mark Taylor, *Alterity* (Chicago: University of Chicago Press, 1987); Zygmunt Bauman, *Postmodern Ethics* (Oxford: Blackwell, 1993); Richard Cohen, *Elevation: The Height of the Good in Rosenzweig and Levinas* (Chicago: University of Chicago Press, 1994); Robert Gibbs, *Correlations in Rosenzweig and Levinas* (Princeton: Princeton University Press, 1992).

3. Emmanuel Levinas, *Otherwise than Being, or Beyond Essence*, trans. Alphonso Lingis (The Hague: Nijhoff, 1981).

4. Emmanuel Levinas, *Time and the Other*, trans. Richard A. Cohen (Pittsburgh: Duquesne University Press, 1987), 94.

5. In this sense, for Levinas, the instincts of self-preservation and even those of pleasure make up the I in its egotism, as "Totality."

6. Hans Jonas, *Das Prinzip Verantwortung* (Nördlingen: G. Wagner, 1982); English version: *The Imperative of Responsibility* (Chicago: University of Chicago Press, 1985).

7. Spinoza's *connatus esse conservandi*. See also Emmanuel Levinas, *Humanisme de l'autre homme* (Montpelier: Fata Morgana, 1972).

8. Emmanuel Levinas, *Totality and Infinity: An Essay on Exteriority*, trans. Alphonso Lingis (Pittsburgh: Duquesne University Press, 1969), 62.

9. *Ibid.*, 63.

10. "The same" is the totality, the system, the Heideggerian "world."

11. Levinas, *Totality and Infinity*, 42–43.

12. Levinas writes, subtly refuting Nietzsche: "Ontology as first philosophy is a philosophy of power. It issues in the State.... Universality presents itself as impersonal.... The 'egoism' of ontology is maintained even when denouncing Socratic philosophy" (*Ibid.*, 46).

13. Emmanuel Levinas, *Existence and Existents*, trans. Alphonso Lingis (The Hague: Martinus Nijhoff, 1978), 85.

14. Immanuel Kant, "An Answer to the Question: What Is Enlightenment," in *Kant: Political Writings*, ed. Hans Reiss, trans. H.B. Nisbet (New York: Cambridge University Press, 1991), 54–60.

15. Levinas's doctoral thesis was *Théorie de l'intuition dans la phénoménologie de Husserl* (Paris: Alcan, 1930).

16. Edmund Husserl, *Cartesian Meditations, An Introduction to Phenomenology*, trans. Dorion Cairns (The Hague: Nijhoff, 1960), 91.

17. In the articles "La trace de l'ature" in *En découvrant l'existence avec Husserl et Heidegger* (Paris: Vrin, 1967), 187–202; "Phenomenon and Enigma," in *Time and the Other*, 61–73; and "Language and Proximity," in *Time and the Other*, 109–39.

18. Levinas, "La trace de l'ature," 196.

19. Emmanuel Levinas, *Existence and Existents*, trans. Alpho Lingis (The Hague: Martinus Nijhoff, 1978).

20. Levinas, *Totality and Infinity: An Essay on Exteriority*.

21. Levinas, "Language and Proximity," 109–39.

22. Emmanuel Levinas, "Sensibility constitutes the very egoism of the I" (*Totality and Infinity*, 59).

23. *Ibid.*, 200–01.

24. Levinas, *Otherwise than Being*, 157, 159.

25. The theme of "ransom" or the "payment to prisoner of war," in other words "redemption," is dealt with at length by Rosenzwieg in Book III of Part II of the *Star of Redemption* (1921, vol. II, 152ff.). A persecuted "hostage" or "prisoner" can offer himself or herself to "redeem" a victim. In this case the "just innocent" one performs a "substitution" for the Other. This is the scenario Levinas has in mind.

26. Levinas, *Totality and Infinity*, 306.

27. "La trace de l'autre" and "Phenomenon and Enigma," in *Time and the Other*, 61–73.

28. Rosenzweig, *Star of Redemption*, 152.

29. For a comparison with Rosenzweig, see Cohen, *Elevations: The Height of the Good in Rosenzweig and Levinas.*

30. Levinas, *Otherwise than Being*, 14–15.

31. *Ibid.*, 48–49.

32. Cf. Spinoza's *Connatus esse conservandi.*

33. Levinas, *Otherwise than Being*, 9, 53, 56.

34. *Ibid.*, 148.

35. *Ibid.*, 125–26, 147, 157ff.

36. *Ibid.*, 161, 165–71.

37. *Ibid.*, 160.

38. The "third party" is an observer, but is also Power: "The third party is other than the neighbor…. It is important to recover all these forms beginning with proximity, in which being, totality, the State, politics, techniques, work are at every moment on the point of having their center of gravitation in themselves, and weighing on their own account" (*Otherwise than Being*, 157, 159).

39. It will be observed that Levinas is sufficiently bold to turn twenty-five centuries of philosophy on its head: philosophy should not be "love of learning" but rather "sophophilia"— "wisdom of love." For the sake of love, the entire order of carnality, sensibility, pain, responsibility for the victim's pain, and only from that starting point "construction," because there is no "re"-construction of the new.

40. Levinas, *Otherwise than Being*, 162–65.

41. Levinas, *Totality and Infinity*, 46.

42. "A philosophy of power, ontology is a philosophy of injustice" (*Ibid.*, 46).

From "Globalization, Organization, and the Ethics of Liberation"[1]

Enrique Dussel
with Eduardo Ibarra-Colado

Introduction: A Crucial Question

I should begin by mentioning three factors which influence, to some degree, the event in which we are taking part. They are related to some of the ideas I wish to share with you. The first has to do with the place we are in, the State of Oaxaca, the birthplace of the Mixtec and Zapotec cultures and the home of the Dominican convent of Santo Domingo. The construction of the latter began in the sixteenth century; exactly at the same moment, we will argue, as the beginning of modernity.[2] I mean to say, of course, the invention of America and the subsequent colonial invasion.

The second aspect is related to the geographical area of the group that has called this meeting. It is a region that competes, day after day, against modern Western nations, directed nowadays from Washington.[3] We are of course referring to those of the Asian Pacific area. Here, we have a mixture of many diverse cultures which shaped the destiny of the first millennium through the achievements of a number of distinguished races and their cultural practices. Some of these were ignored or forgotten by the emerging modern Europe, which had in mind only a supposed civilizing project.

When positioning them in prehistory, it was considered that the cultures and values represented by the Asian Pacific societies had not reached the state of "civilization." This was because the Europeans considered themselves the legitimate heirs of the age of "Reason," and they reserved this idea for themselves during a substantial part of the second millennium. Nevertheless, the last decades of the twentieth century have revealed, and this is indisputable, the strategic role oriental nations are playing in redefining the historical tendency of the planet. Under the shadow of Hiroshima and Nagasaki, in the only way the Occidentals found to reassert their colonial vocation on the world, Japan rose again. From the lands of the rising sun, the Japanese, very promptly, showed their abilities to assimilate, appropriate, and transform occidental technology. Moreover, they created their own and conquered enormous markets. However, this did not imply the renunciation of their own values, forms of organization, collaboration, and life style.

After Japan, other countries such as Taiwan, Hong Kong, Singapore, Malaysia, South Korea, Thailand, the Philippines, and Indonesia followed eagerly. Each of these had its own history and cultural peculiarities. Other countries in the region, such as India or Vietnam, have also demonstrated their tremendous potential. China is now writing the most recent chapter in this story of tigers and dragons, allowing us to see that the third millennium will create spaces in which different races and religions throughout the planet will unite to put limits on modernity. Eurocentrism has refused to accept that its civilizing project is leading us to the destruction of the ecology of the planet along with the annihilation of humankind. Hence, the only way out is to seek, in the world's societies, including Europe, a capacity to live with otherness or difference (alterity). This impulse which is seen in the Asian Pacific is also providing the Arab world, Latin America and African Nations with the possibility of creating a multipolar or *transmodern* cultural world, which protects life and encourages humans to live together instead of simply facilitating profit, private appropriations, and personal benefits.

The third factor that deserves to be mentioned is that this is an academic gathering which sets out to analyze the organization of modernity and yet incorporate certain *critical approaches* which question the received ideas in this area. It is interesting that some of the papers prepared for this encounter show the influence of philosophers such as Foucault, Derrida, or Deleuze, thinkers that have pointed out the inconsistencies in the ideologies of the Modern. Moreover, we must underline the fact that they have done so from the inside, that is to say, from the fruitfulness of these ideas as well as from the limitations that such a line of thought supposes. This, without a doubt, is significant but, as will be explained later, limited in itself because it brings with it the disadvantages inherent to any point of view which remains enclosed within a particular paradigm.

To avoid any possible self-satisfaction of those who consider themselves intellectual critics, I must add one last thing. These papers show clearly how Eurocentrism has not developed solely in the European Center or the United States. It also includes nations of very similar imperial vocation such as Australia and New Zealand from the Asian Pacific area. This ideology has also been cultivated in other regions of the planet such as certain African, Asian and (Latin) American countries. Despite the fact that plenty of the researchers in the colonized countries consider themselves proud critical (or advanced) thinkers, very rarely do they recognize the extent to which they are Eurocentric even though they are not European. This is a crucial question and avoiding it is unforgivable. This shows the limitations of the critical postures mentioned before. In other words, it shows the confusion of some of these researchers.

This is, in fact, another angle of the "conquest." Their minds have been colonized to such an extent that their idea of the "other" is the mirror image of the European or American identity. This problem shows the need to work on a second order criticism. This should not be satisfied with showing the fallacies of Eurocentrism when writing the "history" of humanity. It must seek the limitations that accompany all critical thought which does not question the validity of the "universal history" written from the point of view of the Center.

For this, it is necessary to acknowledge that the planetary dimension is far larger than the European and American concept of "world." Furthermore, when we locate ourselves somewhere else, it should be possible to understand the history of the world from a different perspective. This means that there is the need for an alternative history that emerges from the experience of the victims: the ideas of those who have been invaded and dominated and who have not had the chance to express themselves. Gradually, they are starting to raise their voices because they want to make their presence felt and have their own ideas. Here in Mexico, a clear example would be the Mayan rebellion in the state of Chiapas. There, indigenous communities that had been practically forgotten and existed basically only in [official] history text books and museums, regained visibility by raising their voices after years of living in silence.[4]

In this order of ideas, what should be emphasized, because it is impossible to set out every detail in such a brief space, are the arguments and questions concerning three related issues that have a growing importance in the light of current developments in the contemporary debates on the modern world. These are: *globalization, organization,*[5] and the *ethics of liberation*, which comprise three fundamental aspects necessary for understanding modernity and its future.

First, what will be discussed is the specific meaning that globalization acquires when it is confronted with the prevailing Eurocentrism. The result should be a critical posture which understands the world as a system that goes far beyond Europe. This will enable us to discuss the second point, which is the nature of the problems of organization related to globalization. Finally, the ethics of liberation will allow us to bring both factors together and discuss the elements and determinations that permit their transformation.[6] It may be that these ideas will serve as a useful tool to help stimulate debate about some of the issues of organization of the Modern world, its evolution, and its future.

[...]

The Ethics of Liberation...
The Future of Humanity

Until now, what has been proposed is a different way of understanding modernity. It is seen here as a process of globalization that started over five hundred years ago, and has different forms of organization such as the processes of simplification that require the "managing" of the entire planet and the non-recognition of the "other." We have yet to consider the ethical principles that might guide its transformation into a different and better world by confronting Eurocentrism. This means the recognition of the "otherness" of our nations which have been integrated into the "World" only in their postcolonial, peripheral, and underdeveloped condition. The intention is to reflect on the ways in which globalization and its forms of organization can be transformed. To do this, some of the central ideas of my ethics of liberation will be considered.[7]

This implies acknowledging that so-called global integration is in fact violent and exclusive. There is no place in it for millions of human beings who live unemployed, in poverty, in ignorance, and excluded. These enormous contingents of human beings, which can already be found in the main geographical areas of Western Europe and the United States, do not take part in or benefit from any of the promises of globalization.

If there is any doubt about this, it must be remembered that, after five hundred years of modern Europe, the *Human Development Report* of the United Nations (1992) indicated that the richest 20 percent of mankind (basically located in Western Europe, the United States and Japan) consume over 82 percent of the goods found on earth. On the other hand, the poorest 60 percent (found mostly in the "periphery" from where the riches that permit this "modernity" were plundered) consumes only 5.8 percent of these goods. This concentration is unheard of in human history and it represents a structural unfairness on a world scale. Is this not the result of the modernity Western Europe began and a consequence of its forms of organization based on instrumental reason?

In the end, we are dealing with an ethical problem related to the way we think of the world. This implies, of course, its forms of organization and the way it operates its systems of production, consumption, and social life.

That is, with the different ways in which society has been organized, supposedly with the aim of living better. Thinking of a different world, under different forms of organization, implies thinking about aspects of the ethics of human action. On such a basis, we should be able to elaborate critical principles from which we can transform reality.

The Aspects of Ethical Action

Ethics can be considered under three headings. In the first place, ethics must adopt as a principle the life–death criterion. It must assume that ethical action ought to act normative on *the production, reproduction and development of the life of the community, of humans being.* This is related to the obvious and irrefutable fact that we are living beings. Human beings are material which has organized itself in order to guarantee its own life's reproduction and development. This is done by satisfying the basic material needs—economic, cultural, political, religious, aesthetic—of every individual.

[...]

This leads us to a second aspect of organized human action: who decides on how we should develop life? This question takes us to a well-known discussion about the formal principles that allow decisions and cooperation among individuals. Should only a few make decisions, those who control the organization? Or should those who collectively produce and reproduce the organization with their work have a say? Further still, should individuals that are not directly involved but who are affected by the decisions of the organization be allowed to participate? In the end, is there a formal procedure from which the organization can be built as a collective effort as part of a moral consensus?

The object is to arrive at an intersubjective agreement whose validity rests on consensus, autonomy, and legitimacy. It should also facilitate the application of means and actions that protect and develop life. Such an agreement, in consequence can only be founded on practical–communicative reason and not, as until now, on the violence and exclusion exercised by instrumental reason. There must be a transition; from the imposition of the dominating ego on the "Other" to the intersubjective construction of the reasons of *everyone.*

This second ethical aspect implies not only the construction of a consensus between those who run, control, and conduct the actual organization and those who work. Above all, it also should include those who are affected on the outside, what economists cynically call "externalities." These individuals must be allowed to participate with symmetry in the decision-making of the organization because it affects the development of their lives. All ethical actions thus imply the reciprocal acknowledgment of all the members of a communicative group. They should hence promote the conditions that enable the *symmetric participation* of the affected members in the rational decision-making of such a community.

The third aspect of human ethical action has to do with the fulfillment of both of the prior aspects, that is to say, the *feasibility* of the protection of life and the promotion of symmetric participation in the building of a collective and rational form of organization. Feasibility implies determining in a material fashion what is economically, politically, technically and psychologically possible. We know that there are aims that are logically but not materially possible. Other aims are possible in certain societies, due on some occasions to their levels of prosperity, but impossible in others that have limited growth.

[…]

If organized human action took into consideration these three ethical factors, the defense of life, social consensus, and feasibility would be guaranteed. The reproduction of such a social order would facilitate its diffusion. A permanent cycle of re-organization that acts in favor of life by means of feasible decisions that have been agreed by everyone through consensus and reason would have been established. On the contrary, the non-acceptance of these ideas (the attack on life in order to obtain profit, authority exercised to obtain control over the other, the imposition of methods of development that have been shown to be socially and ecologically harmful) leaves us with forms of organization that act against humans and life, producing through their irrationality the victims whose existence they refuse to acknowledge and silence.

Critical Principles of Transformative Praxis

The factors that guide ethical action, mentioned earlier, find their negative form in the critical principles that guide the *transformative praxis* of reality and its forms of organization. To create different forms of organization requires us, firstly, to recognize the material limits of the modes of organization that are dominant today. It also requires us to show, from the victims' point of view, that their transformation is a matter of urgency.

Although it might seem obvious, it has not always been accepted that *every system is fallible and imperfect*. Thus, every system either produces or will produce consequences that affect someone. If we acknowledge that the system in which we live today is imperfect, then we should also be able to understand that it is a product of human activity from which negative effects inevitably result. Hence, the system and its forms of organization produce, but at the same time ignore, the sufferings of the "other." These manifest themselves in poverty, unhappiness, pain, domination, and/or exclusion.

The utopian aspect of the present system, expressed in its institutions and forms of organization, contains a contradiction. This is because most of those who participate in it are deprived of the possibility of making their rights valid. The right to life as a theoretical concept is in strong contrast with the materiality of many other factors: death, famine, misery, the oppression of corporeity as a result of labor, the repression of the libido and the unconscious, the lack of power of the individual in companies and institutions, curable or preventable diseases, illiteracy, and many other factors. These show up the real situation of the victim even as it is being formally denied.

[...]

Thus, the second critical principle of transformative praxis is based on the premise of the *impossibility of victims taking action until they recognize their own condition.* The consciousness of one's own condition is produced by one's empirical, day-to-day shared experience. This is how wider recognition is reached in one's own communicative group, starting to formalize a possible future that will facilitate liberation. In other words, those excluded can form a community that judges the system by producing a different and improved project. Facing the "impossibility of choosing death" because choosing death is not a choice, the victims need to build new "life options" from definite alternatives.

In spite of the fact that the criticism made by the victims is not taken seriously by the system and the dominant forms of organization, their criticism proves the system to be illegitimate. It reveals the way in which it makes the production, reproduction, and development of human life impossible. The array of examples is vast and is expressed in the emergence of new social movements that fight for recognition and try to achieve different forms of existence: The *Zapatist National Liberation Army* in Mexico, the rural *Sin Tierra movement* in Brazil, the *cocaleros* (coca growers) in Bolivia, or the *piqueteros* (unemployed) in Argentina are examples. Then again, on another level, there are the movements against exploitation in *maquilas* (tax free zone export industries), sweat factories, and the pollution of the environment. Other organized protests include the defense of women, homosexuals, AIDS-infected people, non–Caucasians, illegal immigrants, and old people.

[...]

The third critical principle of transformative praxis is the *liberation principle.* This aims at the implementation of formally planned future alternatives. This means the material transformation of the system, its institutions, and its forms of organization. This will make them function in the service of those who have been excluded. Any form of ethics must look, as a matter of urgency, at the *liberation* of the victims whose lives have been plundered and limited. Anyone who acts critically and ethically should transform the actions, institutions, or systems which currently dominate the world. This implies that their activities should be orientated towards opening up new possibilities in which the life of every victim can be materially transformed, allowing the victim to abandon his state of perpetual anguish.

[...]

Conclusion: A Different World Is Possible

The ideas and questions put forward throughout this paper concern the challenges which globalization represents today. It is a time in which the irrationality of the system is reflected in the flesh of its victims. Everyone can recognize the tremendous problems of poverty, injustice, and exclusion present on the entire planet. This is the other side of the coin from that in which huge profits and great power remain in few hands. We are living in a time of confrontation between the Eurocentric world, exclusive and violent, and the possibility of *a different modernity*. This will be transversal and will allow the planet's social shape to be reinvented.

This is a new type of theoretical possibility which I call *transmodern,*[8] a future utopia not dominated by modernity but in constant dialogue with it. The aim is to build a *pluriverse* (not a universe) in which every culture can conserve its own identity and, at the same time, assimilate the developments of this globalizing modernity. It will have its own criteria so that each person can decide what it is and what one wishes to adopt from this modernity.[9]

In conclusion, an attempt has been made here to outline a few ideas that show the feasibility of a different world project. In this, the modern individual who has been freed from his or her Eurocentrism will reencounter the nonmodern "Other" emancipated from the colonizers. The aim is to build a transition into a different world. We need to be convinced that a different world is possible, *plural, diverse, and symmetrical*. In this new space, all the different world views can be expressed, marking a new departure in the development of Humanity.

NOTES

1. This text came into being at different moments and was the result of three different drafts. It was written for the inaugural conference by Enrique Dussel at the Tenth International Colloquium of APROS that took place in the city of Oaxaca, Mexico, 7–10 December 2003. The second moment consisted of a transcription of the conference made by Eduardo Ibarra-Colado, who accepted the task of structuring and rewriting a new version, including the notes that accompany the text. For this, it was necessary to interpret the sense of the words of Dussel, deciphering the sounds and images on video and revising the published papers of the author. The final moment was again in the hands of Dussel, who revised and corrected the final version, giving it the distinctive form that it has now.

2. The construction of the Convent and College of Santo Domingo was started in 1527, scarcely thirty-five years after the so-called "discovery" of America and six years from its "conquest." Challenging the predominant explanation that assumes the absolute truth of the discovery of the "new world," Dussel has developed a contrasting interpretation. The "discovery" of America should be understood as its invention. The so-called "conquest," likewise, hides and legitimizes a violent *colonization*. For a discussion of this issue, see Dussel, Enrique, *The Invention of the Americas: Eclipse of 'the Other' and the Myth of Modernity* (New York: Continuum International Publishing Group, 1995).

3. Dussel is addressing the gathering of the Asia Pacific Researchers in Organization Studies (APROS), a multidisciplinary research group working on themes of organization in the region. This research network was created in 1982 in Australia and gradually included the other countries of the Asian Pacific, and later the countries of the American Pacific. As of 2007, there have been twelve international colloquia in the following cities: Hong Kong (3), Canberra, Kobe, Hawaii, Cuernavaca, Shanghai, Sydney, Oaxaca, Melbourne, and New Delhi.

4. Dussel refers to the movement begun on January 1, 1994, by the *Zapatist National Liberation Army* (EZLN). This coincided with the coming into effect of the North American Free Trade Association (NAFTA). There is no doubt that history has taken a different turn as a result of this confrontation. On this issue, see Enrique Dussel, "Ethical Sense of the 1994 Maya Rebellion in Chiapas," in *Beyond Philosophy: Ethics, History, Marxism, and Liberation Theology,* ed. Enrique Dussel (Lanham: Rowman & Littlefield, 2003).

5. The term "organization," so popular in the Anglo-Saxon world, does not cease to be an abstraction whose existence allowed functionalism to "dehumanize" the relationship between individuals. This fetishism must be recognized and overcome. If not, it would be impossible to understand that forms of organization—and their problems—are the consequences of power relations affecting humankind's levels of development and well-being. For a discussion, on the issue, see Enrique Dussel, *Ética de la liberación en la edad de la globalización y de la exclusion* (Madrid: Trotta, 1998), 496–500; Enrique Dussel, *Ethics of Liberation in the Age of Globalization and Exclusion* (Durham: Duke University Press, 1998).

6. The reader may consider consulting some other papers by Enrique Dussel, *Underside of Modernity: Apel, Ricoeur, Rorty, Taylor, and the Philosophy of Liberation* (New York: Humanities Press, 1996); Enrique Dussel, *Ética de la liberación en la edad de la globalización y de la exclusion,* 1998; Enrique Dussel, *Hacia una filosofia política crítica* (Bilbao: Desclée de Brouwer, 2001); Enrique Dussel, *Beyond Philosophy: Ethics, History, Marxism, and Liberation Theology* (Lanham: Rowman & Littlefield, 2003); Enrique Dussel, *Philosophy of Liberation* (Pasadena: Wipf and Stock, 2003) for a better appreciation of the problems mentioned throughout his keynote address. A significant part of the philosophical work of Enrique Dussel is available at: http://www.clacso.org and, for a discussion of his work, we recommend Linda-Martin Alcoff and Eduardo Mendieta, eds., *Thinking from the Underside of History: Enrique Dussel's Philosophy of Liberation* (Lanham: Rowman & Littlefield, 2000).

7. Dussel, *Ética de la liberación;* Dussel, *Beyond Philosophy;* Dussel, *Philosophy of Liberation.*

8. Enrique Dussel, "World-System and 'Trans'-Modernity," *Nepantla: Views from the South* 3, no. 2 (2002): 221–44.

9. Thus, various ways of analyzing the world system become possible. The "otherness" of yesterday and today, incorporated in non-modern forms of organization whose existence has been systematically ignored, may be re-examined. For example, the different forms of production, consumption and other human activities, such as education and health, that the Amerindian communities had before their colonization find new meanings. The different types of knowledge, skills, and practices of these cultures gave way to a form of social and ethical organization that emphasized efficiency and which must now be reconsidered. The same thing could be said about alternative forms of organization found in other cultures that, despite their undisputable richness and diversity, have been diminished by presumptuous and "self-sufficient" modernism. Might it not be possible to recreate modernity while conserving everything that it has contributed in favor of life and the planet? Might we not at the same time include in a new civilizing project what it is possible to learn from the Others by recovering from them the knowledge that they have cultivated for thousands of years?

On Pluritopic Hermeneutics, Trans-modern Thinking, and Decolonial Philosophy

MADINA V. TLOSTANOVA *and*
WALTER D. MIGNOLO

I. What Is Behind Encounters with Otherness?

Let us start by questioning the very formula of encountering the other, which is a catchy metaphor to be found in various scholarly publications throughout the world in the last several decades. Although the entire twentieth century experienced a growing painful interest in otherness and was marked by xenophobia often masked as xenophilia, it is starting from European postmodernism that has led otherness to become the focal point of philosophy per se. In today's trans-cultural environment, the narrative of encounter with the other has become central both in theoretical reflections and in contemporary art.

The question of "otherness" is fully a modern/colonial question. We are not saying that the Aztecs did not distinguish themselves from the Chichemecas, or the Greeks from the barbarous—those who did not speak Greek; or the Chinese in Beijing from the people who inhabited the outskirts of the rectangle that enclosed the ruling class. But "otherness," as we sense and think about it today, is a Western construction from the Renaissance on and is constitutive of the Western concept of "modernity." For "modernity" is nothing but a concept and a narrative that originated in and served imperial Western purposes. The fact that today "modernity" is embraced and appropriated in the United Arab Emirates, in China, or in Indonesia means that "modernity" is being expropriated from its place of origin. It is indeed the "/" (slash) that in our formulation divides and unites the "modern" with the "colonial" in which otherness was constructed by and through enunciations always situated in the house of the modern (of *humanitas*, of civilization, of Western Christianity, of science, etc.).

In the modern/colonial world, Western philosophy from the Renaissance on, distinguished, in different guises and masks, *humanitas* from *anthropos*. This distinction was not made by those classified under the domain of *anthropos*; neither were they consulted. The distinction was a pure, sole, and unilateral decision made by those who considered themselves, and their friends, to be *humanitas*. The other-*anthropos* is, then, inevitably linked to the same-*humanitas*. The magic effect here consists in blurring the epistemic and ontological dimensions and in pretending that *humanitas* and *anthropos* is an ontological distinction that the enoncé only describes, but is not an effect of an epistemic and political classification that the enunciation controls. Thus, a dialogue with colonial others (racially and patriarchally classified) is a moot point: why would *anthropos* be interested in talking with *humanitas* when *anthropos* knows that *humanitas* is not interested in dialogue but in domination?

The formulation "trans-cultural environments and encounters" also raises many questions. It should be noted that the trans-cultural is not a concept that has one single frame of reference. If it did, it would have had to be accepted that there is a universal history of the human species, and that the human species organized itself through time in particular cultures defined by memories, languages, rituals, food, knowledge, socioeconomic organization, and the like. But the concept of "culture" entered into the vocabulary of European modern imperial countries—France, England, and Germany—only as late as the eighteenth century. It was in their languages that the universal concept of knowledge (inherited from Christian theology) became global. Consequently, "culture" was already framed in a hierarchical classification. European culture or civilization (depending on whether you prefer German or French legacies) was not just a particular culture among others, but *the* culture. It was so because this concept was an epistemic construct built by agents and institutions that defined culture by the experience of European history. Once created, it legitimized the type of knowledge in which it was embedded. The concept of non–European cultures was a European invention. The difference between European culture and European knowledge that created the concept was organized through the colonial and imperial differential. In this frame, the concept of the trans-cultural as such always presupposes a power difference between cultures and knowledges. This was because it was neither in the Mandarin language and in Chinese society, nor in the Arabic language and in Middle Eastern Muslim societies, that the idea of culture was created and trans-culturally derived.

Otherness and encounters with otherness have acted as a peculiar leitmotif of modernity as such, taking different forms in its different phases—from theology and religion in the sixteenth and seventeenth centuries to national, circular, and globalized today—but always retaining the element of othering as objectifying as one of the main cognitive and rhetorical operations of modernity. The other as a darker side, necessary for the balanced existence and for the successful self-reproduction of culture, helps to define the same as the norm when it is used as a negative reference point and gives birth to the strategies of exclusion and resistance and to multiple reinforcing stereotypes.

The twentieth century was particularly fruitful in its various interpretations of such encounters: Martin Buber and Emanuel Levinas, Jacques Derrida and Mikhail Bakhtin, Paul Ricoeur and Gayatri Spivak, to name just a few.[1] European and wider Western totality is unimaginable without its distorted mirror—the non–European other that is increasingly rendered in modernity as a radically sub-human other. Paul Ricoeur called one of his most famous works *Oneself as Another* (*Soi-même comme un autre*), in a way restating a long-existing Western anxiety expressed a century earlier by Arthur Rimbaud's grammatically incorrect "Je est un autre" (I am an other). Martin Buber in *I and Thou* interpreted existence as encounter, mutuality, exchange, and meeting, and regarded dialogue as a genetic motif for describing the dual modes of being. For him, the I–You dialogue opens up the inherent otherness present in any individual. Bakhtin's dialogic theory developed similarly to Buber's and stressed the constant interaction of self and other. Later the poststructuralist theories of otherness heavily grounded themselves in reconsidered radical Freudian interpretations of fragmented identities and subjects whose "I" is a site of constant struggle between the impulses of the biological unconscious and those of the censuring super-ego. The majority of postmodernist conceptions of otherness dealt with this Freudian understanding of same/other relations, often mediated through Lacan's interpretations.[2]

However, *the other* as a problem for the same has not been solved in modernity or in postmodernity, and remained largely an absolute and insuperable radical otherness. This does not promise anything constructive, but just states once again the absolute relativism and epistemic uncertainty as the staples of postmodernist thinking. So what we have at work here in xenophilic postmodernist theorizing is, in fact, a constant repetition of difference, its endless copying, and the two main ways of treating the other that are typical of the rhetoric of modernity and which are retained in postmodernist thought often in self-reflecting forms. One of these approaches consists of the impossibility of understanding the other, and hence our tendency to translate otherness into sameness in order to be able to treat the other ethically, to communicate with it, to understand it, which is linked with the Levinasian thesis that any contact with otherness ends in violence by means of its appropriation and adjustment to the economy of the same.[3] The other approach rejects absolute otherness, yet clings to the modernist progressivist thinking, claiming that the other represents some previous earlier stage in the development of the same and needs to be condescendingly guided on its way to an enlightened position.

Therefore, we see here that modernist and postmodernist understandings of otherness, and notions of communicating with it, were marked by several philosophic, cognitive, and ethnical limitations, which we would like to further trace in this article, while at the same time attempting to present a different genealogy of otherness as a voice and a reason of the other himself/herself. One of the most fundamental weaknesses of modernist and postmodernist theorizing of otherness lies in the fact that its practitioners have criticized modernity from inside, from the position of sameness or internal non-absolute otherness, and what they criticized was the modern and not the Euro-American element in Western modernity. Therefore, their criticism of modernity remained superfluous or/and was ultimately aimed at redeeming the project of modernity, saving it from itself, and cosmetically redesigning it. More importantly, arguing against an essentialist understanding of identity, postmodernism thus erased the possible agency of an other based on any group affinity, and by doing so it negated the other once again, depriving it of any reason or agency as such.

Defending the authentic relations between people, Levinas offered his well-known concept of responsibility for the other, born beyond the spheres of freedom and Western egology, marked by the asymmetry of intersubjective relations.[4] But the Levinasian understanding of otherness, as well as of Sartrean reciprocity[5] within which both same and other can act as objects for each other at different moments, and of Derridean reflections on the monolingualism and monologism of the other, in fact, are all based on the same othering and objectifying.[6] It is the monology of these positions, their monotopic hermeneutics growing out of Western reason, that becomes obvious in all these interpretations, and not the monology of the other itself as a construct or as reality. The Western deconstruction of modernity from within is minimally and predictably external in relation to the Levinasian totality of European thought, but this thought itself remains the only reference point.

In contemporary Western understanding, the other is no longer eliminated in any violent form. It is overcome by stereotyping, orientalism, and progressivism, by continuing objectification, and, most commonly, by commodification. The culture of immanence (according to Levinas) strives to overcome the otherness of a different individual, a different society, or a different epistemology, while the spiritual is suppressed by the rational and the pragmatic. As a result, the other once again is being taken for the same; it becomes internal for our consciousness, while its ability to question us is ignored, and the Cartesian *ego cogito* turns into *ego consumo.*

Modernity managed to build its entire self-understanding on the rule of contraries where the other—be it a barbarian or a woman, nature or a homosexual—has been incorporated into a complex hierarchy, erected in order to represent the same positively, and also to provide a rationale for ensuring the stability of such divisions.

It is clear that the very idea of encountering and dealing with the "other" presupposes "a same" who enjoys epistemic and discursive privileges and who claims to identify himself/herself as the same in contrast with the other. Thus, the idea of the other assumes a monotopic frame of knowledge—epistemologically, discursively, and visually—that is, the invention of the other was and is always an imperial construct of the same by the colonial difference locating the other. This colonial difference is built into the fundamental asymmetry that was and continues to be sharpened in modernity—between the sameness that has the right to define and categorize the other, to treat it ethically or violently, always using itself as the universal norm, on the one hand, and the muted otherness that does not have the right to define or criticize the same, but is forced to see itself in a deprecating way due to its deficiency within the realm of sameness, on the other hand. If we shift the geography of this imperial reason[7] and look at the world from the perspective of the colonial other, the imperial same emerges in his or her naked privilege and dominant position. This shift requires us to move from monotopic imperial to pluritopic decolonial hermeneutics. Thus, philosophical thinking that can be called other-than-modern, from its very inception, is decolonial, and has to be philosophically decolonial in its trajectory.

II. Monotopic-Diatopic-Pluritopic Hermeneutics

Hermeneutics is generally described as the art of interpretation. It deals with meaning, and characterized the humanities. Hermeneutics has been usually distinguished from epistemology, which is the art of explanation and marks the sciences, both natural and human. There are, however, human sciences, such as history, anthropology, and partly sociology, that prefer interpretation to explanation. In the humanities, hermeneutics has been coupled with the interpretation of tradition. In the example of Hans-Georg Gadamer,[8] hermeneutics and the interpretation of Western traditions become one and the same. But since "the West" starting from the European Renaissance goes hand in hand with colonialism and Western expansion, Western knowledge has managed, controlled, and subsumed non–Western traditions, and, by so doing, taken away from them their own ways of making sense of the past for their own purposes. It was precisely in that cognitive operation (epistemo-logical we can say, using epistemology in a broader sense to refer to the prin-ciples of knowledge making, whether interpretation or explanation) that the idea of *humanitas* was conceived and the self defined in the interpretation of *anthropos*. *Humanitas* and *anthropos* are *two Western concepts*, as Nishitani Osamu has convincingly argued in "Anthropos and Humanitas: Two Western Concepts of 'Human Beings.'"⁹

Let us elaborate some more on pluritopic hermeneutics. It starts and departs from the earlier proposed concept of diatopic hermeneutics offered by Raimundo Panikkar. He defines it as the art of understanding by means of crossing spaces or traditions (dia-topoi), which do not have common mod-els of understanding and understandability.¹⁰ Under diatopic hermeneutics, we do not assume that the other has the same self-understanding as we do. Panikkar rethinks the mechanics of monotopic Western hermeneutics, according to which we can know something only if we acquire a certain degree of pre-understanding (Gadamer's "horizon") and anticipation of meaning. But in intercultural and inter-philosophical contexts, such an antic-ipation, as a basis for a hermeneutic circle, is not possible. Hence, the necessity of diatopic hermeneutics, which helps us understand something that does not belong to our horizon.

Diatopic hermeneutics begins with the realization of pain arising from alienation and radical difference. It becomes an answer to the challenge of an interpretation traversing the cultural and religious boundaries in case the hermeneutic circle has not been created yet. It refuses to colonize the other by its set of preexisting categories and values. In contrast to postmodernists, Panikkar does not think that it is impossible to understand the other. Such an understanding for him is inevitable and necessary. Hence, his method of im-parative (not com-parative) philosophy (from Latin *imparare*, to learn in the atmosphere of plurality), which is a way of dialogic and experiential (not interpretative as in Western hermeneutics) learning from the other, thus enriching our thinking by the other's intuitions and revelations.¹¹ What is important here is that Panikkar still clings to the subject/object and the same/other division, although he takes a huge step in the direction of ques-tioning this rule of modernity.

Last but not least, where is the epistemic location of the understanding subject who operates in a monotopically based hermeneutics (à la Gadamer)? The understanding subject of monotopic hermeneutics is not, and cannot be, *the other,* but is always the same. It is precisely the privilege of controlling knowledge and meaning that allows monotopic hermeneutics to secure the voice of *humanitas* and to define itself by inventing its exteriority, i.e., the other. While dia-topically (and pluritopically) based hermeneutics disobeys the totalitarianism of monotopic hermeneutics, the *other* speaks, reasons, argues, invents, and creates while looking into the eyes of *humanitas*. The difference between *humanitas* with its monotopic hermeneutics, on the one hand, and *anthropos* with its embracing and enacting diatopic and pluritopic hermeneutics, on the other hand, is that *anthropos* has the potential of thinking from his or her own body and experience, subsuming the imperial reason that makes an *other*, an *anthropos* out of him or her. In a way, the epistemic revolt of the *anthropos*, denouncing the non-human of the *humanitas*, enlarges and expands the ideals of the European Renaissance and the Enlightenment beyond their own horizons. The European Renaissance and Enlightenment men and postmodern neoliberal ideologues thought that they had the right to civilize and make the planet after their likeness. But all of a sudden, *anthropos* (the other) decided to take their destiny in their own hands. We are witnessing these reversals unfolding in two directions: de–Westernization and the shift toward the Eastern Hemisphere (as compellingly argued by Kishore Mahbubani),[12] and decoloniality and the shift from Marxism and Liberation Theology toward the global agencies of what Frantz Fanon called *les damnés de la terre*[13]: all those marked by the colonial wound,[14] by being questioned in their/our humanity for their/our religion, skin color, sexual preference, gender, geo-political location, and language. In a nutshell, the *other,* the *anthropos,* is now on the march to decolonize *humanitas* and to build a world in which everyone participates instead of being participated, as *the other* was.

We have already mentioned the crucial meaning of colonial and imperial differentials for conceptualizing "encounters with otherness." This problematic is closely linked with the genealogy of Western comparative studies from the Renaissance on, where the comparison has been always marked by the imperial epistemic and cultural dominance and framed within the false analogy paradigm: the European "apples" were continually compared with the non–European "oranges" and other such strange fruit, only to prove their deviation when opposed to "apples." However, in the colonial space, the strangeness of the other constantly erodes the realm of the same, does not leave it impenetrable, and eventually finds its way to the metropolis, as Anne McClintock has persuasively argued in *Imperial Leather.*[15] Thus, what we have in colonies or semi-colonies in modernity can be called a colonial semiosis,[16] which is based on the interactive production of culture and knowledge by members of different traditions.

What is important here is that in this case, the act of understanding someone else's philosophy, cosmology, ethics, culture, and language presupposes a self-conscious comparison, involving not only the two or more terms that are being compared but also questioning the very act of comparison itself, its mechanisms, its ideologies, and the relativity of its points of view. Instead of Gadamer's monotopic hermeneutic, in which the point of enunciation is always inside the same Western tradition and its linear myth of modernity is invented by the very monotopic understanding and imposed onto the multicultural spaces, in the case of pluritopic hermeneutics, we localize the understanding subject in the colonial periphery, which automatically disturbs the easy and clear rendering of "tradition" or point of reference. Indeed, pluritopic hermeneutics questions the position and the homogeneity of the understanding subject. It moves in the direction of interactive knowledge and understanding, reflecting the very process of constructing the space that is being *known*. The pluritopic approach does not accentuate relativism or cultural diversity. It stresses instead the social, political, and ontological dimensions of any theorizing and any understanding, questioning the Western locus of enunciation masked as universal and out-of-concrete-space. It strives to (re)construct, more specifically, the difference in the loci of enunciation and the politics of knowing beyond cultural relativism. We should not also forget the ethical dimension of pluritopic hermeneutics, which stresses the constant realization that other truths also exist and have the right to exist, but their visibility is reduced by the continuing power asymmetry, which is based on the coloniality of knowledge, power, being, and gender.

III. Trans-modernity Versus Alter-modernity

In the beginning of the 1990s, the Argentinean philosopher Enrique Dussel proposed the concept of trans-modernity.[17] Trans-modernity opened up a spatial dimension in history and in the history of ideas. It occupied a space next to the postmodern. The trans-modern, in other words, brought to the foreground the historical and intellectual presence of the outside of Europe, of some of its colonies in South America and the Caribbean. However, it had the potential of pointing toward multiple trans-modern histories, memories, and knowledges that, being non–European (that is, not based on Greek thought codified by the European Renaissance), had to deal, sooner or later, with the imperial expansion of Europe in the name of modernity and, more recently, postmodernity. To avoid being subsumed under the universal pretenses of the modern and the postmodern, the concept of trans-modernity needed to be backed up as a concept of knowledge geo-politically conceived rather than uni-versally absorbed in a uni-linear time—the time of Europe.

Trans-modernity is the space of the borderlands, the space where exteriority becomes visible. Why does it happen so? Because the subjects who live in exteriority realize that they have been constructed as an exteriority— as the "other." When the other looks into the eyes of the same, realizing that he or she as the other was an invention of the same, and that the same justified himself or herself in creating an exterior to modernity (a space that modernity would conquer or destroy), and when the subject realized that he or she has been made an other by the same that dominates and imposes upon him or her what to do, in the name of modernity, then trans-modernity emerges as another space of thinking and acting, no longer modern, controlled by the same, but trans-modern—the other appropriating, absorbing, and de-linking the emancipating promises of modernity and transforming them into the liberating projects of trans-modernity.

Trans-modernity is the epistemic and ontological dwelling of "the other," taking charge in the decolonial marching. Trans-modernity makes visible the geo- and bio-graphy of knowledge; it shows that postmodernity and alter-modernity in the sense of multiple modernities are regional concepts serving the interests and subjectivities of regional people in particular spaces and, mainly, the internal and imperial history of Europe. The basic question, not asked very often, is the following: who is the same that encounters the other? The question is relevant because it is never the other who encounters the same. If that situation obtained, then the other would become the same who sees the same as the other. The problem with "the other" is that by the very fact of being postulated and enunciated, it ensures the fixity of the enunciation of "the same." "The same," in other words, is he/she/it (human agents and institutions) who/that are in control of the enunciation. At the beginning of the twenty-first century, a radical shift in the geography of knowledge and of reason is taking place: "the other(s)" is/are taking hold and controlling the enunciation and displacing the "Eurocentered same" that created it/them as the "Other(s) of Europe." Decolonial philosophy emerges from this radical shift (from the epistemic regulation of the same to the epistemic disobedience of the other); geo- and body-politics of knowledge disobey imperial theo- and ego-politics, opening up the space for decolonial thinking and decolonial option(s). Decolonial thinking and doing, its very practice, is itself ingrained in the process of shifting the geography of reason and decolonial orientations of actions. It provides arguments that relegate to the past imperial distinctions between the same and the other. While imperial reason (that is, Eurocentrism in Europe as well as in Eastern Europe, its former direct and indirect colonies where local agents promote and enact Eurocentric values—for example, Saakashvili and his supporters in Georgia, or Uribe and his supporters in Colombia) is still in its place and will remain for a while, epistemic pluri-versality and decolonial philosophy are already marching toward a trans-modern (and decolonial) rather than an alter-modern (and newly imperial) future. If this were not the case, the argument we are advancing here could not have been imagined.

There exists a concept of alter-modernity that has become popular lately and needs to be examined vis-à-vis the position that we are defending here. Alter-modernity has become an umbrella term that covers often opposite positions, and is based on the notion of unification. What we mean by this is, for example, the fundamentally different "alternative modernities"[18] and alternatives to modernity itself. In the first case, there is no critical rethinking of modernity as such; it is not questioned but simply imbued with certain local features. However, the alternative modernities model leaves intact the cult of progress, the dichotomy of modernity versus tradition, the vector evolutionary understanding of history, and Eurocentrism. This model has existed for a long time and has been used, to varying degrees of success, by various countries in modernity, as a rule the countries that occupied a secondary position in the hierarchy of modernity and that could not win in its deadly competition. Examples would include some Muslim countries striving to incorporate Western modernity, but at the same time attempting to restrict it to the technology and science areas, while leaving spiritual values intact (which proved to be difficult). They also include the secondary empires of modernity such as Russia, which also has attempted to build an alter-modernity in which the mythology of modernity—completely alien for Russia and not reflected upon by the architects of modernization—has been accompanied by the superfluous entourage of typically Russian elements, which seems to provide the necessary difference from Western modernity and hence to bring solace: we have our own kind of modernity, our own brand of democracy, etc.[19]

The second position—alternative to modernity—is more radical and promising. It is based on the rejection of modernity in both its lighter and darker aspects, in both its attractive and disgusting premises. In other words, it is an epistemic de-linking from modernity, a decolonial epistemic shift leading to pluri-versality. While alter-modernity proposes an "alternative modernity" rather than an "alternative to modernity," decolonial thinking paves the road for decolonial options and "trans-modern" (as Dussel conceptualized it) futures. Trans-modern futures are built on epistemic and aesthetic (*aiesthesis*, sensing) disobedience: the disobedience of the other toward imperial designs of the same, disobedience that transforms and converts the epistemic imperial same into an equal other. This is, in a nutshell, the process of decolonizing epistemology and aesthetics that we are witnessing at the beginning of the twenty-first century.[20]

There is a global march of decoloniality today moving toward a trans-modern, and not a postmodern or alter-modern, world. Postmodern and alter-modern (in the first sense) are mostly regional, and mainly European, visions of their own history that have been projected globally without noticing the imperiality of European history and while seeing it as the history of the world. The foundation of this belief lies in the Bible and in its secular version, Hegel's philosophy of history. Such a vision has not been built on the works of Ibn Khaldun and/or Guamán Poma de Ayala. Alter-modern is a concept that in Europe itself marks the end of the postmodern. While postmodernity presents itself as superseding modernity in the linear time of European history, alter-modernity presents itself as superseding postmodernity by extending its paws to space, to the globe. However, it remains within the confines of monotopic hermeneutics: it is the European observer who, from the hill, looks down on the valley (the rest of the planet). Trans-modernity is used to unveil the imperial pretense of modernity, postmodernity, and alter-modernity. Once again, we are de-linking from monotopic hermeneutics and moving toward dia-topic and pluritopic hermeneutics, essential to understanding "trans-modernity" as both an epistemic and hermeneutic shift when "the other" takes the field and denounces the otherness of "the same" (i.e., *humanitas*), and by so doing, decolonizes the imperial and colonial differences upon which the very idea of the other (the colonial and the imperial other, like China, Russia or Islamic history) was built and sustained.

The illusion that "alter-modernity" in its first understanding runs parallel to "alter-mondisme" as an alternative to "liberal globalization" is just that—an illusion. Alter-modernity, intentionally or not, is an attempt to re-center in Europe what the World Social Forum is trying to do: the "center" is in Porto Alegre, Mumbai, Nairobi, Caracas, Belen and not just and only in Berlin, Paris, London, or New York. Decolonial thinking confronts "alter-modernity," promoting and enacting "barbarian theorizing." To appropriate and remake William Shakespeare's metaphor, it is Caliban who is taking away the reason of Prospero and incorporating it in his own body, in his own sensibility, and in his own reasoning.[21] So Prospero becomes the limited "other" who only feels and knows the reason of the Master, while Caliban knows and feels the reason of the enslaved, and as such knows the reason of the Master. Thus, Caliban inhabits the border, dwells in the border, while Prospero dwells in a territory, and from that territory he only sees the frontiers and the "other" on the "other side." Dwelling in the frontiers, Caliban inhabits double consciousness: the other that all of a sudden becomes the same. At the moment when Caliban shifts the geography of reason, Prospero appears to him as a strange and incomprehensible other: who is this person who believes and assumes that it is natural for a human being to control, exploit, and dominate another human being? Where did Prospero learn that this is the case? By asking such questions, Caliban is already engaged in border thinking, and border thinking is the method of decolonial thinking and the road toward trans-modern and decolonial futures.

IV. Coda: Thinking Decolonially, Decolonial Philosophy

Thinking decolonially cannot be performed from the perspective of the same. This article, therefore, has been written *by the other*. In other words, *we are the other.* We, Madina and Walter, do not and cannot inhabit, for example, the skin of Habermas or Gadamer, or the house of being (which was Europe for Agnes Heller). We, Madina and Walter, inhabit the skin of Fanon or Anzaldúa,[22] not because we are black or brown (actually we are quite white), but because the colonial wound runs deeper than the color of our skin. If you are black in Russia because you are Caucasian, or if you are not quite white in the United States because you are Hispanic, you begin to understand that the question of "the other" cannot be solved by the goodwill of "the same." Thinking decolonially means to decolonize Western control of philosophy as the "correct" way of thinking. In other words, it is necessary to decolonize philosophy to liberate thinking; that is what decolonial thinking means and what decolonial philosophy may look like.

Sir Lloyd Best (1934–2007), the Afro-Caribbean thinker, was not looking at becoming "the same," but called for "independent thought and Caribbean freedom." Independent thought can hardly be achieved by applying or paraphrasing Habermas in the Caribbean. Best knew it. However, since knowledge is controlled by the same (i.e., coloniality of knowledge) and by the same token, the coloniality of being is controlled by imperial knowledge, who would pay attention to Best but the Caribbean people themselves? The reason Habermas has more readers is not necessarily because he has "more important things to say." It is because Habermas speaks on the side of *humanitas* while Best speaks on the side of *anthropos*, according to the dominant perspective imposed by *humanitas*. In his foundational argument on independent thought and Caribbean freedom, Best said:

> It is being proposed here, that being who we are, what we are and where, the kind of action to which we must be committed is determinate […] To acknowledge this is to set ourselves three tasks: The first is to fashion theory on which may be based the clear intellectual leadership for which the nation calls and which it has never had. The second is to conduct the inquiry on which theory can be soundly based. This is what may be called, in the jargon of my original trade, the creation of intellectual capital goods. Thirdly, we are to establish media by which these goods may be transmitted to the rest of us who are otherwise […] We may wish to create a media of direct democratic expression suitable to the native Caribbean imagination.[23]

Muslim-Iranian intellectuals have, of course, different local histories than those of Black Caribbean intellectuals, but there is a deep connection in their decolonial struggle. Here is what an Iranian intellectual, Amr G.E. Sabet, has to say. In introducing his argument, Sabet makes clear that in the investigation he presents he is not making any claims either in favor of any "Islamization of knowledge" or of its secularization. His argument aims, he stresses, at *the integration* of knowledge, "whether secular or religious, through a measure of *intersubjectivity*."[24] Furthermore, and this is crucial for our argument, Sabet notes that beyond looking for an integration of Islamic thought and social theory,

> [...] this study seeks to link the former (i.e., Islamic thought) with *decolonization* in order to underscore Islam's liberating commitment not only toward Muslims but [also] toward humanity at large. The decolonization process that had taken place during the post–World War II era remains, unfortunately, an unfinished, and even a regressing, project.[25]

Decoloniality (to distinguish it from decolonization during the Cold War) refers to a set of projects based on *identities* that are open to humanity at large, in the same way that Christian theology and secular liberalism were, although they did not recognize themselves as *identity*. They recognized themselves as *universality*. For that reason, Sabet argues, "In addition to political, as well as economic, independence[,] there is *the essential need for the independence of thought, of the mental, the psychological, and the spiritual; for the exorcising of souls and liberating of minds.*"[26]

In conclusion, we would like to stress that global decoloniality is marching forward and it is shifting the geo- and bio-graphy of knowledge and understanding[27]: in front of the imperial universality of the same, there emerges the convivial pluri-versality of the other (that is, *us*, connecting through the inter-subjective commonality of the colonial wound). Thinking decolonially means to decolonize Western philosophy management of correct ways of thinking: philosophy remains the thinking of the *same* that invented the *other* to define itself as the *same* (i.e., *humanitas*). To decolonize philosophy means to liberate thinking and to de-link from the philosophical imperialism in the hands of *the same,* reproducing, constantly, *the other.* Decoloniality and pluritopic hermeneutics join forces in moving away from deadly Western imperial distinctions between same and other.

NOTES

1. Martin Buber, *I and Thou*, trans. Ronald Gregor Smith (New York: Charles Scribner's Sons, 1958); Emmanuel Levinas, *Time and the Other*, trans. Richard A. Cohen (Pittsburgh: Duquesne University Press, 1987; also includes *The Old and the New* and *Diachrony and Representation*); Emmanuel Levinas, *Entre Nous: On Thinking-of-the-Other*, trans. Michael B. Smith and Barbara Harshav (New York: Columbia University Press, 1998); Jacques Derrida, *The Gift of Death*, trans. David Wills (Chicago: University of Chicago Press, 1995 [1991]); Jacques Derrida, *Monolingualism of the Other; or, The Prosthesis of Origin*, trans. Patrick Mensah (Stanford: Stanford University Press, 1998); M.M. Bakhtin, *The Dialogic Imagination: Four Essays*, ed. Michael Holquist, trans. Caryl Emerson and Michael Holquist (Austin: University of Texas Press, 1981); Paul Ricoeur, *Oneself as Another* (*Soi-même comme un autre*), trans. Kathleen Blamey (Chicago: University of Chicago Press, 1992 [1990]); Gayatri Chakravorty Spivak, *A Critique of Postcolonial Reason: Toward a History of the Vanishing Present* (Cambridge: Harvard University Press, 1999).

2. Jacques Lacan, *Écrits: The First Complete Edition in English*, trans. Bruce Fink (New York: W.W. Norton & Co., 2006).

3. Emmanuel Levinas, *Totalité et infiniti: essai sur l'extériorité*. [1961] (Paris: Gallimard Livre de Poches, 1990). It is important to remember that Levinas's *other* was not a universal *other* facing the modern universal subject as *the same*, but it was historically and subjectively grounded. Levinas was thinking *as a Jew* about the Jews as internal *others* in Europe. Levinas (after the Holocaust) was confronting Heidegger's *ontology* and its political implications. His

dialogical face-to-face displaces the enunciation from the *same* (the ontology of being, in Heidegger) to the other (the dialogical in Levinas). Dialogical face-to-face disavows ontology and asserts the *other* as "otherwise than being."

4. Levinas, *Totalité et infiniti*.

5. Jean-Paul Sartre, *L'etre et le néant: Essai d'ontologie phénoménologique* (Paris: Gallimard, 1966).

6. See for instance Jacques Derrida, *Le monolinguism de l'autre* (Paris: Galilée, 1996).

7. Lewis R. Gordon, "Prospero's Words, Caliban's Reason," in *Disciplinary Decadence: Living Thought in Trying Times* (Boulder: Paradigm Publishers, 2006), 107–32.

8. Hans-Georg Gadamer, *Truth and Method*, 2nd rev. ed., trans. Joel Weinsheimer and Donald G. Marshall (New York: Crossroad, 1989).

9. Nishitani Osamu, "Anthropos and Humanitas: Two Western Concepts of 'Human Beings,'" in *Translation, Biopolitics, Colonial Difference*, ed. Naoki Sakai and Jon Solomon (Hong Kong: Hong Kong University Press, 2006), 259–74.

10. Raimundo Panikkar, "Cross-Cultural Studies: The Need for a New Science of Interpretation," *Monchanin* 8:3–5 (1975): 12–15.

11. Raimundo Panikkar, "What Is Comparative Philosophy Comparing?," in *Interpreting Across Boundaries: New Essays in Comparative Philosophy*, ed. Gerald James Larson and Eliot Deutsch (Princeton: Princeton University Press, 1988), 116–36.

12. Kishore Mahbubani, *The New Asian Hemisphere: The Irresistible Shift of Global Power to the East* (New York: Public Affairs, 2008).

13. Frantz Fanon, *Les Damnés de la Terre* (Paris: Maspero, 1961).

14. Gloria Anzaldúa, *Borderlands/La Frontera: The New Mestiza* (San Francisco: Aunt Lute Books, 1987).

15. Anne McClintock, *Imperial Leather: Race, Gender, and Sexuality in the Colonial Contest* (New York: Routledge, 1995).

16. Walter D. Mignolo, *The Darker Side of the Renaissance: Literacy, Territoriality, and Colonization* (Ann Arbor: University of Michigan Press, 1995), 11.

17. Enrique Dussel, "Eurocentrism and Modernity (Introduction to the Frankfurt Lectures)," in *The Postmodern Debate in Latin America*, ed. John Beverley, José Oviedo, and Michael Aronna (Durham: Duke University Press, 1995), 65–76.

18. Dilip Parameshwar Gaonkar, ed., *Alternative Modernities*, 2nd ed. (Durham: Duke University Press, 2001).

19. Madina Tlostanova, *A Janus-Faced Empire: Notes on the Russian Empire in Modernity, Written from the Border* (Moscow: Blok, 2003).

20. The next step would be to decolonize the state and the economy, a process that is already being discussed in Bolivia, in the government of Evo Morales, and which was initiated by the Zapatistas in 1994.

21. Paget Henry, *Caliban's Reason: Introducing Afro-Caribbean Philosophy* (New York: Routledge, 2000).

22. Gloria Anzaldúa, *Borderlands/La Frontera: The New Mestiza* (San Francisco: Aunt Lute Books, 1987).

23. Lloyd Best, "Independent Thought and Caribbean Freedom," *New World Quarterly*, 3:4 (1967), 13–34; Lloyd Best, "Independence and Responsibility," in *The Critical Tradition of Caribbean Political Economy: The Legacy of George Beckford*," ed. Kari Levitt and Michael Witter (Kingston, Jamaica: Ian Randle Publishers in association with the George Beckford Foundation, 1996).

24. Amr G.E. Sabet, *Islam and the Political: Theory, Governance and International Relations* (London: Pluto Press, 2008), 4.

25. *Ibid.*, 4.

26. *Ibid.*, 5.

27. Walter D. Mignolo and Madina V. Tlostanova, "Theorizing from the Borders: Shifting to Geo- and Body-Politics of Knowledge," *European Journal of Social Theory* 9, no. 2 (2006): 205–21.

From "Levinas's Hegemonic Identity Politics, Radical Philosophy, and the Unfinished Project of Decolonization"

NELSON MALDONADO-TORRES

It is no secret that Levinas's work acquired particular value in the Global North as a way to infuse poststructuralism and deconstruction with a seemingly irrefutable ethical character in the face of the also irrefutable continued violence, domination, and exploitation that raised questions about the power and reach of poststructuralist and postmodern theses. Initial criticisms about the way in which the "turn to ethics" easily came to signify not much more than an evasion of politics gave way to even stronger criticisms that depicted deconstruction and Levinasian ethics as philosophies that not only failed to critically respond to capitalism, but that actually fomented erroneous discourses and practices.[1] These include multiculturalism, identity politics, relativism, and the ethics of difference, all of which are said to be grounded on or fomented by the prime value of the relation with an other.

Leading the charge against Levinas have been post–Marxist philosophers such as Alain Badiou and Slavoj Žižek, both of whom also oppose the politics of multiculturalism, difference, and identity. As the translator of Badiou's *Ethics* puts it, "Badiou's book does nothing less than *evacuate* the foundation upon which every deconstructive, 'multicultural,' or 'postcolonial' ethics is built: the (ethical) category of alterity."[2] And Badiou is explicit that his target is the very idea of the other, rooted of course in Levinas's philosophy: "The truth is that, in the context of a system of thought that is both a-religious and genuinely contemporary with the truths of our time, the whole ethical predication based upon recognition of the other should be purely and simply abandoned."[3] For his part, Žižek aims to respond "to the burning question of how we are to reformulate a leftist, anti-capitalist political project in our era of global capitalism and its ideological supplement, liberal-democratic multi-culturalism."[4] And for him, the main coordinates are not Judaism or alterity, but Christianity and universality. As he puts it in *The Ticklish Subject*: "What we need today is the gesture that would undermine capitalist globalization from the standpoint of universal Truth, just as Pauline Christianity did to the Roman global Empire."[5] In *The Puppet and the Dwarf* he further expands on this point by clarifying that "to become a true dialectical materialist, one should go through the Christian experience."[6] This position leads Žižek to establish a dialogue with radical orthodoxy, and to claim that true radicalism is closer to orthodoxy than many would want to admit. Referring to G.K. Chesterton's 1908 book *Orthodoxy*, Žižek writes: "In a properly Leninist way, [Chesterton] asserts that the search for true orthodoxy, far from being boring, humdrum, and safe, is the most daring and perilous adventure (exactly like Lenin's search for the authentic Marxist orthodoxy—how much less risk and theoretical effort, how much more passive opportunism and theoretical laziness, is in the easy revisionist conclusion that the changed historical circumstances demand some 'new paradigm'!)."[7] Just as Chesterton was standing in his time against the onslaught of the then "heresies" and new spiritualisms, Žižek stands now against discourses of difference, deconstruction, identity, and multiculturalism.[8]

From these responses to Levinas's work and the politics of difference we see how recent European political philosophy has turned against any ethics grounded on the relation with an other, as well as how this opposition includes multiculturalism and subaltern identity politics—which is significant in a context where Europe confronts an increase in ethno-racial populations and related forms of organizing. It is therefore not surprising that the notion of "being radical" has been changed to correspond more with an "orthodox" response to the problems that we face today. This new orthodoxy asks us to return to Western or Christian sources and delink from deconstruction and from minority politics that seek the recognition of cultural difference. In a sense, since these post–Marxist philosophers attack the centrality of the very category of the Other, any effort to render Levinas's work relevant for political matters becomes almost impossible, unless, of course, one can show that the conclusion of this work coincides with their judgments about contemporary political matters. In a way, the challenge consists in showing not only that Levinas's philosophy of the other provides an essential and nonrelativistic ethical core to discourses such as deconstruction, and that this can help to understand politics and justice, but also that Levinas's philosophy can do that without collapsing into anything like identity politics, something like multiculturalism, or the search for cultural recognition. This strategy, it turns out, is not too difficult, as Levinas's work clearly provides elements that go in this direction.

As any Levinasian scholar would know, the irony of the post–Marxist critique of Levinas is that Levinas was critical of cultural relativism, and that he can be construed as a critic of the politics of identity. Levinas was also a defender of universalism, and he believed that European, Christian, and Jewish cultures participated in a conceptual and cultural universe that was particularly attuned to this universalism. Also, to some extent ironic, in spite of the critique of Levinas, it is clear that Badiou and Žižek share with him a view of the universal that transcends the particular while they all posit and follow the idea that this universal is best expressed or contained by a particular culture or set of cultures, among which European culture is included. Whether one is faced by Žižek's orthodoxy or Levinas's philosophy of the other, one begins and ends with either Europe, Christianity, and/or Judaism. The reason for this agreement, I would like to posit, lies in an identity discourse that is not so much criticized by the critics of identity politics, even though it is one of the most brutal forms of identity discourse. It is an identity politics from the position of hegemony, or hegemonic identity politics. It is this form of identity politics that will become the main object of analysis here, as found in Levinas and in recent Levinas scholarship.[9]

The problem of such hegemonic identity politics needs to be discussed alongside the elements of a politics of decolonization, which is often part of minority political discourses but is portrayed negatively as "identity politics" (i.e., as a politics concerned with the recognition of cultural identity over and beyond distribution of resources or any fundamental structural change, for instance) from the standpoint of those who practice their own form of hegemonic identity politics. Decolonial politics are concerned about the material conditions of existence, yet they are not necessarily Marxist, and definitely not post–Marxist in the sense indicated above. They also share the Levinasian focus on alterity, gift giving, sociality, and the sense of a scandal in the face of murder and genocide, but they are not merely Levinasian either. If they deserve a name, perhaps, it should be Fanonian, making reference to the also Francophone writer (but this time from the Caribbean), Frantz Fanon. But we do not have to find a name for it other than decolonial politics itself, which has been forged by multiple subjects and formulated in different forms since the inception of modernity/coloniality.[10]

Levinas's Hegemonic Identity Politics

> "I often say, although it is a dangerous thing to say publicly,
> that humanity consists of the Bible and the Greeks. All the
> rest can be translated: all the rest—all the exotic—is dance."
> —Emmanuel Levinas, *French Philosophers*
> *in Conversation*

There is a skewed form of identity politics in Levinas. While he rightly wishes to demonstrate the relevance of Jewish thought for philosophizing about human reality at large, and while he also insightfully spells out Judaic elements in European culture, he generally succumbs all too easily to the temptations of Eurocentrism, at least in its ethnocentric dimensions, and Orientalism. He is most harsh about Europe when it comes to condemning Nazism and anti–Semitism, but less critical when it comes to understanding Cold War politics and the politics of decolonization. There is also his understanding of the Israeli-Palestinian conflict and his reaction to the death of Palestinians, which has appalled even some of his supporters.[11] In the following, I provide a brief summary and commentary of some of Levinas's most notable interventions, more or less in chronological order, which have already been identified and commented on by a number of interpreters.

Howard Caygill dedicates a short section of his book *Levinas and the Political* to Levinas's view of "Threatening Others."[12] He includes an analysis of Levinas's 1960 essay "The Russo-Chinese Debate and the Dialectic" that, according to him, "must rank as Levinas's ugliest and most disturbing published work."[13] In this essay, Levinas voices concern over Russia's increasing departure from the West and its relationship with China. He writes: "The exclusive community with the Asiatic world, itself a stranger to European history to which Russia, in spite of all its strategic and tactical denials, has belonged for almost a thousand years, would this not be disturbing even to a society without classes?" Levinas elaborates on his view of the "disturbing" element of the formation of a Russian-Chinese community: "The yellow peril! It is not racial, it is spiritual. It does not involve inferior values; it involves a radical strangeness, a stranger to the weight of its past, from where there does not filter any familiar voice or inflection, a lunar or Martian past."[14] As Caygill points out "It is difficult to imagine any circumstance in which the phrase 'the yellow peril' cannot be racist, let alone in the context set by Levinas that consigns a phantasm of Asia to the moon or another planet, thus figuratively stripping Asians of their humanity."[15]

This is not the only text where Levinas speaks negatively of people from Asia. In an essay from 1961, he writes about "the rise of countless masses of Asiatic and underdeveloped peoples ... peoples and civilizations who no longer refer to our holy history, for whom Abraham, Isaac and Jacob no longer mean anything."[16] Levinas continues this line of thinking in another article of 1967 where he advocates Jewish-Christian solidarity in face of the "innumerable masses advancing out of Asia. In the eyes of these crowds who do not take holy history as their frame of reference, are we Jews and Christian anything but sects quarrelling over the meaning of a few obscure texts?"[17]

It is most interesting in the passages above that the otherness of China, in relation to Russia and Europe, is depicted negatively as a "radical strangeness," and not, for instance, as an opportunity to further put into question the centrality of philosophies and cultures that value the Same, or self-preservation, over an encounter with an other, for instance. It is as if there is a hermeneutic plasticity around concepts of the Other that Levinas can turn into positive ethical injunctions, fundamentally passive figures (e.g., the feminine), or menacing elements, depending on his particular view of a situation—heteronormativity or a form of identity politics, for example. On this point Levinas remained quite close to other phenomenologists, even as phenomenology itself is supposed to be a philosophy "without presuppositions." In Husserl, for instance, there is the attempt to rethink philosophy anew, starting with "the things themselves" and without naturalistic or psychologistic presuppositions, and yet when it comes to speaking of Europe as a historical phenomenon and idea, he cannot do away with strong doses of Eurocentrism and Orientalism.[18] Heidegger put in question some of Husserl's ideas while transforming others, and yet, if anything, his work is even more heavily marked by Eurocentrism. Eurocentrism has multiple ways of making a mark in a philosophical project, whether its fundamental cornerstone or point of departure is the phenomenon, Being, or the Other. In a moment of European crisis, the task at hand was to engage in an internal critique of Europe while also claiming its universal value in ways that presupposed the misrecognition of other cultures and geopolitical forms, including Europe itself. How Levinas differs from Husserl and Heidegger on this point is that he is also responding to Nazi genocide, and his project is deeply involved with demonstrating the relevance of Judaism to Europe. But this does not necessarily make him more critical of Eurocentrism or Orientalism.

When these issues are raised, it is often said that the most fundamental contributions by these thinkers are their abstract theoretical reflections, and that these can be isolated from their more concrete analyses. It is also said that these thinkers are just showing the prejudice of their time, suggesting that they could not avoid but having these opinions and perceptions. While prejudicial ideas of the kind that Levinas expresses above cannot be used without further reflection to discard his methodological and more abstract reflections, the idea that there is nothing in the method and in such abstract reflections that leads, opens the door, or fails to address the problems in the more concrete opinions is equally problematic. On this point, what is arguably needed is careful inquiry by determining the elements in any given theoretical model or object of investigation that either foment or are complicit with problematic presuppositions and ideas. What is needed is not merely a "reduction" of the phenomenon or theoretical apparatus that one needs to carefully describe and examine, but, more precisely a "decolonial reduction."[19] By this I mean an investigation into how the *said* of, in this case, theory, can get to the point of betraying the *saying* of responsibility not simply by creating synchronicity and leading to the autoreferentiality of the Same, but, more radically than that, by creating a new layer of nonsynchronous difference between being and a newly created "zone of nonbeing."

The notion of a "zone of nonbeing" comes from the work of Frantz Fanon, a Martiniquean and Algerian thinker and revolutionary.[20] The zone of nonbeing is a phenomenological term, but it is also, to some extent a geographical or geopolitical one, since the condition of nonbeing is systematically spread and found in colonized territories. This leads to another thought regarding the context that explains why figures such as Husserl, Heidegger, and Levinas continued to hold on to Eurocentric premises. Yes, it was the time, but also the place from where they thought. Both time and place are relevant when contextualizing anything, and so here one cannot disregard the differences between living, thinking, and writing in Europe vis-à-vis doing the same in places with long histories and systematic structures that promote dehumanization. This is what Walter Mignolo has aimed to capture in his concept of "colonial difference" and more recently in the idea, "We are where we think."[21] The colonial context is most relevant here, as the very existence of the colony is premised on its inferiority or lack of full human status, demonstrated by its lack of autonomy and self-determination in a context where the right for both of those features are taken as fundamental traits of humanity. Similar features constitute the being, or rather nonbeing, of the racialized body: "color" and other features are taken precisely as a mark of nonhumanity. The "colonial difference" refers to the particular traits in the colonies that emerge and can be explained, not with reference to differences in nature or culture, but in relation to the very dynamics of imperial and colonial power, in short, in relation to the coloniality of power, knowledge, and being.

The existence of "colonial difference," which is a dimension or result of what W.E.B. Du Bois called "the color-line," does not imply a total estrangement between the zone of being and the zone of nonbeing, between civilized and colonial realities. In fact, the colony is constitutive of the being of the "civilized," and always remains as a challenge or question.[22] It is this challenge and question that Eurocentrism aims to mute or translate as a request for further dependence. There are also techniques and forms of govermentality from civilization that are taken to the colonial world, and once there, they take on new dimensions. Other times, it is techniques from the colonies that are taken back to the civilized world. Therefore, civilization and colony are different but mutually imbricated. And the imbrication is enough to provide the condition that civilized subjects could get to identify and diagnose a number of problems that are relevant, not only to the civilized context, but to the colonial as well. There also exists the possibility of transgressing the line of colonial difference and of a civilized subject understanding and thinking from the other side of the colonial difference itself. Yet such admission can only come with a confession, which is that subjects in that other line of the colonial difference are in general more attuned to the subtle and not so subtle forms that colonial difference takes, and so their art, theory, and praxis provide indispensable elements to understand and diagnose not only the colonial context but the entire arrangement of civilization/coloniality. This would imply the need to "shift the geography of reason,"[23] which is, of course, what Eurocentrism impedes. Both the confession and the project of shifting the geography of reason are precisely what are absent in the discussion when Levinas describes Asia as he does, as well as when he describes decolonization.

Levinas was aware of decolonization, but his response to it was ambivalent and largely Eurocentric. In "Meaning and Sense,"[24] for instance, he recognizes the value of the appreciation of cultural diversity that was often seen as an outcome of the decolonization process, but clarifies that this recognition is anchored in a more fundamental characteristic of humanity, a characteristic that is best spelled out, not by advocates of decolonization or by the multiplicity of cultures that they celebrate, but by European culture, and particularly Judaism:

> One reasons as though the equivalence of cultures, the discovery of their profusion, and the recognition of their riches were not themselves the effects of an orientation and of an unequivocal sense in which humanity stands. One reasons as though the multiplicity of cultures from the beginning sunk its roots in the era of decolonization, as though incomprehension, war, and conquest did not derive just as naturally from the contiguity of multiple expressions of being—the numerous assemblages or arrangements which it takes on in the diverse civilizations. One reasons as though peaceful coexistence did not presuppose that in being there is delineated an orientation which gives it a unique sense.[25]

For Levinas, the appreciation of cultural diversity by itself can lead to war or to a fundamental miscommunication and disorientation. Instead of spelling out decolonization in terms of the challenge to shift the geography of reason, Levinas focuses instead on its potential to open the door to renewed conflict or excessive fragmentation, as if decolonization was no more than what French ethnographers took it to be. Decolonization therefore appears here as an ambivalent and derivative historical occurrence instead of as a historical event that takes the challenge implicit in the existence of the colony to new heights, and that therefore creates the conditions for widespread opposition and overcoming of Eurocentrism.

Levinas renders decolonization and its positive dimensions secondary in relation to the "unique sense" that being carries with it, notwithstanding its multiple and diverse expressions. For him, "sense" is transcendent, while decolonization is temporal and contextual. Yet, one could argue that the fact there could be something such as a transcendent "sense" does not mean there might not be ideas or historical moments when its ineluctable presence is shown forth most strongly. Levinas concedes as much, but this concession only becomes an opportunity to further express his Eurocentrism. This is evinced in an interview of 1984, when Levinas is told that, in addition to there being a multiplicity of human beings, there are also a multiplicity of cultures, such as the Bororo of the Mongols, and the culture of the Indians. His reply is: "To be sure, but it is Europe which, alongside its numerous atrocities, invented the idea of 'de-Europeanization.' This represents a victory of European generosity. For me, of course, the Bible is the model of excellence; but I say this knowing nothing of Buddhism."[26]

While in the 1964 essay Levinas refused talk of a victory of decolonization by rendering the idea of the multiplicity and riches of cultures a "unique sense" that transcends history, twenty years later recognition of the riches of the multiplicity of cultures is traced back to history, in the form of a European victory that takes place in spite of its violence. European history, however, is not elevated beyond the transcendent unique sense that is ahistorical. Rather, what happens is that European history has a peculiar relation with that transcendent sense, which is why Levinas mentions the Bible.[27] The idea is that European history and culture have been infused by the Bible—which Levinas takes as "the model of excellence"—as well as with the language of the Greeks. Levinas spells out the significance of Greek and the Judeo-Christian tradition in a 1981 interview:

> For me the essential characteristic of philosophy is a certain, specifically Greek, way of thinking and speaking. Philosophy is primarily a question of language; and it is by identifying the subtextual language of particular discourses that we can decide whether they are philosophical or not. Philosophy employs a series of terms and concepts—such as *morphe* (form), *ousia* (substance), *nous* (reason), *logos* (thought) or *telos* (goal), etc.—which constitute a specifically Greek lexicon of intelligibility. French and German, and indeed all of Western philosophy is entirely shot through with this specific language; it is a token of the genius of Greece to have been able to thus deposit its language in the basket of Europe. But although philosophy is essentially Greek, it is not exclusively so. It also has sources and roots which are non–Greek. What we term the Judeo-Christian tradition, for example, proposed an alternative approach to meaning and truth.[28]

And he is even more extreme in an interview in 1989: "I always say— but under my breath—that the Bible and the Greeks present the only serious issues in human life; everything else is dancing…. There is no racism intended."[29] Here adding that "there is no racism intended" functions similarly to when he referred to the "yellow peril" but then added, "It is not racial. It is spiritual," as if racism were strictly an issue of natural difference. Fanon made clear decades before that racism can also be cultural, and in this case also epistemic.[30]

What one finds in these statements from the 1980s is not only consistent, but to some extent a more radical form of Eurocentrism than twenty years earlier. And this happens even as he makes rhetorical gestures that point to his developing a sense of "the fraternal West" as imperial and Israel as a nation that could and should unite with the Third World. Santiago Slabodsky has identified and commented on these and other gestures that suggest an opening of Levinas toward the Third World and the politics of decoloniza- tion.[31] He has done a good service by distilling elements in Levinas's work that provoke his interpreters and Jewish philosophers interested in Levinas's work to break away from the tendency to read Levinas only in relation to other European thinkers or problems that are defined in the North.

And yet it is not only Levinas's interpreters and Jewish philosophers who are challenged by elements of Levinas's thought; other aspects of Lev- inas's own work are challenged as well. In a sense, if Levinas had a serious understanding of decolonization and of its relevance to politics and knowl- edge, that would have made the views of the multiplicity of cultures and phi- losophy that he made through the 1980s more unconscionable. But it could also be that he had a very limited understanding of decolonization, and that his critiques of the West in relation to the Third World as well as his showing of solidarity with the Third World are rhetorically suggestive but ultimately artificial or cosmetic. In a way, his view of the continuity between ancient empires and the "fraternal West" reveals Levinas's desire to launch a decolo- nial critique, but also his inability to understand colonization in its own terms and with a genealogy of its own, delinked from the long Eurocentric scope of understanding Europe as a unity of sorts from ancient times to the present. As a result, he can only see in colonization the repetition of themes that already appeared in the (ancient) West itself, thereby making the politics of decolonization part of the drama of the West and reducing the importance of the non–West to the level of the strictly political, but not to political think- ing or to thinking at large. Levinas is missing a genealogy that can capture the specificity of modern colonization and decolonial processes, say, one more focused on the "discovery" of the New World and the unfolding expan- sion of the West, than on the vices of Rome, for instance. This is precisely one of the chief contributions of one of the Third World interlocutors of Levinas that Slabodsky identifies, that is, Enrique Dussel. Unfortunately, Levinas did not take Dussel too seriously, and there is no evidence that he paid serious attention to Dussel's genealogy. The problem for Levinas is that, without a proper genealogy, and with only vague allusions to 1492 as a crucial point for Jews in Spain and for the Americas, his philosophy of the other is bound to, at best, remain limited when it comes to thinking about decolonization, the otherness of the colonial subject, or even the very meaning of other concepts that he takes for granted, including European and Jew. Still, identifying decolonial gestures in Levinas's work remains an important challenge to Levinas and Levinasians, although one that we would find more consistently addressed elsewhere or in combination with elements found in works by other authors.

In identifying "overlooked conversations between rabbinical and Third World decolonialisms," Slabodsky has provided an important point of reference for Levinasian scholarship concerned with the question of radicalizing Levinas. Part of the reason for this is that he distances himself from the narrow dual identity politics in Levinas's work and adopts another point of view, one far more open and less provincial. Unfortunately, Levinasian scholarship in the United States and Europe has tended to reproduce instead of substantially challenge this problematic element in Levinas's work and of his reception in the Global North. Admissions and denunciations of Levinas's Eurocentrism are not too difficult to make. What remains relatively nonexistent, however, is the formulation of alternative frameworks that allow for the exploration of problems and the examination of sources that are not exclusively those found in hegemonic intellectual sectors of the Global North.

[…]

Toward a Decolonial Humanities

Levinas does contribute to identity discourse and to postcolonial studies in the view of the constitutive ethical character of the self and through his analysis of some of the ways in which philosophical positions can intentionally or unintentionally promote violence. Particularly relevant are his analyses of war, which can be coupled with the idea that colonization can be seen as the naturalization of a death ethics of war.[32] This situation is what creates the "zone of nonbeing" that Fanon analyzes. Yet, as a contrast with Fanon's work also makes clear, Levinas was not the only one thinking about the philosophical dimensions of colonial violence, and he did not develop his thinking about these matters in a substantial decolonial form. Also, without a sociogeny or genealogy that attends to the particularities of modern forms of colonization, Levinas was blinded when it came to determining modes of alterity and different concrete expressions of his own philosophical themes. That is why he poses Asians as a threat without a careful consideration of the Orientalist legacy that was part and parcel of the "ethos" of European empires. This same Orientalism plays a role in his view of Palestinians.

Levinas's view of the Palestinians came very powerfully to light in his response to the massacre of Sabra and Shatila in Lebanon in 1982. This massacre happened while the Israeli military controlled the entrance to the camps and while it learned of the initial assassinations. There was a scandal following the massacre, and many believed that Israel at least had some responsibility for, if not complicity with, the murders.[33] In that context, Levinas was asked "Isn't history, isn't politics the very site of the encounter with the 'other,' and for the Israeli, isn't the 'other' above all the Palestinian?" to which he replied,

> My definition of the Other is completely different. The Other is the neighbor, who is not necessarily kin, but who can be. And in this sense, if you are for the Other, you are for the neighbor. But if your neighbor attacks another neighbor or treats him unjustly, what can you do? Then alterity takes on another character, in alterity we can find an enemy, or at least then we are faced with the problem of knowing who is right and who is wrong, who is just and who is unjust. There are people who are wrong.[34]

Levinas, the great philosopher of alterity, not only seems to evade giving a full account of responsibility toward the Palestinian at the precise moment when hundreds of Palestinians and Lebanese civilians were killed, but demonstrates a profound inability to think sophisticatedly about alterity and its varied forms and manifestations.

Levinas's response to the question about whether Palestinians are "the 'other' above all" for the Israeli corrects the perception that one can simply apply his categories to any relation of difference. After all, every one is an other, even if they are part of one's group. Also, that one person belongs to another group does not necessarily mean that one has increased responsibilities toward her or him. One can observe a similar point in Fanon's conception of decolonial and identity politics: even when they focus on the defense or liberation of a particular group, participants should be oriented by the desire to respond to an oppressed other, and sometimes one belongs to the very group of the affected, against a given or a multiplicity of oppressors.[35] But this implies that one has an understanding of oppression and a clear way to point to certain groups or structures as oppressive. This is, in a way, what coloniality theory aims to elucidate, but this is precisely what Levinas misses. Instead, he appeals to justice and to a determination of "who is just and who is unjust." But, as John Drabinski has pointed out, Levinas's appeal to justice makes it appear as if different groups find each other in a symmetrical plane in the context of which one has a discussion about specific just or unjust actions.[36] What if the sociopolitical plane is fundamentally asymmetrical?

Much relevant to our discussion, Drabinski considers Levinas not only as *not* a radical, but a "conservative" by failing to take into account asymmetrical relations in a state—and, we can add here, asymmetrical relations in the geopolitical arena.

In a context defined by asymmetry, and even more in a context of naturalized war, one cannot consider questions of ethics and justice as taking place just between selves and others. Questions that emerge here are: are there just neighbors and enemies, as two distinct categories, in most conflicts? And, if we were to think seriously about what constitutes an enemy, would we not have to think more generally about what constitutes an enemy in our world, and how modern forms of colonization and, particularly, racism are premised on the idea of an other not only as inferior in some way, but also ultimately as a perpetual enemy in a naturalized war? If so, then the main object of critique should be the politics and thought of colonization, dehumanization, and racial elimination, anchored in the unfolding of European empires and their history, on the one hand, and of any group relying on similar ways of thinking or acting. And for better understanding this one needs a sociogeny and a genealogy. In contrast to developing or seeking the assistance of discourses and analysis such as the ones provided by Fanon's decolonial sociogeny or Dussel's decolonial genealogy, Levinas emphasizes the idea of the significance of Holy History, a universal responsibility due to the "victims of Hitlerism"—everyone having to assume responsibility for the Holocaust, including the Palestinians—and in erasing the specificity of Palestinians (portraying them as part of a large mass of Arabs in the region) and evading an analysis of their condition and struggle.[37] Once again, whether abstract or material, Levinas's conception of alterity is plastic, and lends itself easily to problematic formulations that rely on, at most, creative extensions of old prejudices. But not only is Levinas's conception of the other plastic, but, as Jason Caro remarks, "Because the criteria for the consideration of justice are theoretically underdeveloped, the Levinasian and Levinas himself run the risk and temptation of serving partisan aims instead of the obligations inescapably owed to the Other."[38] A view of the ethical sense undergirding human reality and of how it implies the necessity of justice cannot by itself offer an indication of the multiple ways in which injustice, and the denial of certain subjects to be considered candidates for raising the question of justice or injustice in the first place, can come to define ordinary life in any given context and the responses needed to critically engage that situation. No matter how much one radicalizes Levinas, Levinasian discourse alone cannot provide the sufficient elements for radical thought. How to overcome the limits of Levinas's discourse?

In her essay on Levinas's view of alterity, [Diane] Perpich follows Judith Butler in calling for a view of the human as "the refusal of representation," to be understood as "recognitions that *bear the visible marks of their own failure.*"[39] While Perpich seeks to mobilize Butler's argument as support for her critique of identity politics, Butler is arguably most concerned in her recent work with contemporary modes of representation that all too quickly lend themselves to produce a view about an enemy, or people whose deaths are not grieveable. These are also images that portray humans by taking away that which is most human in them and that which would awake a sense of responsibility. This is not the context to provide an analysis of images connected with identity movements, but one could find plenty of images that demonstrate both fragility as well as power and agency—that is to say, full humanity, among the dehumanized groups that they aim to portray. Sometimes, the images depict the inhuman character of the dominant prejudices, and sometimes they seek to complicate the idea of identity as a closed set of practices, behaviors, symbols, and meanings. That is, if anything, representations linked to identity movements would further contribute to spelling out the ways in which representations do not have to become obstacles, but can actually contribute to the task of affirming the complex and rich humanity of different groups.

In addition to providing a lucid analysis of dehumanization through representation, Butler believes that her analysis is relevant to the work of the humanities. She argues, "If the humanities have a future as cultural criticism, and cultural criticism has a task at the present moment, it is no doubt to return us to the human where we do not expect to find it, in its frailty and at the limits of its capacity to make sense."[40] While Levinas's analysis of the Other helps us to define the humanities and cultural criticism in this way, a consideration of the limits and pitfalls in his work points to the equal need of carefully analyzing the inhuman and dehumanization at large, as well as the Orientalisms and forms of Eurocentrism that marked his work. We also need analyses such as Fanonian sociogenesis and Dusselian genealogies, in order to understand the predicament and implications of coloniality, understood as naturalized war, and of decolonization in the modern world. In brief, we need decolonial humanities, or rather, decolonial forms of thinking that combine the humanities and the social sciences, and that are ultimately not confined by either of those two discourses or ways of producing knowledge. This project can be referred to, at least in part, as an effort to "shift the geography of reason," which serves as an important activity in the effort at radicalizing any figure, particularly one as embedded in and committed to hegemonic identity politics as Levinas.[41] Shifting the geography of reason can also be taken as a necessary part in the effort of truly radicalizing theory. [. . .] Without the larger enterprise of decolonizing thought, the elaboration of sophisticated sociogenic analysis and the projection of decolonial genealogies, and without shifting the geography of reason, we risk images of the other becoming as plastic as they were for Levinas and having Eurocentric and other forms of prejudice take over our interpretations of different situations and parties when it comes to theorizing justice. Having these other forms of analysis will not guarantee that we will always have it right, but it can go a long way toward making it as difficult as possible for us to continue the same problematic trends through the continued forgetfulness of the multiple dimensions of coloniality.

NOTES

1. For a consideration of various angles of the "ethical turn" see Marjorie Garber, Beatrice Hanssen, and Rebecca L. Walkowitz, eds., *The Turn to Ethics* (New York: Routledge, 2000); Todd F. Davis and Kenneth Womack, eds., *Mapping the Ethical Turn: A Reader in Ethics, Culture, and Literary Theory* (Charlottesville: University Press of Virginia, 2001). For the more radical critiques of Levinasian ethics and deconstruction see Alain Badiou, *Ethics: An Essay on the Understanding of Evil*, trans. Peter Hallward (London: Verso, 2001); Slavoj Žižek, *The Puppet and the Dwarf: The Perverse Core of Christianity* (Cambridge: The MIT Press, 2003).

2. Badiou, *Ethics*, xxxv.

3. *Ibid.*, 25.

4. Slavoj Žižek, *The Ticklish Subject: The Absent Centre of Political Ontology* (London: Verso, 2000), 4.

5. Žižek, *The Ticklish Subject*, 211.

6. Žižek, *The Puppet*, 7.

7. *Ibid.*, 35.

8. I explore Žižek's orthodoxy more in depth in Nelson Maldonado-Torres, review of "The Regressive Kernel of Orthodoxy," *The Puppet and the Dwarf: The Perverse Core of Christianity*, by Slavoj Žižek, *Radical Philosophy Review* 6, no. 1 (2003): 59–70.

9. I have also examined this issue in Nelson Maldonado-Torres "Decolonization and the New Identitarian Logics After September 11: Eurocentrism and Americanism Against the Barbarian Threats," *Radical Philosophy Review* 8, no. 1 (2005): 35–67.

10. For an elaboration of the concept of the modern/colonial see Walter Mignolo and Arturo Escobar, eds., *Globalization and the Decolonial Option* (London: Routledge, 2009); Walter Mignolo, *Local Histories/Global Designs: Coloniality, Subaltern Knowledges, and Border Thinking* (Princeton: Princeton University Press, 2000).

11. This and related points are discussed in a section on "Threatening Others" in Howard Caygill, *Levinas and the Political* (London: Routledge, 2002), 182–94. See also, for instance, Jason Caro, "Levinas and the Palestinians," *Philosophy and Social Criticism* 35 (2009): 671–84.

12. Caygill, *Levinas and the Political*, 182–94.

13. *Ibid.*, 183.

14. Levinas's statement is quoted in Caygill, *Levinas and the Political*, 184. See also Emmanuel Levinas, *Les imprévus de l'histoire* (Montpellier: Fata Morgana, 1994), 171.

15. Caygill, *Levinas and the Political*, 184.

16. Emmanuel Levinas, *Difficult Freedom: Essays on Judaism* (Baltimore: Johns Hopkins University Press, 1997), 165; Also quoted in Caygill, *Levinas and the Political*, 182.

17. Emmanuel Levinas, *Alterity and Trancendence*, 1995, 17. Also quoted in Caygill, *Levinas and the Political*, 183.

18. I develop further these problematic elements in Husserl's and Heidegger's philosophies in Nelson Maldonado-Torres, "Post-Imperial Reflections on Crisis, Knowledge, and Utopia: Transgresstopic Critical Hermeneutics and the 'Death of European Man,'" *Review: A Journal of the Fernand Braudel Center for the Study of Economics, Historical Systems, and Civilizations* 25, no. 3 (2002): 277–315; and Nelson Maldonado-Torres, *Against War: Views from the Underside of Modernity* (Durham: Duke University Press, 2008).

19. See Maldonado-Torres, *Against War*, 100ff.

20. See Frantz Fanon, *Black Skins, White Masks*, trans. Richard Wilcox (New York: Grove Press, 2008); and Lewis R. Gordon, "Through the Zone of Nonbeing: A Reading of *Black Skin, White Masks* in Celebration of Fanon's Eightieth Birthday," *The C.L.R. James Journal* 11, no. 1 (2005): 1–43.

21. See Walter Mignolo, *The Darker Side of Western Modernity: Global Futures, Decolonial Options* (Durham: Duke University Press, 2012).

22. W.E.B. DuBois, *The Souls of Black Folk: Authoritative Text, Contexts, Criticism*, ed. Henry Louis Gates, Jr., and Terri Hume Oliver (New York: W.W. Norton & Company, 1999).

23. For more on this theme see Lewis Gordon, "Shifting the Geography of Reason in an Age of Disciplinary Decadence," *Transmodernity* 1.2 (Fall 2011): 95–103. This is also the motto of the Caribbean Philosophical Association. For more on the Caribbean Philosophical Association, see the website of the association (www.caribbeanphilosophicalassociation.org) and the annotated bibliography "Caribbean Philosophical Association" that is part of Oxford Bibliographies Online (oxfordbibliographiesonline.com/view/document/obo-9780199766581/obo-9780199766581-0024.xml).

24. Emmanuel Levinas, "Meaning and Sense," in *Basic Philosophical Writings*, ed. Adriaan T. Peperzak, Simon Critchley, and Robert Bernasconi (Bloomington: Indiana University Press, 1996).

25. Levinas, *Basic Philosophical Writings*, 39.

26. Emmanuel Levinas, *Is It Righteous to Be? Interviews with Emmanuel Levinas*, ed. Jill Robbins (Stanford: Stanford University Press, 2001), 164.

27. For an analysis of how Levinas's view of "sense" is used to establish a substantial difference between European and non–Western culture see Ma Lin, "All the Rest Must be Translated: Levinas's Notion of Sense," *Journal of Chinese Philosophy* 35, no. 4 (2008): 599–612.

28. Emmanuel Levinas, "Ethics of the Infinite," in *Dialogues with Contemporary Continental Thinkers*, ed. Richard Kearney (Manchester: Manchester University Press, 1984), 54–55.

29. Levinas, *Is It Righteous to Be?*, 149.

30. See Frantz Fanon, "Racism and Culture," *Toward the African Revolution*, trans. Haakon Chevalier (New York: Grave Press, 1988), 29–44.

31. Santiago Slabodsky, "Emmanuel Levinas's Geopolitics: Overlooked Conversations between Rabbinical and Third World Decolonialisms," *The Journal of Jewish Thought and Philosophy* 18, no. 2 (2010): 147–65.

32. See Steve Martinot, "Patriotism and Its Double," *Peace Review* 15, no. 4 (2003): 405–10; Martinot, "Pro-Democracy and the Ethics of Refusal," *Socialism and Democracy* 19, no. 2 (2005). Available at sdonline.org/38/; Maldonado-Torres, *Against War*.

33. Caygill, *Levinas and the Political*, 161.

34. Emmanuel Levinas, "Ethics and Politics," in *The Levinas Reader*, ed. Seán Hand (Oxford: Blackwell) 289–297.

35. For a development of this point see chapters three and four in Maldonado-Torres, *Against War*.

36. John Drabinski, "The Possibility of an Ethical Politics: From Peace to Liturgy," *Philosophy and Social Criticism* 26, no. 4 (2000): 62.

37. See Jason Caro, "Levinas and the Palestinians." *Philosophy and Social Criticism* 35, no. 1 (2009): 678–79; Caygill, *Levinas and the Political*, 182, 87; *DF* 131.

38. Caro, "Levinas and the Palestinians," 678.

39. Diane Perpich, "Levinas, Feminism, and Identity Politics," in *Radicalizing Levinas*, eds. Peter Atterton and Matthew Calarco (Albany: SUNY Press, 2010), 66.

40. Judith Butler, "Precarious Life," in *Radicalizing Levinas*, eds. Peter Atterton and Matthew Calarco (Albany: SUNY Press, 2010), 18.

41. "Shifting the geography of reason" is the organizing theme of the Caribbean Philosophical Association. For more on this, see note 23 above.

SECTION 4

Posthuman Ethics

From "The Animal That Therefore I Am (More to Follow)"

Jacques Derrida

In the beginning, I would like to entrust myself to words that, were it possible, would be naked.

Naked in the first place—but this is in order to announce already that I plan to speak endlessly of nudity and of the nude in philosophy. Starting from Genesis. I would like to choose words that are, to begin with, naked, quite simply, words from the heart. [...]¹

And to speak from that point in time, so long ago, as one says,² a time that for me becomes fabulous or mythical. [...]

[E]verything in what I am about to say will lead back to the question of what "to follow" or "to pursue" means, as well as "to be after," back to the question of what I do when "I am" or "I follow," when I say "*Je suis*," if I am to follow this suite then, I move from "the ends of man," that is the confines of man, to "the crossing of borders" between man and animal. Passing across borders or the ends of man I come or surrender to the animal, to the animal in itself, to the animal in me and the animal at unease with itself, to the man about which Nietzsche said (I no longer remember where) something to the effect that it was an as yet undetermined animal, an animal lacking in itself. Nietzsche also said, at the very beginning of the second treatise of *The Genealogy of Morals,* that man is a promising animal, by which he meant, underlining those words, an animal that is permitted to make promises (*das versprechen darf*). Nature is said to have given itself the task of raising, domesticating, and "disciplining" (*heranzuchten*) this animal that promises.

Since time, since so long ago, hence since all of time and for what

187

remains of it to come, we would therefore be in passage toward surrendering to the promise of that animal at unease with itself.

Since time, therefore.

Since so long ago, can we say that the animal has been looking at us?[3]

What animal? The other.

I often ask myself, just to see, who I am—and who I am (following) at the moment when, caught naked, in silence, by the gaze of an animal, for example the eyes of a cat, I have trouble, yes, a bad time,[4] overcoming my embarrassment.

Whence this malaise?

I have trouble repressing a reflex of shame. Trouble keeping silent within me a protest against the indecency. Against the impropriety [malséance] that comes of finding oneself naked, one's sex exposed, stark naked [...] before a cat that looks at you without moving, just to see. The impropriety of a certain animal nude before the other animal, from that point on one might call it a kind of animalséance: the single, incomparable and original experience of the impropriety that would come from appearing in truth naked, in front of the insistent gaze of the animal, a benevolent or pitiless gaze, surprised or cognizant. The gaze of a seer, visionary, or extra-lucid blind person. It is as if I were ashamed, therefore, naked in front of this cat, but also ashamed for being ashamed. [...]

Ashamed of what and naked before whom? Why let oneself be overcome with shame? And why this shame that blushes for being ashamed? Especially, I should make clear, if the cat observes me frontally naked, face to face, and if I am naked faced with the cat's eyes looking at me as it were from head to toe, just to see, not hesitating to concentrate its vision—in order to see, with a view to seeing—in the direction of my sex. To see, without going to see, without touching yet, and without biting, although that threat remains on its lips or on the tip of the tongue. Something happens there that shouldn't take place—like everything that happens in the end, a lapsus, a fall, a failure, a fault, a symptom (and "symptom," as you know, also means "fall": case, unfortunate event, coincidence, what falls due [échéance], mishap). It is as if, at that instant, I had said or were going to say the forbidden, something that shouldn't be said. As if I were to avow what cannot be avowed in a symptom and, as one says, wanted to bite my tongue.

Ashamed of what and before whom? Ashamed of being as naked as a beast. [...] It is generally thought, although none of the philosophers I am about to examine actually mention it,[5] that the property unique to animals, what in the last instance distinguishes them from man, is their being naked without knowing it. Not being naked therefore, not having knowledge of their nudity, in short without consciousness of good and evil.

[...]

The animal, therefore, is not naked because it is naked. It doesn't feel its own nudity. There is no nudity "in nature." There is only the sentiment, the affect, the (conscious or unconscious) experience of existing in nakedness. Because it *is* naked, without *existing* in nakedness, the animal neither feels nor sees itself naked. And it therefore is not naked. At least that is what is thought. For man it would be the opposite, and clothing derives from technics. We would therefore have to think shame and technicity together, as the same "subject." And evil and history, and work, and so many other things that go along with it. Man would be the only one to have invented a garment to cover his sex. He would only be a man to the extent that he was able to be naked, that is to say to be ashamed, to know himself to be ashamed because he is no longer naked. And knowing *himself* would mean knowing himself to be ashamed. On the other hand, because the animal is naked without consciousness of being naked, modesty would remain as foreign to it as would immodesty. As would the knowledge of self that is involved in that.

[...]

To follow and *to be after* will not only be the question and the question of what we call the animal. We shall discover in the follow-through the question of the question, that which begins by wondering what *to respond* means, and whether an animal (but which one?) ever replies in its own name. And by wondering whether one can answer for what "I am (following)" means when that seems to necessitate an "I am inasmuch as I am *after* [*aprés*] the animal" or "I am inasmuch as I am *alongside* [*auprès*] the animal."

Being *after*, being *alongside*, being *near* [*près*] would appear as different modes of being, indeed of *being-with*. With the animal. But, in spite of appearances, it isn't certain that these modes of being come to modify a preestablished being, even less a primitive "I am." In any case they express a certain order of the being-huddled-together [*être-serré*] (which is what the etymological root, *pressu*, indicates, whence are derived the words *près, auprès, après*), the being-pressed, the being-with as being strictly attached, bound, enchained, being-under-pressure, compressed, impressed, repressed, pressed-against according to the stronger or weaker stricture of what always remains pressing. In what sense of the neighbor [*prochain*] (which is not necessarily that of a Biblical or Greco-Latin tradition) should I say that I am close or near to the animal and that I am (following) it, and in what type or order of pressure? Being-with-it in the sense of being-close-to-it? Being-alongside-it? Being-after-it? *Being-after-it* in the sense of the hunt, training, or taming, or *being-after-it* in the sense of a succession or inheritance? In all cases, if I am (following) *after* it, the animal therefore comes before me, earlier than me [...]. The animal is there before me, there close to me, there in front of me— I who am (following) after it. And also, therefore, since it is before me, it is behind me. It surrounds me. And from the vantage of this being-there-before-me it can allow itself to be looked at, no doubt, but also—something that philosophy perhaps forgets, perhaps being this calculated forgetting itself— it can look at me. It has its point of view regarding me. The point of view of the absolute other, and nothing will have ever done more to make me think through this absolute alterity of the neighbor than these moments when I see myself seen naked under the gaze of a cat.

What is at stake in these questions? One doesn't need to be an expert to foresee that they involve thinking about what is meant by living, speaking, dying, being, and world as in being-in-the-world or being towards the world, or being-with, being-before, being-behind, being-after, being and following, being followed or being following, there where *I am,* in one way or another, but unimpeachably, *near* what they call the animal. It is too late to deny it, it will have been there before me who is (following) after it. *After* and *near* what they call the animal and *with* it—whether we want it or not and whatever we do about it.

I'll be obliged to return more than once to the malaise of this scene. I beg your forgiveness for it. I shall do all I can to prevent its being presented as a primal scene: this deranged theatrics of the *wholly other that they call animal, for example, a cat.* Yes, the wholly other, more other than any other that *they* call an animal, for example a cat, when it looks at me naked, at the instant when I introduce myself, present myself to it—or, earlier, at that strange moment when, before the event, before even wanting it or knowing it myself, I am passively presented to it as naked, seen and seen naked, before even seeing *myself* seen by a cat. Before even seeing myself or knowing myself seen naked. I am presented to it before even introducing myself. Nudity is nothing other than that passivity, the involuntary exhibition of the self. Nudity gets stripped to bare necessity only in that frontal exhibition, in that face-to-face. Here, faced with a cat of one *or* the other sex, or of one *and* the other sex. And faced with a cat that continues to see me, to watch me leave when I turn my back on it, a cat that, from that moment on, because I no longer see it seeing me still, from behind, I thus risk forgetting.

I have just attributed passivity to nudity. We could nickname this denuded passivity with a term that will come back more than once, from different places and in different registers, namely, *the passion of the animal, my* passion *of* the animal, my passion of the animal other: seeing oneself seen naked under a gaze that is vacant to the extent of being bottomless, at the same time innocent and cruel perhaps, perhaps sensitive and impassive, good and bad, uninterpretable, unreadable, undecidable, abyssal, and secret. Wholly other, like the (every) other that is (every bit) other found in such intolerable proximity that I do not as yet feel I am justified or qualified to call it my fellow, even less my brother. For we shall have to ask ourselves, inevitably, what happens to the fraternity of brothers when an animal enters the scene. Or, conversely, what happens to the animal when one brother comes after the other, when Abel is *after* Cain who is *after* Abel. Or when a son is *after* his father. What happens to animals, surrogate or not, to the ass and ram on Mount Moriah?

What does this bottomless gaze offer to my sight [*donne à voir*]? What does it "say" to me, demonstrating quite simply the naked truth of every gaze, given that that truth *allows me to see and be seen* through the eyes of the other, in the *seeing* and not just *seen* eyes of the other? I am here thinking of those seeing eyes, those eyes of a seer whose color must at the same time be *seen and forgotten*. In looking at the gaze of the other, Levinas says, one must forget the color of his eyes, in other words see the gaze, the face that gazes before seeing the visible eyes of the other. But when he reminds us that the "best way of meeting the Other is not even to notice the color of his eyes,"[6] he is speaking of man, of one's fellow as man, kindred, brother; he thinks of the other man and this, for us, will later be revealed as a matter for serious concern.

As with every bottomless gaze, as with the eyes of the other, the gaze called "animal" offers to my sight the abyssal limit of the human: the inhuman or the ahuman, the ends of man, that is to say the bordercrossing from which vantage man dares to announce himself to himself, thereby calling himself by the name that he believes he gives himself. And in these moments of nakedness, under the gaze of the animal, everything can happen to me, I am like a child ready for the apocalypse, *I am (following) the apocalypse itself*, that is to say the ultimate and first event of the end, the unveiling and the verdict. I am (following) it, the apocalypse, I identify with it by running behind it, after it, after its whole zoology. When the instant of extreme passion passes, and I find peace again, then I can relax and speak of the beasts of the Apocalypse, visit them in the museum, see them in a painting (but for the Greeks zoography referred to the portraiture of the living in general and not just the painting of animals); I can visit them at the zoo, read about them in the Bible, or speak about them as in a book.

If I began by saying, "the wholly other they *call* the 'animal,' and for example a 'cat,'" if I underlined the call [*appel*] and added quotation marks, it was to do more than announce a problem that will henceforth never leave us, that of appellation—and of the *response* to a call.

Before pursuing things in that direction, let me confide in you the hypothesis that crossed my mind the first time my gaze met that of a cat-pussycat that seemed to be imploring me, asking me clearly to open the door for it to go out, as she did, without waiting, as she often does, for example when she first follows me into the bathroom then immediately regrets her decision. It is moreover a scene that is repeated every morning. The cat follows me when I wake up, into the bathroom, asking for her breakfast, but she demands to be let out of that very room as soon as it (or she) sees me naked, ready for everything and resolved to make her wait. However, when I am found naked under the gaze of what they call the animal, a fictitious tableau is played out in my imagination, a sort of classification after Linnaeus, a taxonomy of the *point of view of animals*. Other than the difference [...] between poem and philosopheme, one can only find, at bottom, two types of discourse, two positions of knowledge, two grand forms of theoretical or philosophical treatise regarding the animal. What distinguishes them is obviously the place, indeed the body of their signatories, that is to say the trace that that signature leaves in a corpus and in a properly scientific, theoretical, or philosophical thematics. In the first place there are those texts signed by people who have no doubt seen, observed, analyzed, reflected on the animal, but who have never been *seen seen* by the animal. Their gaze has never intersected with that of an animal directed at them (forget about their being naked). If, indeed, they did happen to be seen seen furtively by the animal one day, they took no (thematic, theoretical, or philosophical) account of it. They neither wanted nor had the capacity to draw any systematic consequence from the fact that an animal could, facing them, look at them, clothed or naked, and in a word, without a word, *address them*. They have taken no account of the fact that what they call animal could *look at* them and *address* them from down there, from a wholly other origin. That category of discourse, texts, and signatories (those who have never been seen seen by an animal that addressed them) is by far the most frequent. It is probably what brings together *all* philosophers and all theoreticians *as such*. At least those of a certain *epoch*, let's say from Descartes to the present, but I will say later why the word "epoch" and even this historicism leaves me quite uneasy or dissatisfied. Clearly all those (all those males but not all those females, and that difference is not insignificant here) whom I will later situate in order to back up my thesis, arranging them within the same configuration, for example Descartes, Kant, Heidegger, Lacan, and Levinas, belong to this quasi-epochal [...] category. Their discourses are sound and profound, but everything goes on as if they themselves had never been looked at, and especially not naked, by an animal that addressed them. At least everything goes on as though this troubling experience had not been theoretically registered, supposing that they had experienced it at all, at the precise moment when they made of the animal a *theorem*, something seen and not seeing. The experience of the seeing animal, of the animal that looks at them, has not been taken into account in the philosophical or theoretical architecture of their discourse. In sum they have denied it as much as misunderstood it. Henceforth we can do little more than turn around this immense disavowal whose logic traverses the whole history of humanity, and not only that of the quasi-epochal configuration I just mentioned. It is as if the men representing this configuration had seen without being seen, seen the animal without being seen by it, without being seen seen by it; without being seen seen naked by someone who, from the basis of a life called animal, and not only by means of the gaze, would have obliged them to recognize, at the moment of address, that this was their affair, their lookout [*que cela les regardait*].

But since I don't believe, deep down, that it has never happened to them, or that it has not in some way been signified, figured, or metonymized, more or less secretly, in the gestures of their discourse, the symptom of this disavowal remains to be deciphered. This figure could not be the figure of just one disavowal among others. It institutes what is proper to man, the relation to itself of a humanity that is above all careful to guard, and jealous of, what is proper to it.

As for the other category of discourse, found among those whose signatories are first and foremost poets or prophets, in the situation of poetry or prophecy, those men and women who admit taking upon themselves the address of an animal that addresses them, before even having the time or the power to take themselves off [*s'y dérober*], to take themselves off with clothes off or in a bathrobe, I know of no *statutory representative* of it, that is to say no subject who does so as theoretical, philosophical, or juridical man, or even as citizen. I have found no such representative, but it is in that very place that I find myself, here and now, in the process of searching.

That is the track I am following, the track I am ferreting out [*la piste que je dépiste*], following the traces of this "wholly other they *call* 'animal,' for example 'cat.'"

Why rename that appellation? Why say "the wholly other they *call* 'animal,' for example 'cat'"? In order to recall a scene of name-calling, beginning at the beginning, namely in Genesis—and at least a type of new beginning, a second beginning in what is distinguished in Bereshit as the *second* narrative. For one must indeed specify that that story is a second "Heading" ("*Entête*" in Chouraqui's translation).[7] The man who, in that rendering, calls the animals by name is not only Adam, the man of the earth, the husbandman [*glébeux*]. He is also Ish preceding Ishah, man before woman. It is the man Ish, still alone, who gives names to the animals created before him: "The husbandman cried out the name of each beast," one translation (Chouraqui) says; another (Dhormes): "Man called all the animals by their names."

Let me repeat: it is only recorded thus in the *second* narrative. If one believes what is called the *first* narrative, God creates man in his image but he brings male and female into the world at the same time. Naming will thus have been the fact of man as a couple, if it can be put that way. The original naming of the animals does not take place in the first version. It isn't the man-woman of the first version but man *alone* and *before* woman who, in that second version, gives their names, his names, to the animals. On the other hand it is said in the first version that the husbandman, created as God's replica, and created male-female, man-woman, immediately receives the order to subject the animals to him. In order to obey he is required to mark his ascendancy, his domination over them, indeed his power to tame them. Having created the living animals on the fifth day (the beasts, that is to say animals for domestication, birds, fish, reptiles and wild beasts), and having blessed them:

> Elohim said: "Let us make man in our image, in our likeness! Let them [note the sudden move to the plural] *have authority* [my italics] over the fish of the sea and the birds of the heavens, over the cattle, over all the wild beasts and reptiles that crawl upon the earth!" Elohim therefore created man in his image, in the image of Elohim he created him. Male and female he created them. Elohim blessed them and said, "Be fruitful and multiply, fill the earth and subdue it, *have authority* [my italics again] over the fish of the sea and the birds of the heavens, over every living thing that moves on the earth" [Dhormes]. [...]
>
> Elohim said: "We will make Adam the husbandman—/As our replica, in our likeness./They will *subject* [my italics] the fish of the sea, the flying creatures of the heavens,/The beasts, the whole earth, every reptile that crawls upon the earth."/Elohim created the husbandman as his replica,/As a replica of Elohim he created him,/Male and female he created them./Elohim blessed them. Elohim said to them:/"Be fruitful, multiply, fill the earth, conquer it./*Subject* [my italics again] the fish of the sea, the flying creatures of the heavens,/Every living thing that crawls on the earth" [Chouraqui]. [...]

That is the first narrative. God commands man-woman to command the animals, but not yet to name them. What happens next, in the second narrative? There occurs something, a single and double thing, twice at the same time, something that, it seems to me, gets little notice in most readings of this Genesis that is infinite in its second breath.

On the one hand, the naming of the animals is performed *at one and the same time*, before the creation of Ishah, the female part of man, *and*, as a result, before they perceive themselves to be naked; and they are at first naked without shame ("The two of them are naked, the husbandman and his wife; they don't blanch on account of it"). After a certain serpent—one we shall return to—comes by, they will perceive themselves to be naked, and not without shame.

On the other hand, and this is especially important, the public announcing of names remains *at one and the same time* free *and* overseen, under surveillance, under the gaze of Jehovah who does not for all that intervene. He lets Adam, he lets man, man alone, Ish without Ishah, the woman, freely call out the names. He lets him go about naming alone. But he is waiting in the wings, watching over this man alone with a mixture of curiosity and authority. God observes: Adam is observed, within sight, he names under observation. In Chouraqui's translation: "He has them come towards the husbandman *in order to see* what he will call out to them." [...] He has them come forward, he summons them, the animals that, according to the first narrative, he had created—and I firmly underline this factor that is fundamental to what concerns us—he summons them in order to "subject" them to man's command, in order to place them under man's "authority." More precisely, he has created man in his likeness *so that* man will *subject, tame, dominate, train,* or *domesticate* the animals born before him and assert his authority over them. God destines the animals to an experience of the power of man, *in order to see* the power of man in action, in order to see the power of man at work, in order to see man take power over all the other living beings. Chouraqui: "He has them come towards the husbandman *in order to see* what he will call out to them"; Dhormes: "He brings them to man *in order to see* what he will call them."

The "in order to see" that I have emphasized twice seems full of meaning. It is the same expression in both translations. God gives Ish alone the freedom to name the animals, granted, and that represents at the same time his sovereignty and his loneliness. However, everything seems to happen as though God still wanted to oversee, keep vigil, maintain his right of inspection over the names that were about to echo out and by means of which Ish, Ish all alone, Ish still without woman, was going to get the upper hand with respect to the animals. God wanted to oversee but also abandon himself to his curiosity, even allow himself to be surprised and outflanked by the radical novelty of what was going to occur, by this irreversible, welcome or unwelcome event of naming whereby Ish would begin to see them and name them without allowing himself to be seen or named by them. God lets him, Ish, speak on his own, call out on his own, call out and nominate, call out and name, as if he were able to say, "I name," "I call." God lets Ish call the other living things all on his own, give them their names in his own name, these animals that are older and younger than him, these living things that came into the world before him but were named after him, on his initiative according to the second narrative. In both cases, man is in both senses of the word *after* the animal. He follows him. This "after," which determines a sequence, a consequence, or a persecution, is not in time, nor is it temporal; it is the very genesis of time.

God thus lets Ish do the calling of his own accord, he accords him the right to give them names in his own name—but just in order to see. This "in order to see" marks at the same time the infinite right of inspection of an all-powerful God *and* the finitude of a God who doesn't know what is going to happen to him with language. And with names. In short, God doesn't yet know what he really wants; this is the finitude of a God who doesn't know what he wants with respect to the animal, that is to say with respect to the life of the living as such, a God who sees something coming without seeing it coming, a God who will say *"I am that I am"* without knowing what he is going to see when a poet enters the scene to give his name to living things. This powerful yet deprived "in order to see" that is God's, the first stroke of time, before time, God's exposure to surprise, to the event of what is going to occur between man and animal, this time before time has always made me dizzy. As if someone said, in the form of a promise or a threat, "you'll see what you'll see" without knowing what was going to end up happening. It is the dizziness one feels before the abyss opened by this stupid ruse, this feigned feint, what I have been feeling for so long [*depuis le temps*] whenever I run away from an animal that looks at me naked. I often wonder whether this vertigo before the abyss of such an "in order to see" deep in the eyes of God is not the same as that which takes hold of me when I feel so naked in front of a cat, facing it, and when, meeting its gaze I hear the cat or God ask itself, ask *me*: is he going to call me, is he going to address me? What is he going to call me, this naked man, before I give him woman, before I lend her to him in giving her to him, before I give her to him or before he gives her to himself by taking upon himself, from under him, from at his side? Or even from his rib?

Since time.

For so long now it is as if the cat had been recalling itself and recalling that, recalling me and reminding me of this awful tale of Genesis, without breathing a word. Who was born first, before the names? Which one saw the other come to this place so long ago? Who will have been the first occupant, and thus the master? Who the subject? Who has remained the despot, for so long now?

[...]

The animal, what a word!

The animal is a word, it is an appellation that men have instituted, a name they have given themselves the right and the authority to give to another living creature.

At the point at which we find ourselves, even before I get involved, or try to drag you after me [...] or in pursuit of me upon an itinerary that some of you will no doubt find torturous, labyrinthine, even aberrant, leading us astray from lure to lure, I will attempt the operation of disarmament that consists in *posing* what one could call some hypotheses in view of theses; posing them simply, naked, frontally, as directly as possible, *pose* them as I said, by no means in the way one indulgently poses in front of a spectator, a painter of portraits, or a camera, but "pose" in the sense of situating a series of "positions."

First hypothesis: for about two centuries, intensely and by means of an alarming rate of acceleration, for we no longer even have a clock or a chrono-logical measure of it, we, we who call ourselves men or humans, we who recognize ourselves in that name, have been involved in an unprecedented transformation. This mutation affects the experience of what we continue to call imperturbably, as if there were nothing wrong with it, the animal and/or animals. I intend to stake a lot, or play a lot on the flexible separation of this *and/or*. This new situation can be determined only on the basis of a very ancient one. We must continuously move along this coming and going between the oldest and what comes of the exchange among the new, the "again," and the "anew" of a repetition. Far from appearing, simply, within what we continue to call the world, history, life, and so on, this unheard-of relation to the animal or to animals is so new that it should oblige us to worry all those concepts, more than just problematize them. That is why I would hesitate to say that we are *living through* that (if one can still confidently call *life* the experience whose limits tremble at the bordercrossings between *bios* and *zoē*, the biological, zoological, and anthropological, as between life and death, life and technology, life and history, and so on). I would therefore hesitate just as much to say that we are living through a historical turning point. The figure of the turning point implies a rupture or an instantaneous mutation for which the model or the figure remains genetic, biological, or zoological, and which therefore remains, precisely, to be questioned. As for history, historicity, even historicality, those motifs belong precisely—as we shall see in detail—to *this* auto-definition, *this* auto-apprehension, *this* auto-situation of man or of the human *Dasein* with respect to what is living and with respect to animal life; they belong to this auto-biography of man that I wish to call into question today.

Since all these words, in particular "history," belong in a constitutive manner to the language, interests, and lures of this autobiography, we should not be overhasty in giving them credence or in confirming their pseudo-evidence. I will therefore not be speaking of a historical turning point in order to name a transformation in process, an alteration that is at the same time more serious and less recognizable than a turning point in the relation to the animal, in the being-with shared by man and by what man calls the animal: the *being* of what calls itself man or the *Dasein with* what he himself calls, or what we ourselves call, what we still dare, provisionally, to name in general but in the singular, *the animal*. However one names or interprets this alteration, no one could deny that it has been accelerating, intensifying, no longer knowing where it is going, for about two centuries, at an incalculable rate and level.

[Over the last two centuries] traditional forms of treatment of the animal have been turned upside down by the joint developments of zoological, ethological, biological, and genetic *forms of knowledge* and the always inseparable *techniques* of intervention with respect to their object, the transformation of the actual object, its milieu, its world, namely, the living animal. This has occurred by means of farming and regimentalization at a demographic level unknown in the past, by means of genetic experimentation, the industrialization of what can be called the production for consumption of animal meat, artificial insemination on a massive scale, more and more audacious manipulations of the genome, the reduction of the animal not only to production and overactive reproduction (hormones, genetic crossbreeding, cloning, and so on) of meat for consumption but also of all sorts of other end products, and all of that in the service of a certain being and the so-called human well-being of man.

All that is well known; we have no need to dwell on it. However one interprets it, whatever practical, technical, scientific, juridical, ethical, or political consequence one draws from it, no one can deny this event any more, no one can deny the *unprecedented* proportions of this subjection of the animal. Such a subjection, whose history we are attempting to interpret, can be called violence in the most morally neutral sense of the term and even includes a certain interventionist violence that is practiced, as in some very minor and in no way dominant cases, let us never forget, in the service of and for the protection of the animal, most often the human animal. Neither can one seriously deny the disavowal that this involves. No one can deny seriously, or for very long, that men do all they can in order to dissimulate this cruelty or to hide it from themselves, in order to organize on a global scale the forgetting or misunderstanding of this violence that some would compare to the worst cases of genocide (there are also animal genocides: the number of species endangered because of man takes one's breath away). One should neither abuse the figure of genocide nor consider it explained away. For it gets more complicated here: the annihilation of certain species is indeed in process, but it is occurring through the organization and exploitation of an artificial, infernal, virtually interminable survival, in conditions that previous generations would have judged monstrous, outside of every supposed norm of a life proper to animals that are thus exterminated by means of their continued existence or even their overpopulation. As if, for example, instead of throwing people into ovens or gas chambers (let's say Nazi) doctors and geneticists had decided to organize the overproduction and overgeneration of Jews, gypsies, and homosexuals by means of artificial insemination, so that, being more numerous and better fed, they could be destined in always increasing numbers for the same hell, that of the imposition of genetic experimentation or extermination by gas or by fire. In the same abattoirs. I don't wish to abuse the ease with which one can overload with pathos the self-evidences I am drawing attention to here. Everybody knows what terrifying and intolerable pictures a realist painting could give to the industrial, mechanical, chemical, hormonal, and genetic violence to which man has been submitting animal life for the past two centuries. Everybody knows what the production, breeding, transport, and slaughter of these animals has become. Instead of thrusting these images in your faces or awakening them in your memory, something that would be both too easy and endless, let me simply say a word about this "pathos." If these images are "pathetic," if they evoke sympathy, it is also because they "pathetically" open the immense question of pathos and the pathological, precisely, that is, of suffering, pity, and compassion; and the place that has to be accorded to the interpretation of this compassion, to the sharing of this suffering among the living, to the law, ethics, and politics that must be brought to bear upon this experience of compassion. For what has been happening now for two centuries involves a new experience of this compassion. In response to the irresistible but unacknowledged unleashing and the organized disavowal of this torture, voices are raised—minority, weak, marginal voices, little assured of their discourse, of their right to discourse and of the enactment of their discourse within the law, as a declaration of rights—in order to protest, in order to appeal (we'll return to this) to what is still presented in such a problematic way as *animal rights*, in order to awaken us to our responsibilities and our obligations with respect to the living in general, and precisely to this fundamental compassion that, were we to take it seriously, would have to change even the very basis (and that basis is what I wish to discuss today) of the philosophical problematic of the animal.

It is in thinking of the source and ends of this compassion that about two centuries ago someone like Bentham, as is well known, proposed changing the very form of the question regarding the animal that dominated discourse within the tradition, in the language of both the most refined philosophical argument and everyday acceptation and common sense. Bentham said something like this: the question is not to know whether the animal can think, reason, or talk, something we still pretend to be asking ourselves. (From Aristotle to Descartes, from Descartes, especially, to Heidegger, Levinas, and Lacan, this question determines so many others concerning *power* or *capability* [*pouvoirs*] and *attributes* [*avoirs*]: being able, having the power to give, to die, to bury one's dead, to dress, to work, to invent a technique, and so on, a power that consists in having such and such a faculty, thus such and such a power, as an essential attribute). Thus the question will not be to know whether animals are of the type *zōon logon echon*, whether they *can* speak or reason thanks to that *capacity* or that *attribute* implied in the *logos*, the *can-have* [*pouvoir-avoir*] of the *logos*, the aptitude for the *logos* (and logocentrism is first of all a thesis regarding the animal, the animal deprived of the *logos*, deprived of the *can-have-the-logos*: this is the thesis, position, or presupposition maintained from Aristotle to Heidegger, from Descartes to Kant, Levinas, and Lacan). The *first* and *decisive* question will rather be to know whether animals *can suffer*.

"Can they suffer?" asks Bentham simply yet so profoundly.

Once its protocol is established, the form of this question changes everything. It no longer simply concerns the *logos*, the disposition and whole configuration of the *logos*, having it or not, nor does it concern more radically a *dynamic* or *hexis*, this having or manner of being, this *habitus* that one calls a faculty or "power," this can-have or the power one possesses (as in the power to reason, to speak, and everything that that implies). The question is disturbed by a certain *passivity*. It bears witness, manifesting already, as question, the response that testifies to a sufferance, a passion, a not-being-able. The word *can* [*pouvoir*] changes sense and sign here once one asks "can they suffer?" The word wavers henceforth. As soon as such a question is posed what counts is not only the idea of a transitivity or activity (being able to speak, to reason, and so on); the important thing is rather what impels it towards self-contradiction, something we will later relate back to auto-biography. "Can they suffer?" amounts to asking "can they *not be able?*" And what of this inability [*impouvoir*]? What of the vulnerability felt on the basis of this inability? What is this nonpower at the heart of power? What is its quality or modality? How should one account for it? What right should be accorded it? To what extent does it concern us? Being able to suffer is no longer a power, it is a possibility without power, a possibility of the impossible. Mortality resides there, as the most radical means of thinking the finitude that we share with animals, the mortality that belongs to the very finitude of life, to the experience of compassion, to the possibility of sharing the possibility of this nonpower, the possibility of this impossibility, the anguish of this vulnerability and the vulnerability of this anguish.

With this question—"can they suffer?"—we are not standing on the rock of indubitable certainty, the foundation of every assurance that one could, for example, look for in the *cogito*, in *Je pense donc je suis*. But from another perspective we are here putting our trust in an instance that is just as radical, however different it may be, namely, what is undeniable. No one can deny the suffering, fear or panic, the terror or fright that humans witness in certain animals. (Descartes himself was not able to claim that animals were insensitive to suffering.) Some will still try—this is something else we will come to—to contest the right to call that *suffering* or *anguish*, words or concepts that they would still reserve for man and for the *Dasein* in the freedom of its being-towards-death. We will have reason to problematize that discourse later. But for the moment let us note the following: the response to the question "can they suffer?" leaves no doubt. In fact it has never left any room for doubt; that is why the experience that we have of it is not even indubitable; it precedes the indubitable, it is older than it. No doubt either, then, for the possibility of our giving vent to a surge of compassion, even if it is then misunderstood, repressed, or denied, held in respect. Before the *undeniable* of this response (yes, they suffer, like us who suffer for them and with them), before this response that precedes all other questions, the problematic changes ground and base. Perhaps it loses all security, but in any case it no longer rests on the old, supposedly natural (its ground) or historic and *artifactual* (its base) foundation. The two centuries I have been referring to somewhat approximately in order to situate the present in terms of this tradition have been those of an unequal struggle, a war being waged, the unequal forces of which could one day be reversed, between those who violate not only animal life but even and also this sentiment of compassion and, on the other hand, those who appeal to an irrefutable testimony to this pity.

[...]

Here now, in view of another thesis, is the *second hypothesis* that I think must be deduced without hesitation. It concerns or puts into effect another logic of the limit. [...] Let's allow that word to have both a general and strict sense: what abuts onto limits but also what feeds, is fed, is cared for, raised, and trained, what is cultivated on the edges of a limit. In the semantics of *trephō, trophē,* or *trophos,* we should be able to find everything we need to speak about what we should be speaking about [with regard to] the autobiographical animal: feeding, food, nursing, breeding, offspring, education, care and keeping of animals, training, upbringing, culture, living and allowing to live by giving to live, be fed, and grown, autobiographically. *Limitrophy* is therefore my subject. Not just because it will concern what sprouts or grows at the limit, around the limit, by maintaining the limit, but also what *feeds the limit,* generates it, raises it, and complicates it. Whatever I will say is designed, certainly not to efface the limit, but to multiply its figures, to complicate, thicken, delinearize, fold, and divide the line precisely by making it increase and multiply. Moreover, the supposed first or literal sense of *trephō* is just that: transform by thickening, for example, in curdling milk. So it will in no way mean questioning, even in the slightest, the limit about which we have had a stomachful, the limit between Man with a capital M and Animal with a capital A. It will not be a matter of attacking frontally or antithetically the thesis of philosophical or common sense on the basis of which has been built the relation to the self, the presentation of the self of human life, the autobiography of the human species, the whole history of the self that man recounts to himself, that is to say the thesis of a limit as rupture or abyss between those who say "we men," "I, a man," and what this man among men who say "we," what he *calls* the animal or animals. I won't take it upon myself for a single moment to contest that thesis, nor the rupture or abyss between this "I-we" and what we *call* animals. To suppose that I, or anyone else for that matter, could ignore that rupture, indeed that abyss, would mean first of all blinding oneself to so much contrary evidence; and, as far as my own modest case is concerned, it would mean forgetting all the signs that I have sought to give, tirelessly, of my attention to difference, to differences, to heterogeneities and abyssal ruptures as against the homogeneous and the continuous. I have thus never believed in some homogeneous continuity between what calls *itself* man and what *he* calls the animal. I am not about to begin to do so now. That would be worse than sleepwalking, it would simply be too asinine [*bête*].[8] To suppose such a stupid memory lapse or to take to task such a naive misapprehension of this abyssal rupture would mean, more seriously still, venturing to say almost anything at all for the cause, for whatever cause or interest that no longer had anything to do with what we claimed to want to talk about. When that cause or interest begins to profit from what it simplistically suspects to be a biologistic continuism, whose sinister connotations we are well aware of, or more generally to profit from what is suspected as a geneticism that one might wish to associate with this scatterbrained accusation of continuism, the undertaking in any case becomes so aberrant that it neither calls for nor, it seems to me, deserves any direct discussion on my part. Everything I have suggested so far and every argument I will put forward today stands overwhelmingly in opposition to the blunt instrument that such an allegation represents.

There is no interest to be found in debating something like a discontinuity, rupture, or even abyss between those who call themselves men and what so-called men, those who name themselves men, call the animal. Everybody agrees on this, discussion is closed in advance, one would have to be more asinine than any beast [*plus bête que les bêtes*] to think otherwise. Even animals know that (ask Abraham's ass or ram or the living beasts that Abel offered to God; they know what is about to happen to them when man says, "Here I am" to God, then consent to sacrifice themselves, to sacrifice their sacrifice or to forgive themselves). The discussion is worth undertaking once it is a matter of determining the number, form, sense, or structure, the foliated consistency of this abyssal limit, these edges, this plural and repeatedly folded frontier. The discussion becomes interesting once, instead of asking whether or not there is a discontinuous limit, one attempts to think what a limit becomes once it is abyssal, once the frontier no longer forms a single indivisible line but more than one internally divided line, once, as a result, it can no longer be traced, objectified, or counted as single and indivisible. What are the edges of a limit that grows and multiplies by feeding on an abyss? Here is my thesis in three paragraphs:

1. This abyssal rupture doesn't describe two edges, a unilinear and indivisible line having two edges, Man and Animal in general.
2. The multiple and heterogeneous border of this abyssal rupture has a history. Both macroscopic and microscopic and far from being closed, that history is now passing through the most unusual phase in

which we find ourselves and for which there is no scale. Indeed, one can only speak here of history, of an historic moment or phase, from one of the supposed edges of the said rupture, the edge of an anthropocentric subjectivity that is recounted or allows a history to be recounted about it, autobiographically, the history of its life, and that it therefore calls *History*.

3. Beyond the edge of the *so-called* human, beyond it but by no means on a single opposing side, rather than "the Animal" or "Animal Life," there is already a heterogeneous multiplicity of the living, or more precisely (since to say "the living" is already to say too much or not enough) a multiplicity of organizations of relations between living and dead, relations of organization or lack of organization among realms that are more and more difficult to dissociate by means of the figures of the organic and inorganic, of life and/or death. These relations are at once close and abyssal, and they can never be totally objectified. They do not leave room for any simple exteriority of one term with respect to another. It follows from that that one will never have the right to take animals to be the species of a kind that would be named the Animal, or animal in general. Whenever "one" says, "the Animal," each time a philosopher, or anyone else says, "the Animal" in the singular and with-out further ado, claiming thus to designate every living thing that is held not to be man (man as *rational animal*, man as political animal, speak-ing animal, *zōon logon echon*, man who says "I" and takes himself to be the subject of a statement that he proffers on the subject of the said ani-mal, and so on), each time the subject of that statement, this "one," this "I" does that he utters an *asinanity* [*bêtise*]. He avows without avowing it, he declares, just as a disease is declared by means of a symptom, he offers up for diagnosis the statement "I am uttering an *asinanity*." And this "I am uttering an *asinanity*" should confirm not only the animality that he is disavowing but his complicit, continued, and organized involvement in a veritable war of the species.

Such are my hypotheses in view of theses on the animal, on animals, on the word *animal* or *animals*.

Yes, *animal*, what a word!

Animal is a word that men have given themselves the right to give. These humans are found giving it to themselves, this word, but as if they had received it as an inheritance. They have given themselves the word in order to corral a large number of living beings within a single concept: "the Animal," they say. And they have given themselves this word, at the same time accord-ing themselves, reserving for them, for humans, the right to the word, the name, the verb, the attribute, to a language of words, in short to the very thing that the others in question would be deprived of, those that are corralled within the grand territory of the beasts: the Animal. All the philosophers [...] from Aristotle to Lacan, and including Descartes, Kant, Heidegger, and Levinas [...] say the same thing: the animal is without language. Or more precisely unable to respond, to respond with a response that could be precisely and rigorously distinguished from a reaction, the animal is without the right and power to "respond" and hence without many other things that would be the property of man.

Men would be first and foremost those living creatures who have given themselves the word that enables them to speak of the animal with a single voice and to designate it as the single being that remains without a response, without a word with which to respond.

That wrong was committed long ago and with long-term consequences. It derives from this word or rather it comes together in this word *animal* that men have given themselves at the origin of humanity and that they have given themselves in order to identify themselves, in order to recognize themselves, with a view to being what they say they are, namely men, capable of replying and responding in the name of men.

I would like to try and speak of a certain wrong or evil that derives from this word, to begin with by stammering some chimerical aphorisms.

The animal that I am (following), does it speak?

That is an intact question, virginal, new, still to come, a completely naked question.

[...]

We are following, we follow ourselves. I shall not impose upon you a complete exposition of this theory of *animots* that I am (following) or that follow me everywhere and the memory of which seems to me inexhaustible. Far from resembling Noah's ark it would be more like a circus, with an animal trainer having his sad subjects, bent low, file past. The multiple *animot* would still suffer from always having its master on its back. It would have it up to the neck [*en aurait plein le dos*] with being thus domesticated, broken in, trained, docile, disciplined, tamed. Instead of recalling the menagerie that some who badmouth me might characterize as my autobibliography, I shall simply recall the idea, or rather the troubling stakes of a philosophical bestiary, of a bestiary at the origin of philosophy. It was not by chance that it first imposed itself in the region of an undecidable *pharmakon*. Concerning the Socratic irony that "precipitates out one *pharmakon* by bringing it in contact with another *pharmakon*," that is to say "reverses the *pharmakon*'s powers and turns its surface over," I tried (in 1968, that is thirty years ago) to imagine what the program of a Socratic bestiary on the eve of philosophy might be, and more precisely (I note in the context of Descartes) how that would appear in a place where the demonic, the cunning, indeed the evil genius has some affinity with the animal: a malign and hence perverse beast, at one and the same time innocent, crafty, and evil. Keeping myself to the program, let me refer to the note that made explicit, right in the middle, in the very center, in the binding between the two parts of "Plato's Pharmacy," this alternating border crossing:

> Alternately and/or all at once, the Socratic *pharmakon* petrifies and vivifies, anesthetizes and sensitizes, appeases and anguishes. Socrates is a benumbing stingray but also an animal that needles [this is a reference to well-known texts]: we recall the bee in the *Phaedo* (91c); later we will open the *Apology* at the point where Socrates compares himself precisely to a gadfly. This whole Socratic configuration thus composes a bestiary. [Of course, since this is a matter of animal figures in Socrates' presentation of the self, the question is indeed that of Socrates as autobiographical "animal."] Is it surprising that the demonic inscribes itself in a bestiary? It is on the basis of this zoopharmaceutical ambivalence and of that other Socratic *analogy* that the contours of the *anthropos* are determined.[9]

At the risk of being mistaken and of having one day to make honorable amends [...], I will venture to say that never, on the part of any great philosopher from Plato to Heidegger, or anyone at all who takes on, *as a philosophical question in and of itself*, the question called that of the animal and of the limit between the animal and the human, have I noticed a protestation *of principle*, and especially a protestation of consequence against the general singular that is *the animal*. Nor against the general singular of an animal whose sexuality is as a matter of principle left undifferentiated—or neutralized, not to say castrated. Such an omission is not without connection to many others that form either its premise or its consequence. This philosophical or metaphysical datum has never been required to change philosophically speaking. I indeed said "philosophical" (or "metaphysical") datum for the gesture seems to me to constitute philosophy as such, the philosopheme itself. Not that all philosophers agree on the definition of *the* limit separating man in general from the animal in general (although this is an area that is most conducive to consensus and is no doubt where we find the dominant form of consensus on the matter). But in spite of that, through and beyond all their disagreements, philosophers have always judged and *all* philosophers have judged that limit to be single and indivisible, considering that on the other side of that limit there is an immense group, a single and fundamentally homogeneous set that one has the right, the theoretical or philosophical right, to distinguish and mark as opposite, namely, the set of the Animal in general, the animal spoken of in the general singular. It applies to the whole animal realm with the exception of the human. Philosophical right thus presents itself as that of "common sense." This agreement concerning philosophical sense and common sense that allows one to speak blithely of the Animal in the general singular is perhaps one of the greatest, and most symptomatic idiocies [*bêtises*] of those who call themselves humans. We shall perhaps speak of *bêtise* and of bestiality later, as that from which beasts are in any case exempt by definition. One cannot speak—moreover, it has never been done—of the *bêtise* or bestiality of an animal. It would be an anthropomorphic projection of something that remains reserved to man, as the single assurance finally, and the single risk, of what is "proper to man." One can ask why the ultimate fallback of what is proper to man, if there is such a thing, a property that could never in any case be attributed to the animal or to God, thus comes to be named *bêtise* or bestiality.

Interpretive decisions (in all their metaphysical, ethical, juridical, and political consequences) thus depend on what is presupposed by the general singular of this word *Animal*. I was tempted, at a given moment, in order to indicate the direction of my thinking, not just to keep this word within quotation marks, as if it were a citation to be analyzed, but without further ado to change the word, indicating clearly thereby that it is indeed a matter of a word, only a word, the word *animal* [*du mot "animal"*], and to forge another word in the singular, at the same time close but radically foreign, a chimerical word that sounded as though it contravened the laws of the French language, *l'animot*.

Ecce animot. Neither a species nor a gender nor an individual, it is an irreducible living multiplicity of mortals, and rather than a double clone or a portmanteau word, a sort of monstrous hybrid, a chimera waiting to be put to death [...]

[...]

Ecce animot—that is what I was saying before. In order not to damage French ears too sensitive to spelling and grammar I won't repeat the word *animot* too often. I'll do it several times but each time that, henceforth, I say the animal [*l'animal*] or the animals [*animaux*] I'll be asking you to silently substitute *animot* for what you hear. By means of the chimera of this singular word, the *animot*, I bring together three heterogeneous elements within a single verbal body.

1. I would like to have the plural of animals heard in the singular. There is no animal in the general singular, separated from man by a single indivisible limit. We have to envisage the existence of "living creatures" whose plurality cannot be assembled within the single figure of an animality that is simply opposed to humanity. This does not of course mean ignoring or effacing everything that separates humankind from the other animals, creating a single large set, a single great, fundamentally homogeneous and continuous family tree going from the *animot* to the *homo* (*faber, sapiens,* or whatever else). That would be an *asinanity*, even more so to suspect anyone here of doing just that. [...] Among non-humans and separate from nonhumans there is an immense multi-

plicity of other living things that cannot in any way be homogenized, except by means of violence and willful ignorance, within the category of what is called the animal or animality in general. From the outset there are animals and, let's say, *l'animot*. The confusion of all nonhuman living creatures within the general and common category of the animal is not simply a sin against rigorous thinking, vigilance, lucidity, or empirical authority; it is also a crime. Not a crime against animality precisely, but a crime of the first order against the animals, against animals. Do we agree to presume that every murder, every transgression of the commandment "Thou shalt not kill" concerns only man (a question to come) and that in sum there are only crimes "against humanity?"

2. The suffix *mot* in *l'animot* should bring us back to the word, namely, to the word named a noun [*nommé nom*]. It opens onto the referential experience of the thing *as such*, as what it is in its being, and therefore to the reference point by means of which one has always sought to draw the limit, the unique and indivisible limit held to separate man from animal, namely the word, the nominal language of the word, the voice that names and that names the thing *as such*, such as it appears in its being (as in the Heideggerian moment in the demonstration that we are coming to). The animal would in the last instance be deprived of the word, of the word that one names a noun or name.

3. It would not be a matter of "giving speech back" to animals but perhaps of acceding to a thinking, however fabulous and chimerical it might be, that thinks the absence of the name and of the word otherwise, as something other than a privation.

Ecce animot, that is the announcement of which I am (following) something like the trace, assuming the title of an autobiographical animal, in the form of a risky, fabulous, or chimerical response to the question "But me, who am I?" that I have bet on treating as that of the autobiographical animal. Assuming that title, which is itself somewhat chimerical, might surprise you. It brings together *two times two* alliances, as unexpected as they are irrefutable.

[...]

The animal in general, what is it? What does that mean? Who is it? To what does that "it"[10] correspond? To whom? Who responds to whom? Who responds in and to the common, general, and singular name of what they thus blithely call the "animal?" Who is it that responds? The reference made by this what or who regarding me in the name of the animal, what is said in the name of the animal when one appeals to the name of the animal, that is what needs to be exposed, in all its nudity, in the nudity or destitution of whoever, opening the page of an autobiography, says, "here I am."

"But as for me, who am I (following)?"

NOTES

1. This article represents the first part of a ten-hour address Derrida gave at the third Cerisy-la-Salle conference devoted to his work, in July 1997. The title of the conference was "L'Animal autobiographique"; see *L'Animal autobiographique: Autour de Jacques Derrida*, ed. Marie-Louise Mallet (Paris, 1999); [...] Later segments of the address dealt with Descartes, Kant, Heidegger, Lacan, and Levinas, as note 4 explains and as other allusions made by Derrida suggest. [...] The French title of Derrida's article is "*L'Animal que donc je suis* (à suivre)." An obvious play on Descartes's definition of consciousness (of the thinking animal as human), it also takes advantage of the shared first-person singular present form of *être* (to be) and *suivre* (to follow) in order to suggest a displacement of that priority, also reading as "the animal that therefore I follow after." [...]—Trans.

2. The adverbial fragment *depuis le temps*, which is not usually used as such in French, is repeated throughout the text. The relative form, *depuis le temps que*, has the sense of "for so long now" [or] "since so long ago." [...] In all cases the reader should bear in mind Derrida's reference to the mythological and philosophical "prehistory" of conceptualizations of the animal that he is calling into question.—Trans.

3. "Que l'animal nous regarde": also "that the animal has been our concern."—Trans. Derrida plays on this double sense of *regarder* ("to look at" and "to concern") in various cases below.

4. "J'ai du mal": the expression also evokes the sense of evil or a curse. Here and below Derrida implies a recasting of the Genesis myth whereby it is an animal that brings man to consciousness of his nakedness and of good and evil, rather than being the cause (via woman) of his fall.—Trans.

5. Later the same day, and on the next day, this introduction was followed by four sessions during which I proposed readings of Descartes, Kant, Heidegger, Levinas, and Lacan. Those interpretations, as close and patient as possible, were designed to test the working hypotheses that I am outlining here, on the threshold of a work in progress.

6. Emmanuel Levinas, *Ethics and Infinity: Conversations with Philippe Nemo*, trans. Richard A. Cohen (1982; Pittsburgh, 1985), 85.

7. In this section Derrida consistently compares two authoritative French translations of Genesis (Bereshit), those by Chouraqui (Desclée de Brouwer) and Dhormes (Pleiade). My translations lose some of the subtleties. For comparison, readers can consult the King James Version, The Jerusalem Bible, or *The JPS Torah Commentary (Genesis)* (Philadelphia: Jewish Publication Society, 1989).—Trans.

8. In modern French, the noun *une bête* is normally used to mean "animal" with a slightly familiar sense; as adjective *bête* means stupid. *Une bêtise*, which I have taken the liberty of translating below with the neologism asinanity, means a "stupid mistake" or "idiocy."—Trans.

9. Derrida, *Dissemination*, trans. Barbara Johnson (Chicago: University of Chicago Press, 1981), 119n, 52.

10. Ça, also "Id."—Trans.

From "Posthuman Ethics and the Becoming Animal of Emmanuel Levinas"

Mary Bunch

Emmanuel Levinas knew what it was like to be treated as an animal. The philosopher was detained in a Nazi camp as a Jewish prisoner of war from 1940 to 1945, and he reflects on this dehumanizing experience in *Difficult Freedom*. The prisoners, he writes, were "looked at" by both camp guards and villagers as if they were "subhuman, a group of apes."[1] They became what Giorgio Agamben terms *homo sacer*, a figure of political life that has been returned ambiguously to nature and exposed to violence.[2] The Germanic version of this Roman outlaw figure has been quite literally dehumanized, exiled from the community as a wolf. This process of dehumanization, Agamben argues, survives today as the logic of biopolitics, in which everyone is stripped of subjectivity and exposed to political power. Yet today, no less than yesterday, certain groups are more likely than others to suffer dehumanization and the ethical violations associated with it. Recall, for instance, the dehumanizing souvenir photographs taken by American soldiers of prisoners at Abu Ghraib, some of whom were posed as dogs; or the mainstream public disregard for the poverty and vulnerability to violence of marginalized groups from transsexuals to undocumented migrant workers. Levinas's answer to radical dehumanization is an ethical humanism of the other. But can humanism provide the cure for dehumanization? Levinas's tale of the dog shows us that biopolitics makes beasts of us all, in one way or another. The solution, at first glance, is to find our way back to being human subjects. But it seems as though we perpetually fail to accomplish this without creating limits that exclude and dehumanize some group or other, and at great cost. Is there, alternatively, an ethical politics that we might possess *as* bare life, outside of the autonomous, individualizing conditions of the humanist subject?

In this essay, I take Agamben's link between *homo sacer* and the wolf ban as a starting place to look for an ethico-political response to biopolitics in the very space that is produced by its dehumanizing gestures. Levinas introduces the possibility of a biopolitical ethics, for his ethics takes place "outside of the law." Yet this transcendence of the law divides ethics from the political sphere. Thus, while Levinas lays the ground for a posthuman ethics, his face-to-face ethics is challenged by the ethical demands introduced by biopolitics because it remains bound by humanism, and is restricted to singular, nonpolitical encounters.

Levinas's ethics demands responsibility to the other, based on a singular, pure alterity. While Levinas intends this ethics to disrupt politics, readers of Levinas are by now quite familiar with the criticism that his ethical program fails in this regard, remaining instead at the level of personal or religious responsibility. I am likewise concerned that the radical potential of the ethics of alterity becomes somehow misplaced when it comes to politics; indeed, I am not the first to be dismayed by political remarks on the part of this philosopher that show a marked failure to meet the standards of his own ethical program. This dismay is all the more pronounced because the ethics of alterity has so much appeal as a response to the limits of Kantian ethics (the requirement of sameness for ethical recognition) and enlightenment models of national and biological fraternity (which found their horrific conclusion in the dehumanizing biopolitics of National Socialism). This essay responds to these critiques of Levinas's politics by looking for strategies to apply an ethics of alterity to the political realm. In this effort I turn to the concept of becoming animal developed by Gilles Deleuze and Felix Guattari in *A Thousand Plateaus*. These authors set out to cross the threshold between alterity and politics or, in other terms, between singularity and collectivity. When read alongside Levinas, becoming animal offers some useful strategies for crossing the ethics/politics divide. Their decidedly posthuman approach not only explicitly blurs the borders between human subject and the animal, expanding the field of ethical consideration; it also politicizes the ambiguity between subjection and abjection and sets out a model for passing from the singular to the multiple.

Biopolitics and Dehumanization

Agamben's four-part series on *homo sacer* rethinks our political categories in light of biopolitics, a form of politics that administrates life, rather than governing subjects.[3] Agamben points to the link between biopolitics and dehumanization in *Homo Sacer: Sovereign Power and Bare Life*.[4] Foucault, he reminds us, refers to biopolitics as the "bestialization of man."[5] Agamben argues that sovereignty has always been conceptualized as power over life, whereas for Foucault, he specifies, the "growing inclusion of natural life in the mechanisms and calculations of power" is a modern phenomenon.[6] He intends this thesis to "correct or complete" Foucault's biopolitical conceptualization of modern politics as the inclusion of *zoē* (natural life) in the *polis*. His investigation circulates around the political function of *homo sacer*, an obscure outlaw figure from Roman law that he argues represents the new biopolitical citizen.[7] It is Agamben's particular contribution to link biopolitics, which for Foucault is a function of governance, to modern forms of sovereignty, which are informed by Carl Schmitt's understanding of the sovereign as "he who decides on the state of exception."[8] For Agamben, the sovereign is outside of, or above, the law, but so is *homo sacer*, as the figure of bare life that emerges as a remainder produced by the sovereign exception. Notably, where in the past *homo sacer* was an exceptional category, today everybody is *homo sacer*, because, Agamben argues, the exception has become the rule.

Agamben further links *homo sacer* to an animalized figure produced by archaic legal structures banning lawbreakers as wolves. This originary lawbreaker is poised in a liminal status at the boundary between nature and culture, held in "a threshold of indistinction and of passage between animal and man, *physis* and *nomos*, exclusion and inclusion: the life of the bandit is the life of the *loup garou*, the werewolf, who is precisely *neither man nor beast*, and who dwells paradoxically within both while belonging to neither."[9] By making biological life political, bare life, for Agamben, survives today as the logic by which people are stripped of subjectivity and exposed to political power, for the politics of life in Western sovereignty revolves around this inclusive exclusion.[10] This has horrific consequences that Agamben describes *vis-à-vis* the analogy of the concentration camp, the model according to which the bare life of the citizen constitutes the new "biopolitical body of humanity."[11] On the one hand, sovereign entities—whether national, transnational, or corporate—are characterized by the power to act outside of the law, whereas populations are marked by their sheer vulnerability and exposure to death. Human life is stripped of its meaning, and sovereign entities treat their extra-legal activities as if they are legitimate and deal with citizens and non-citizens alike as objects of bare life, leaving the door wide open for abuses. In response, Agamben proposes an ethical approach that questions the moral distinction made between human and inhuman, and reconceptualizes the political domain as a "coming politics" structured by a Benjaminian imperative of "pure means."[12] However, just how this politics takes form is not entirely clear.

My discussion takes as its point of departure these discourses of biopolitics that are, for good reason, enjoying so much currency. This essay attempts to understand how a political ethics might disrupt the seemingly all-encompassing infiltration of the techniques of power in our lives and the administration of our exposure to death. For it seems to me that *homo sacer* and the animalized subjects of the ban possess a potency that is lost in modern conceptualizations of dehumanization. Perhaps something of an ethics of life itself can be found in the terrain in which humans become indistinct from animals, an ethics with a political potency and a claim to justice that exceeds the law that tries to capture it in its biopolitical grip.

The Human Ethics of Faciality

Levinas's ethics are an apropos starting point for a study of ethics that transcends the limits of humanism, even though he locates his approach as a "humanism of the other."[13] For his philosophical insights locating ethics in relation to alterity spring from his actual experience of dehumanization in what for Agamben is the paradigmatic metaphor of biopolitics: the concentration camp. The Shoah left a lasting imprint on Levinas's thought. He describes his work as being "dominated by the presentiment and memory of the Nazi horror."[14] As Howard Caygill outlines, Levinas's thought was, as a consequence, "unambiguously aligned … with the thinking of political horror."[15] Thus, while there may not be consensus among commentators as to how easily his ethics might be applied to politics, nor how ethical his political views are (on women and minority groups, for instance), there is general agreement that his philosophical program constitutes an ethical response to the politics of his time.

Levinas's primary objective is thus to critique modernity's totalitarian tendencies and explore the ethics of singular relationships. Yet scholars disagree regarding the degree to which Levinas keeps to the prevailing norms of modern humanism in working through these questions. Derrida, for instance, suggests that although Levinas's ethics don't follow traditional humanism, they treat only human life as sacred.[16] Likewise John Llewelyn argues that Levinas restricts ethics to humanity, specifying that he is Kantian in the respect that he reserves an ethical response for rational beings with the capacity for language and a recognizable face.[17] Yet others contend that Levinas clearly engages in a critique of liberal humanism. For instance, Caygill points to the critique of humanism implicit in Levinas's concept of fraternity. Where humanism specifies a concept of liberty based on the autonomy and rationalism of the subject, Levinas locates freedom as a relational experience, rethinking "fraternity" through the ethics of alterity and a promise of peace.[18] Catherine Chalier reads Levinas as sharing with Kant an emphasis on a human subject with a moral obligation that extends beyond theoretical knowledge,[19] thus placing Levinas inside a humanist framework that derives from Enlightenment thought, although she also shows how he departs from this approach. This tradition is exemplified in the Kantian regulative ideal. In this view, we are human subjects to the extent that we transcend our particularities and share a common identity as rational autonomous beings, a common identity that also grounds our rights in the political sphere. The subject is thus constituted in its finitude: one finds within oneself the human rationality that grounds one's good will and makes one a good community member.[20] This view is in keeping, to a limited extent, with Llewelyn's view, but where Llewelyn outlines an anthropocentric Levinas who is strongly Kantian, Chalier makes a distinction between Levinas's ethics and his politics in terms of an affinity with Kant. She argues that where for Kant both ethical and political judgment are based on rational autonomy mediated by universal laws, Levinas sees politics as mediated by such generalizations, but ethics as instead based in singularity, heterogeneity, and infinitude; indeed, as Chalier points out, for Levinas "the infinite dwells within the subject's finitude."[21] In general, Levinas was skeptical about the moral autonomy of the finite subject and found the notion of a universal moral law to be homogenizing and violent.[22] On this basis, Levinas disrupts the totalizing tendency of Kantian logic by shifting the emphasis from identity to alterity. He subverts the inside/outside dichotomy whereby Kant asserts an ethical relation to the extent that we share a common moral law. For Levinas, we are responsible to the Other not because the Other is like us, but because the Other is absolutely different. We come to ethics, in other words, through openness to heterogeneity, rather than its foreclosure. One does not become an ethical subject by turning inward. On the contrary, through the ethical relation, the unity of the subject is disrupted and emphasis is placed on what is exterior to the self.

While affirming that Levinas does reveal some affinities with Kant by making ethics central to both philosophy and human dignity, Diane Perpich argues against strong Kantian readings of Levinas. She specifies that those aspects of Levinasian thought that are sometimes read along the lines of a regulative ideal are political, not ethical.[23] Yet what she finds most meaningful cannot be so easily separated by a division between normative humanism and what surpasses human limits. Rather, the meaning of Levinas's ethics arises in the tension between these competing demands: "between the necessity and demand for representation and the equal impossibility and inadequacy of every such representation."[24] As to the question of who or what is included in ethical consideration, for Perpich, the answer lies in the unanswerability of the question: "it is the uncertainty of responsibility that is constitutive of ethical life."[25]

Indeed, as we shall see, it is this very uncertainty that opens a pathway by which the ethics of alterity might disrupt the political realm. The openness of the ethical is made possible by exposure to the face of the other, but the face is an ambiguous territory with respect to identity (politics) and alterity (ethics). Indeed, for Levinas, subjectivity becomes visible through faciality, for through the face, both one's uniqueness as an "incomparable subject" and an "other for the others" is established. Levinas writes in *Otherwise than Being*: "as a subject incomparable with the other, I am approached as an other by the others, that is, 'for myself.'"[26] Ethical openness also depends on speech, which is conceived not as mediating or universalizing but instead as what makes possible a "breach" of the finite totality of the subject.[27] "Speech proceeds from absolute difference,"[28] writes Levinas, continuing, "Language is a relation between separated terms."[29] Being in language is not a total experience, an identity with the Same, but instead is the experience of being Other with Others. Ethics is thus communicative, derived from the face-to-face relation, but only with the human other: a relation of "a living presence," an "expression" that speaks to another expressive living presence that speaks.[30]

This visual and articulate face-to-face relationship introduces a breach instead of simply recreating the shared moral space identified by Kant. But it always seems to happen in relation to this shared space, which for Levinas is political space. He calls it *le tiers*, the third party. In contrast to ethics, the third-party relation refers specifically to law and the state, which tend always toward totalization. Third-party relations are always already ethically unjust because they are unable to account for the specificity of the face-to-face encounter and must generalize for the good of all citizens. As a consequence of this unifying function, Levinas equates the political with violence and war. Politics is "the art of foreseeing war and of winning it by every means ... the very exercise of reason. Politics is opposed to morality, as philosophy is to naiveté."[31] As he continues, Levinas links war, and implicitly politics and political subjects, to totalization: "[t]he visage of being that shows itself in war is fixed in the concept of totality, which dominates Western philosophy. Individuals are reduced to being bearers of forces that command them unbeknown to themselves. The meaning of individuals (invisible outside this totality) is derived from the totality."[32]

The political sphere is situated in relation to totality, rather than the infinite embrace of the other. Ethics disrupts such finitude, as an expression of the infinite, which is defined by Levinas as what exceeds totality.[33] Levinas thus shifts between an emphasis on the interiority of ethical rationality to the fact of exteriority and from identity to difference. Ethics takes place as a shock when that exterior, singular alterity puts the rational self and the normative basis of the shared community of subjects into question. A political subject is a subject-in-common, whereas an ethical subject is an other-among-others. Already there is some disruption of the political field when the subject is divided in this way, for neither commonality nor subjection are any longer a requirement for the agency of an ethical subject. Of the ethical subject Levinas writes: "Subjectivity realizes these impossible exigencies—the astonishing feat of containing more than it is possible to contain ... subjectivity [is] welcoming the Other, as hospitality; in it the idea of infinity is consummated."[34] Ethics, in other words, is openness to exteriority. But a political subject cannot open toward the Other. This openness only happens in the ethical sphere. The ethical relation, it follows, transcends politics, which invokes identity and reduces even difference to the terms of identity.

A kind of transcendental disruption of politics is possible, but the disconnect between ethics and politics diminishes the political usefulness of ethics as a concept. Indeed, as Simon Critchley elaborates, Levinasian politics, in accordance with the Schmittian friend/enemy divide, is derived from the antagonism between friends and enemies. His ethics, however, is shaped by monotheism and a concept of fraternity that contradicts this division, for on an ethical level "all humanity is my friend and no one is my enemy," as Critchley phrases it.[35] In other words, for Levinas, humanity is a spiritual fraternity mediated through the presence of God. The difficulty then, is that the ideal transcendence of the face-to-face encounter is impossible in the plurality of beings that comprise the political sphere. In other words, ethical responsibility is incompatible with politics. Today, if Foucault and Agamben are correct, biopolitics depletes subjects of political responsibility as well, for totalization is so all-encompassing that it is no longer possible to be a political actor at all. The outcome of biopolitics, in this respect, seems to be that no one is any longer responsible for the political sphere. This withdrawal of human responsibility for politics makes the task of ethics even more urgent. In response to this problematic, Agamben calls for a new kind of politics.[36] The task here is to imagine how such a new kind of politics might open itself to ethics. Levinas's approach promises some possibilities in this effort, since the aim of Levinasian ethics is to reconstitute political space by repeatedly interrupting all claims at totalization, including those hidden in liberal concepts of freedom and autonomy, as Critchley points out.[37] In such an approach, a recognition of and responsibility to the Other disrupts the hatred of the Other on which political unity is organized. But it is unclear whether an ethical politics is achievable.

Indeed, somewhat ironically, when it comes to politics, Levinas sometimes fails to live up to his own ethical ideal. His politics are fraught with difficulties. First of all, as we have seen, Levinas's view of what counts as political is very narrow.[38] Indeed, his approach appears similar to Schmittian political concepts in which the state's role is to distinguish friend from enemy and foreclose all difference in the name of unity. Moreover the political, as Levinas conceptualizes it, has further traces of the Schmittian decisionism that for Agamben produces a biopolitical state of exception. As Critchley elaborates,

Levinas sees politics as archic: "it is obsessed with the moment of foundation … linked to the act of government, of sovereignty, most of all of decision that presupposes and initiates a sovereign political subject capable of self-government and the government of others."[39] As a result, the political sphere is a realm where only the sovereign has agency and modern political subjects find themselves limited by a prescribed social role, yet exposed to the extra-legal violence of the sovereign decision. This is precisely the condition for the biopolitical state of exception.

To be clear, these similarities do not by any means align Levinas with Schmitt, either ethically or politically: where Schmitt recommends decisive totalitarian politics as an ideal political system, Levinas is intent on disrupting such totalizing forces with what lies outside the political realm. Yet his ethical challenge to politics has limits that have been widely discussed. For as Critchley points out, Levinasian ethics leaves no room for progressive political action: the disruptive moment transforms into the archic founding gesture, instituting a new third party.[40] In other words, when ethics engages politics, it becomes political, which is to say it takes on a unifying, totalizing impulse and erasure of the ethics that founded it. If this is the case, can we put Levinasian ethics to the task of disrupting biopolitics?

Critchley advises that politics is Levinas's "Achilles heel."[41] His positioning of the feminine as a preethical opening to the other is well known since, for example, Simone de Beauvoir's criticism of the Levinasian view of the feminine other.[42] Levinas, moreover, sometimes falters in his own embrace of difference, as is demonstrated in the following troubling quote, which surfaced in a 1991 interview: "I often say, although it is a dangerous thing to say publicly, that humanity consists of the Bible and the Greeks. All the rest can be translated: all the rest—all the exotic—is dance."[43] It is difficult to rationalize this dismissal with the thinking of a philosopher whose entire ethical program hinges on the embrace of alterity. For Critchley, this view is symptomatic of a disconnect between Levinas's ethics and the realm of politics.

Perpich, alternatively, suggests that Levinas's insensitive treatment of non–Western cultures, minority groups and women reflects a failure to meet the standards of his own ethics rather than a failure of his ethical program to be of use to various emancipatory struggles.[44] Critiques that conflate his political views with his ethical program, she suggests, confuse Levinasian ethics with a normative imperative that is marked by a slippage between the specific and the universal, by conflating respect for difference with the erasure of difference. She turns to the example of contemporary multicultural identity politics, which depends on a Kantian politics of recognition that problematically transforms difference into identity. The problem of identity politics, she specifies, is that even as it seeks recognition for an oppressed group, it re-marks the group according to the very categories that marginalize it, while reaffirming the privilege of the dominant position.[45] Levinas, she argues, may have found his own ethics difficult to always live up to, but his ethics nevertheless do hold promise for an emancipatory politics of alterity. She writes that "when Levinas's conception of alterity is understood as a concern for singularity rather than difference, we see that his philosophy reflects in important ways our concern to do justice both to the uniqueness of individual lives and to the ways in which those lives are embedded, for better or for worse, within social, cultural, and religious communities and within social categories such as race, gender, class, and disability."[46] In other words, his conception of alterity refers not to the difference of the other but to singularity, which can be applied to politics and can help us move beyond the limits of identity politics precisely because it disrupts identity with a responsibility to other.[47]

In the following sections, I look more closely at the biopolitical example of Levinas's experience in the camp, where for him ethics and politics collide, linking Levinas's experience of becoming animal (in the sense of dehumanization), and the becoming-ethical of the dog Bobby, with Deleuze and Guattari's effort to devise an ethical politics. I suggest that, in part, the difficulties in Levinas's political content point to the limits of the analogy of the face-to-face encounter, particularly its anthropocentric and humanist seductions. As such I return to questions that several commentators have asked in relation to the meeting of Levinas and Bobby in biopolitical conditions. How does one respond ethically to Others whose faces are unrecognizable to us or whose language is incomprehensible? Moreover, I contend that there is some difficulty with the hospitality model of ethics that Levinas forwards. We only affirm our own subjectivity when we posit disenfranchised Others as recipients of an ethical response, rather than as subjects of their own ethical and political agency.

Notwithstanding the importance of an ethics of the subject, can we also conceive of an ethics that does not reside in the subject, via the face-to-face encounter between the self and Other, nor in the specifically singular relation? Is there an ethics of "the people" of biopolitics, the dehumanized masses, the disenfranchised and the dispossessed? Indeed, exclusion from the polis demands a disruption of politics by the dispossessed themselves. In the modern era, this imperative operates on two levels: that of the specific groups that are disenfranchised and dehumanized on transnational and local scales (poor people, those who have been colonized, gender and sexual minorities, and so on) for the stranger that coexists in a world where resources are distributed in ways that are categorically unequal; and the biopolitical world order in which everyone is somehow cut off from political subjectivity. In the latter sense, a posthuman ethics is a call to reclaim responsibility for the political sphere (in which some continue to be treated as less human than others), as much as it is a demand that life, human and otherwise, should matter. A posthuman approach, such as the one forwarded by Deleuze and Guattari, addresses both local and global biopolitical trends by shifting the focus from ethics directed toward those who are excluded to the ethics *of* those who are excluded, whose politics are disruptive of the status quo. This is not out of line with Levinas's ethics of alterity, which operates on the very principle of disruption from the outside; as such, becoming animal helps transport Levinasian ethics into a relation with the political sphere.

Levinas and the Ethics of Bare Life

Although Levinas does not articulate an ethics that pertains to the dispossessed masses, he does point the way in an article in *Difficult Freedom* titled "The Name of a Dog; or Natural Rights." In this reflection on his experience as a Jewish prisoner of war during the Shoah, the only ethical being encountered by the prisoners is "Bobby," the dog whom Levinas nominates as "the last Kantian in Nazi Germany."[48] Where Bobby is anthropomorphized in this work, Levinas and the other prisoners are dehumanized by both camp guards and villagers as "subhuman, a group of apes."[49] He describes how, in the camp, those qualities that make him a subject, that imbue life with meaning and form identity, are bracketed: "Our comings and goings, our sorrow and laughter, illnesses and distractions, the work of our hands and the anguish of our eyes, the letters we received from France and those accepted for our families—all that passed in parentheses."[50] The Jewish prisoners were instead "beings entrapped in their species; despite all their vocabulary, beings without language."[51] The dog was more "human"—that is, ethical—than the camp guards and the villagers who demonstrated no concern for the life the Other: "[Bobby] would appear at morning assembly and was waiting for us as we returned, jumping up and down and barking in delight. For him, there was no doubt we were men."[52] Where the humans rob the prisoners of their humanity, the animal thus restores it.

Levinas's discussion pinpoints the very ambiguous space in which the differences between human and animals blur, since what is animal about humans—the beastliness of the Nazis and the villagers—is in fact not animal-like at all, as the example of an ethical dog demonstrates. Moreover, in the narrative, ethics, which is otherwise proper to humans for Levinas, is embodied by an animal in a case where all the humans have been animalized as the subject or object of a beastly action. This simultaneous bestialization of ethical justice (Bobby) and injustice (the Nazis) raises questions, not only about the subject of ethics, but also about the relationship of ethics to concepts of humanity and animality. While conventionally we might ascribe a negative value to animality as such—it is what is unreasonable, nonconceptual, simple, mechanical, bereft of signification, brute and violent—the notion of an ethical dog returns some of the natural purity of *zoē* to the ethical realm. Might there be an ethics in life itself, as it occurs as a creative force?

This concept of an ethical dog denotes a rather curious departure from Levinas's usual ethical stance, which is ambivalent in its relation to animals. Indeed, the segment on Bobby has been interpreted in several ways, as have his statements on animals more generally.

[...]

But I am letting the tale get ahead of the dog. Bobby's ethics—the ethics *of* animals—are not really at issue here. It is the becoming animal of Levinas himself, during that period when he finds himself excluded from ethical consideration, that launches this moment of ethical becoming. Levinas extends his ethics to Bobby (he recognizes Bobby as an ethical being) at the instant of his own desubjectivation. Indeed, this is his most ethical moment if we are to truly locate ethics outside of the knowing ego. It is thus a form of politics from which his ethical thought springs. More specifically, his development of an ethics of alterity is motivated by biopolitical exclusion from the polis. Thus taking my cue from Levinas's own anomalous encounter with Bobby, the ethical dog, I wonder if the ethical/political relation may *not* properly be that of the human subject at all; at least not as subjectivity has been understood, since Aristotle, as what comes to be through a negation of animality. Instead, perhaps ethical politics derives from the margins—including the margins of humanity itself. By "margins of humanity" I mean not only those humans who are politically *marginalized*. I also mean the limit that demarcates our humanity, the threshold where subjectivity borders on abjection, in Kristeva's sense of abjection as simultaneous dejection and resistance.[53] It is in this zone of indistinction that politics becomes biopolitics.

The Posthuman Ethics of Becoming Animal

Levinas's theorization of his experience in relation to this ethical dog points to a way to dislodge Levinasian ethics from the limits of the human yet retains, at its center, Levinas's commitment to an openness to alterity and the creation of openings toward nonfascist politics. In "becoming animal," Deleuze and Guattari forward a posthuman concept that might further these aims. Becoming animal replaces the subject as the figure of political agency with a kind of bare life. Becoming animal thus signals a movement toward a new kind of ethical politics: as bare life, becoming animal is vulnerable in its exclusion from the polis but nevertheless acts to counter the law. Such becoming is ethical, in Levinas's sense, because of its relationship to Otherness, and the disruption of finitude that constitutes it. But it differs from Levinasian ethics, because the ethics does not arise through facial recognition (identity), and it extends from singularity to multiplicity. This approach has its own limits. Indeed, becoming animal has been criticized for its obscurity and for erasing the specificity of real minority positions, and thus undermining political movements.[54] Yet, it nonetheless offers a view to what posthumanism has to offer in terms of bridging the ethical and biopolitical political spheres.

Deleuze and Guattari question the affiliation of ethics with faciality, in an implicit critique of Levinas that precedes their discussion of the concept of becoming animal. While they agree with Levinas that alterity is essential to ethics, they find that faciality contradicts this effort, for the face is the seat of identity. They argue that we are ethical only insofar as we move away from the assimilating "horrors" of the face, which they tie to an aversion to difference. They propose that "[f]rom the viewpoint of racism there is no exterior, there are no people of the outside. There are only people who should be like us and whose crime it is not to be."[55] This is a response to a logic that would appropriate what is outside the law, through assimilation or by extermination. They write: "Racism never detects the particles of the other; it propagates waves of sameness until those who resist identification have been wiped out…."[56] Faciality, in their analysis, is a fiction, a mask that is imposed as a condition of humanity. The face is an artifice that limits and restricts our possibilities.

What Levinas represents as "ethics"—that is, the face—in this view might be reconceived as a "politics" in Levinas's own sense. It is a totalizing force through which we represent ourselves and establish our relation to structures of power: the face is the vehicle for signification and subjectivation.[57] Becoming animal, in contrast, shifts the emphasis to an acting body. Moreover, it explicitly expands the field of ethical consideration beyond the human subject, an area of ambiguity in Levinas that has been the subject of much debate, as we have seen. Dehumanization signals, or even demands, the emergence of a posthuman ethics because it exposes the limits of humanism: one can always disregard the ethical demands of humanism by treating others as animals or as objects. If, on the other hand, ethics extends to nonhuman others, then humanism loses its prioritizing exclusions. This is the moment that we glimpse when Levinas reflects on his relation to Bobby, which signifies the becoming animal of Levinas. A political ethics of the Other became possible when Levinas found himself stripped of subjectivity and relegated to the sphere outside of the law.

Deleuze and Guattari argue that a more ethical politics would derive from a movement toward the outside, leaving the safety of the familiar and the similar, and casting off privilege and dominance. […] [T]hey argue that ethics not only derives from exteriority, but it is an exteriority of self-transformation and alliance. In such becomings, politics and ethics shift from the face—that is, from logos, signification, and subjectivation—to the natural life of the body, linking it implicitly to biopolitics. Elsewhere Deleuze emphasizes the animality of humans: "the face is a structured spatial organization which covers the head, while the head is an adjunct of the body, even though it is its top. It is not that it lacks a spirit, but it is a spirit which is body, corporeal and vital breath, an animal spirit; it is the animal spirit of man...."[58] In effect, Deleuze deconstructs the mind/body dualism that has structured Western metaphysics since antiquity, positioning spirit as an aspect of political life, although in a different sense from what we find in Agamben. Unlike conceptions of spirit as political (logos or rationality) or theological, spirit and body are interconnected here as a force of sheer vitality, a kind of *zoē*. Deleuze and Guattari's approach in "Becoming Animal" thus shifts the ethical apparatus from face to figure, and from reason to passion.

It is not clear if Deleuze and Guattari were thinking of Levinas when they outlined a structure for the ethical politics of becoming animal. However, when read alongside the ethics of alterity, it seems as though becoming animal might represent an effort to bridge the rift between singularity and commonality that divides ethics from politics for Levinas. The politics of becoming animal includes both the macro elements of Levinas's *Le Tiers* and the micro elements of the ethics of alterity, furthermore encompassing both singularity and multiplicity. In a sense, becoming animal thus represents the very terrain on which ethics disrupts politics. Deleuze and Guattari position becoming animal as a form of what they term minoritarian politics, a politics of the Other that is evoked through an "Anomalous" phenomenon of bordering. The Anomalous (*anomal*) refers to "that which is outside rules or goes against the rules" and moreover "*an-omalie* ... designates unequal, the coarse, the rough, the cutting edge of deterritorialization."[59] The concept dislodges the dominant subject-position of the "self-conscious white male of the occident" and dismantles the human ideal inherited from Western metaphysics.[60] [...] Becoming animal thus expresses a politics of the posthuman subject, an ethical politics of those who are disenfranchised and situated outside of the law. This might include both dehumanized minorities and the biopolitical masses.

While this approach holds potential for disrupting (bio)politics with an ethics of alterity, it also been criticized for undermining political movements. Some feminist scholars, for instance, question the emergence of a post-subject politics just as women (and by implication other minorities) consolidate status as subjects. [...] Braidotti critiques Deleuze and Guattari for destabilizing "woman" as a specific category. Braidotti is concerned that the shift from specificity to multiplicity in becoming-minoritarian will "result in women's disappearance from the scene of history, their fading-out as agents of history."[61] [...] [T]he approach is more of a critique of identity politics than of feminism proper. Indeed, Deleuze and Guattari challenge the very binaries around which sexed identities are crystallized: "It is as deplorable to miniaturize, internalize the binary machine as it is to exacerbate it; it does not extricate us from it."[62] Thus it is precisely when women consolidate a status as subjects that feminists must consider a post-subject politics, a politics by and for the Other. While identity groups must at times consolidate (establish a state, struggle for recognition, demand rights, etc.), such archic approaches ought not constitute the entire political field, or they may become counterrevolutionary forms that mimic their very oppressors. Political struggle takes molecular as well as molar forms, forms that dismantle institutions and decentralize the flow of power. Deleuze and Guattari write that: "It is thus necessary to conceive of a molecular women's politics that slips into molar confrontations, and passes under or through them."[63] In other words, politics exceeds the accumulation of status in the present system, the gaining of rights and participation in the polis to include a disruption and reconfiguration of the political system. Because molar and molecular politics are not opposed to one another, it does not constitute a contradiction for both forms of politics to occur simultaneously. This allows for an ethical politics that possesses the mobility to itself be multiple, to transform, and to engage in alliances with other identities and non-identities along the lines of Levinas's opening toward the other.

The capacity of becoming animal to cross the distinctions made by Levinas between the singularity of ethics and the generalizations of politics also situates it as an ethico-political response to biopolitics. Like ethics, biopolitics is a condition in which the mediating forces of politics have been stripped away, but where exposure to difference takes place as exposure to death instead of as recognition of responsibility. To be sure, Levinas wanted nothing more than to see ethical responsibility disrupt the killing machine of fascist biopolitics, but he is restricted because ethics as a singular event is divided from politics as a universalizing structure. Yet Deleuze and Guattari offer a route to an ethical politics by destabilizing such polarizations: the realm of the political includes both singular and general qualities. They resolve the limit that blocks ethics from entering the realm of politics by constructing a concept that instantiates a movement between these very spheres, through a shift from the ontology of "being" to one of "becoming." The focus shifts from fixed terms of identification to what passes between such terms.

Deleuze and Guattari thus retain the emphasis on singularity that is necessary to an ethics of pure alterity, yet they position that singularity in relation to both the multiplicity of singularities and mediated forms of politics. Indeed, Deleuze and Guattari explicitly depart from traditions that oppose the total to the multiple, asserting that we are always both molar and molecular (or, in Levinas's terms, political and ethical). Moreover, they distinguish between different kinds of multiplicity—of selves, of states, and of political movements, those that condense in molar forms and others that disperse in the direction of infinity. They move away from always conceiving of the multiple in its totalizing form as an archaic or future unity and instead conceive of it in its "pure state" of sheer multiplicity.[64]

The relationship of singularities to multiplicity is not the same as the subject's relation to the state, for these authors. The self is a threshold between multiplicities that are always transforming, multiplicities that are "composed of heterogeneous terms in symbiosis."[65] The self occupies various positions along the borderline of these shifting multiplicities, desiring both the otherness of the other and desiring to become the other. Fascinated selves form and dispel into collectives with other diverse elements, and act back in relation to the molar forms of power that it meets in its bordering capacities. These relationships are not dialectical, and they may be simultaneous. For on the one hand, these collectives interact with state political forms: "they continually work them from within and trouble them from without, with other forms of content, other forms of expression."[66] And on the other, multiplicities may transform from one form to the other "replacing pack effects with family feelings or State intelligibilities."[67]

Deleuze and Guattari are thus interested in process, metamorphosis, and connection, rather than how, or what, things *are*. Where dichotomies depend on fixed positions and oppositional relations, in this ontology of becoming, the borders between oppositions are put under question. Becoming animal takes place on a "vanishing line" or a "line of flight." Minor politics as such act on and reconstitute the more structured third-party political sphere. For however singular an urge for becoming may be, becoming animal is qualitatively affective: becomings pull beings together, one to the other, under conditions of ethical possibility (sheer alterity) without binding them under conditions of sameness.

Conclusion

A posthuman ethics is necessary if Agamben is correct in his diagnosis that in modernity, politics has been replaced with biopolitics. Instead of finding a subject at its center, biopolitics circulates around the figure of bare life, signaling a mass dehumanization of populations and further exacerbating the limits of humanism. This concern has been central to Levinas all along, for his entire ethical project is a response to the biopolitics of National Socialism. My aim in this essay was to put Levinasian ethics to the task of disrupting biopolitics. Deleuze and Guattari describe just such an ethical shock when they outline the affective pull to become animal: "the affect is not a personal feeling, nor is it a characteristic; it is the effectuation of the power of the pack that throws the self into upheaval and makes it reel. Who has not known the power of these animal sequences, which uproot one from humanity, if only for an instant?"[68] The affect pulls Levinas, Bobby, the camp guards, and the people of the town into a becoming that is a critical desubjectivation; it launches them each into a border position between human and animal, although in several different ways at once. Along these deterritorialized borders, passages open by which ethics might infiltrate the political sphere (although not necessarily).

The irony of the association of ethics with bare life should not be ignored. For, while bare life is life that has been stripped of its politics, we are most *un*ethical when we dehumanize others. So how can the very terms of dehumanization—bare life, or animal life—become a site for ethics and political action? Perhaps the question should be *how can it not*? For those at the center of politics, ethics responds to a demand to undo one's own subjectivity and commonalities, to open oneself to transformation from the outside, and to break down borders without striving for sameness. For those at the margins who make this demand, politics takes the singularly ethical form of disruption. These are not the demands of logic and reason, but rather of ethical justice, which falls outside such normative constraints. Bobby "knows" how to respond ethically with respect to bare life, and he knows it without reason. Perhaps this makes Bobby not the last Kantian in Nazi Germany, but the first Levinasian. He needs no mediating term to recognize the prisoners as deserving of ethical consideration, and his mode of being ethical is transferred to Levinas as a shock that forever changes him.

Indeed, Bobby launches Levinas into a series of becomings, whereby the ethics of alterity is born, despite (and because of) the violence of biopolitical dehumanization under which they each suffer. Becoming animal thus sheds a different light on Levinasian ethics as it intersects with biopolitics, by presenting a posthuman, rather than merely anthropocentric or dehumanized figure, that can be both ethical and political. Moreover, rather than referring to some individual who flouts the law in isolation, becoming animal shares an affective relation with other entities as part of a multiplicity, a collective that crosses the boundaries between human and animal. Yet how does this connect to politics? For Levinas, the camp is total mediation—biopolitics is thus the ultimate politics—such that singularity (that is, ethics) becomes impossible for anyone *but* a dog, revealing (bio)politics itself as ultimately inhumane. Deleuze and Guattari, in contrast, situate ethics in terms of a different kind of political relation via the liminal, in-between concept of becoming animal. Such a political ethics moves between same and other, interior and exterior, finite and infinite, reason and passion, singular and multiple, through transformation and alliance. In other words, it builds connections between and among sites of difference without eradicating that difference, and it provides a route by which what is excluded might undo or transform dominant structures. Thus these thinkers offer us a way to conceive of alterity politics: a politics of minorities insofar as they are other to a "majority," but in which neither position—minority or majority—is fixed. The ethical shock that Levinas specifies, when one's ego is shattered by sheer otherness, is thus brought to a political conclusion.

NOTES

1. Emmanuel Levinas, *Difficult Freedom: Essays on Judaism*, trans. Seán Hand (London: Althone, 1990), 48.

2. Giorgio Agamben, *Homo Sacer: Sovereign Power and Bare Life*, trans. Daniel Heller-Roazen (Stanford: Stanford University Press, 1995).

3. Michel Foucault, *History of Sexuality Volume I: An Introduction*, trans. Robert Hurley (New York: Vintage Books, 1978).

4. The series that follows *Homo Sacer* expands Agamben's analysis of the sovereign state of exception (2005), the ethics of testimony and the *muselmann* as a limit-figure of the human (1999), and an elaboration of *homo sacer* in the figure of the refugee (2000).

5. Agamben, *Homo Sacer*, 3.

6. *Ibid.*, 119.

7. *Ibid.*, 8.

8. Carl Schmitt, *Political Theology: Four Chapters on the Concept of Sovereignty*, trans. George Schwabb (Cambridge: MIT Press, 1985), 11.

9. Agamben, *Homo Sacer*, 105.

10. To be clear, bare life is not synonymous with natural life, but is, rather, produced when natural life is politicized through its very exclusion from politics.

11. *Ibid.*, 9.

12. Giorgio Agamben, *Means Without End: Notes on Politics*, trans. Vincenzo Binetti and Cesare Casarino (Minneapolis: University of Minneapolis Press, 2000), 89, 119.

13. Emmanuel Levinas, *Humanism of the Other*, trans. Nidra Poller (Champaign: University of Illinois Press, 2003).

14. Levinas, *Difficult Freedom*, 291.

15. Howard Caygill, *Levinas and the Political* (New York: Routledge, 2002), 5.

16. Jacques Derrida, "Eating Well, or the Calculation of a Subject: An Interview with Jacques Derrida." *Who Comes After the Subject*, ed. Eduardo Cadava, Peter Connor, and Jean-Luc Nancy (New York: Routledge, 1991), 96–119.

17. John Llewelyn, *The Middle Voice of Ecological Consciousness: A Chiasmic Reading of Responsibility in the Neighbourhood of Levinas, Heidegger, and Others* (New York: St. Martin's Press, 1991), 199.

18. Caygill, *Levinas and the Political*, 3, 9, 35.

19. Catherine Chalier, *"What Ought I to Do?": Morality in Kant and Levinas*, trans. J.M. Todd (Ithaca: Cornell University Press, 2002).

20. *Ibid.*, 5.

21. *Ibid.*

22. *Ibid.*, 6.

23. Diane Perpich, *The Ethics of Emmanuel Levinas* (Stanford: Stanford University Press, 2008), 14.

24. *Ibid.*

25. *Ibid.*

26. Emmanuel Levinas, *Otherwise than Being, or Beyond Essence*, trans. Alphonso Lingis (Pittsburgh: Duquesne University Press, 1981), 158.

27. Emmanuel Levinas, *Totality and Infinity*, trans. Alphonso Lingus (Pittsburgh: Duquesne University Press, 1969), 23.

28. *Ibid.*, 194.

29. *Ibid.*, 195.

30. *Ibid.*, 66.

31. *Ibid.*, 21.

32. *Ibid.*, 21–22.

33. *Ibid.*, 26.

34. *Ibid.*, 27.

35. Simon Critchley, "Five Problems in Levinas's View of Politics and the Sketch of a Solution to Them," *Political Theory* 32, no. 2 (2004): 174.

36. Agamben, *Means Without End*, 8.

37. Simon Critchley, *Ethics and Deconstruction: Derrida and Levinas* (Oxford: Blackwell, 1992), 223.

38. Critchley, "Five Problems," 173.

39. *Ibid.*, 182.

40. Critchley, *Ethics and Deconstruction*.

41. Critchley, "Five Problems," 181.

42. Simone de Beauvoir, *The Second Sex*, trans. H.M. Parshley (New York: Vintage Books, 1989).

43. Critchley, "Five Problems," 175–6.

44. Perpich, *The Ethics*, 15, 180.

45. *Ibid.*, 183–84.

46. *Ibid.*, 185–86.

47. *Ibid.*, 180.

48. Emmanuel Levinas, "The Name of a Dog, or Natural Rights," in *Difficult Freedom: Essays on Judaism*, trans. Seán Hand (Baltimore: Johns Hopkins University Press, 1990), 51.

49. *Ibid.*, 48.

50. *Ibid.*

51. *Ibid.*

52. *Ibid.*, 49.

53. Julia Kristeva, *Powers of Horror: An Essay on Abjection* (New York: Columbia University Press, 1982).

54. Alice Jardine, "Woman in Limbo: Deleuze and his Br(others)," *SubStance* 44/45, no. 1 (1984): 46–60, and Rosi Braidotti, *Patterns of Dissonance*, trans. Elizabeth Guild (Cambridge: Polity Press, 1991).

55. Gilles Deleuze and Félix Guattari, *A Thousand Plateaus: Capitalism and Schizophrenia*, trans. Brian Massumi (Minneapolis: Minnesota University Press, 1987), 197.

56. *Ibid.*, 178.

57. *Ibid.*, 181.

58. Gilles Deleuze, "The Body, the Meat and the Spirit: Becoming Animal," *The Artist's Body*, ed. Tracy Warr, trans. Liz Heron (London: Phaidon, 2000), 197–98.

59. Deleuze and Guattari, *Kafka: Toward a Minor Literature* (Minneapolis: University of Minnesota Press, 1986), 244.

60. Stephan Günzel, "Immanence and Deterritorialization: The Philosophy of Gilles Deleuze and Félix Guattari," in *Twentieth World Congress of Philosophy* (Boston, MA, August 1998), 9.

61. Braidotti, *Patterns of Dissonance*, 111.

62. Deleuze and Guattari, *Kafka*, 276.

63. *Ibid.*

64. Deleuze and Guattari, *Kafka*, 32.

65. *Ibid.*, 249.

66. *Ibid.*, 242.

67. *Ibid.*, 256.

68. *Ibid.*, 240.

From "Articulating Ecological Ethics and Politics"

MICK SMITH

> If ethics without politics is empty, then politics without
> ethics is blind.
> —Simon Critchley, *Infinitely Demanding:*
> *Ethics of Commitment, Politics of Resistance*

How might the relations between political action and ecological (ethical) responsibility begin to be envisaged in such a way that each informs the other and yet neither is made subject to the other? How do we dissolve the claims of sovereignty and yet retain a politics informed by the Good where each is understood as an expression of natality and diversity (plurality) and as exemplifying the appearance of those individuals who feel, speak, and act? Another way of posing the question would be to ask whether an ecological ethics might come to delimit, but not dictate, how political communities choose to act in the world.

There is an understandable but regrettable tendency in environmental ethics to translate ethical concerns for nonhuman others into more or less fixed moral frameworks—often on the basis of naturalistic claims about supposedly objective (intrinsic) moral value attaching to certain species[1]—values that are then regarded as imposing constraints on the freedoms of human-centered politics. [...]

[E]thics and politics as such, and the relation between them, should be understood anarchically, that is, in terms of the rejection of any principle (*archē*) of sovereignty altogether. And one way of attending to the myriad possible paths among ethics and politics as such might be by elucidating further connections between Levinas's understanding of ethical responsibility (and ethics as such) and Arendt's understanding of political responsibility.

The emphasis in what follows is on Levinas [...] first because despite the (metaphysical and ecological) drawbacks of Levinas's philosophical approach, his work provides a [detailed account] of just how ethical responsibility arises; and second, because there is already a body of secondary material that has attempted, however unsuccessfully, to draw out the political implications of his ethics. Unfortunately, although successfully undercutting the claims of sovereignty within ethics, especially in relation to the (supposedly sovereign) individual, Levinas too tends to fall back into this same language of (individual and state) sovereignty where politics is concerned, and this is because he lacks the kind of understanding of politics as such that Arendt provides. Understanding this failure, its ecological implications, and its possible solution requires reiterating and expanding on some of the core aspects of Levinas's and Arendt's positions.

Politics and Ethics as Such

> That man is more of a political animal than bees or any
> other gregarious animals is evident.
> —Aristotle, *The Politics*

Most people influenced by the Western philosophical tradition would concur with Aristotle's statement, for humans are, as he argued, *bios politikos*, beings who constitute themselves as (differently) human within and through their political forms of life. But this is not, as Hannah Arendt[2] points out, an attempt to define humanity as a particular kind of biological species (an early iteration of the anthropological machine) so much as a claim about the importance of sustaining a political life for the expression of human freedoms. Politics is, in this sense, the worldly medium of human beings' different possibilities, of how, in certain circumstances, they can come to freely express themselves as themselves, as individuals and not simply as beings constrained by biological necessities (by their work) or as functionaries fulfilling productive roles dictated by social conventions (by their labor). Remember, for Arendt, the words and deeds that comprise (political) action express *who*, not *what*, we are. As Giorgio Agamben argues, the *bios* in *bios politikos* refers to a "form of human living [that] is never prescribed by a specific biological vocation, nor is it assigned by whatever necessity; instead, no matter how customary, repeated, and socially compulsory, it always retains the character of a possibility; that is, it always puts at stake living itself."[3]

This is why politics, on this reading, is not at all a *means to an end*, especially not an end predetermined by some essential human nature, whether selfless altruism, selfish genes, or selfish instincts, as so many political theorists have argued. Politics is, in Agamben's[4] terminology, a "means without end," a pure means, a practice valuable not for what it produces but only insofar as we value human freedom itself. We (that is, those who are so concerned) must also recognize that there are consequently no guarantees that human lives will always have a political aspect, since this is not a fact of nature but something that we, through our own actions, must strive to sustain. Such freedoms are all too easily lost. As Agamben[5] argues, the principle used to justify exercising political authority over others, the principle of sovereignty, is precisely a claim to be able to strip those subject to it of their political possibilities, their freedom of expression and association, to reduce them to the condition of "bare life."

This understanding of politics as a tenuous but vital freedom of self-expression through words and deeds in the face of others, as an opening on the infinite possibilities of being (differently) human, seems far removed from those practices often labeled "politics." It might also seem unduly utopian in many respects, not least in the sense that action is never entirely freed from the requirements of work and labor or from our other necessary involvements in nature and culture. But this is, one might argue, how we might delimit politics as such, as an event that, while dependent on, is nonetheless irreducible to, work and labor. And the value of this understanding can be seen precisely because every other conception of politics as a (relatively) autonomous practice, and every attempt to claim political authority, is parasitic on this prior understanding—an understanding, we might say, that comes before, or better, lies *beyond*, all of its constitutional manifestations. The constitutive power (the associative potential) of politics as such to create a community in and through the differences between us lies beyond, even as it underlies, attempts by political authorities to constitutionally control, define, channel, utilize, and constrain the power of "free association."

All this has already been said, but clearly one implication of this understanding is that the state (polis) is not, as Aristotle[6] claims, "a creation of nature"; rather, it is revealed *before all* as a *political* creation, even though every state retroactively tries to naturalize itself, to reimagine itself as the natural repository of all (authorized) political action. Aristotle,[7] of course, argues that the "proof that the state is a creation of nature and prior to the individual is that the individual, when isolated, is not self-sufficing: and therefore he is like a part in relation to the whole." But if this insufficiency is understood just as a matter of *survival*, then bees would be no less, and given their degree of dependence and "social" integration, perhaps *more* political than humans, which is quite contrary to Aristotle's intent. Once again we see that the political *life*, the *bios politikos*, cannot be simply a matter of an individual's capacity to survive or not: it is not reducible to bare life; rather, it has to do with having the potential to initiate, participate in, and sustain politics as such. And this requires, Aristotle argues, a "sense of good and evil, of the just and unjust and the like, and the association of living beings that have this sense makes a family and a state."[8]

This understanding of politics as such has much in common with, and in many senses complements, Levinas's understanding of ethics as "first philosophy," as a regard for and an infinite responsibility toward Others that emerges through our face-to-face encounter with these (differently) human individuals. I argue that, in many respects, Levinas's understanding of ethics is not only compatible with but could be considered *constitutive* of such an understanding of politics, that what Arendt refers to as the "in between" of politics as such is, at least to some extent, dependent on the "between us"[9] of ethics as such, and vice versa. This, of course, is a much stronger claim and has to be interpreted carefully to avoid any temptation to regard ethics or politics as such as either equivalent, reducible, or in a hierarchical relation to each other: they are not. However, Levinas's understanding of ethics as such is complementary to an Arendtian take on the political in several ways, all of which relate to their attempts to articulate this "as suchness," the singularity of these relations that always lies before, beyond, and still exceeds its subsequent crystallization in, for example, a body of moral or legal codes or a particular political ideology. They each understand ethics or politics as such as *constitutive* of human associations and of who we are as (differently) human individuals, and only secondarily, if at all, as *constitutionally* defined limits on such expressions: they emphasize the anarchic aspects of ethics and politics.

Levinas and Arendt: Anarchē, Ethics, and Politics

> The notion of anarchy we are introducing here has a meaning prior to the political (or anti-political) meaning currently attributed to it.
> —Emmanuel Levinas, *Essay on Thinking-of-the-Other*

Although Levinas often refers to his understanding of ethics as anarchical,[10] and the anarchical strand of Arendt's work too has sometimes been noted,[11] neither are anarchists in the usual political sense. However, we might say that ethics as such are anarchic in at least three inseparable ways. First, Levinas rejects the idea that ethics as such can be captured within or ruled over by any overarching moral principles and concepts, focusing instead on the interruptive power of the ethical event. This, I argue, links to Arendt's critique of the (political) dangers of simply adhering to dominant moral norms and also to that systematization (and bureaucratization) of the political sphere that seeks to replace political action as such with rules and processes. Second, and closely linked to this, Levinas claims that ethical responsibility arises without and before any definable point of origin; it has no *archē* (beginning) in the ontology of the world; it is beyond or otherwise than Being. This, I suggest, resembles Arendt's understanding of the "miraculous" initiating power she associates with politics as such, its natality—the liberating power to engender new beginnings despite what are often portrayed as the unchangeable "givens" of a social situation. Third, Levinas regards the ethical relation to the Other as Arendt regards politics, as a matter that "concerns the individual in his singularity."[12] The connections here are complicated, but the point is that political action and ethical responsibility are what constitute the individual as an individual and that ethics and politics *as such* are constituted through attentive responses to those Other individuals with whom we become associated.

The theoretical inseparability of these anarchic aspects makes it impossible to treat them in isolation. The issue of singularity inevitably introduces the question of ontology and also of the resistance of ethics and politics to inscription in rules and codes. Nonetheless, singularity offers an initial way to link Levinas's thought to Arendt's, since each argues that ethics and politics are initiated and sustained through intimate face-to-face encounters between singular individuals, encounters in and through which we come to glimpse something of *who* the Other/other facing us is without ever fully knowing her or him. Both also argue that such encounters require the acceptance of the Others'/others' radical differences from ourselves, a refusal to see them only (or at all, in Levinas's case) in the light of our desires (as fulfilling what *we* need or in terms of what they can do for *us*) or to subsume them under preconceived categories that reduce them to abstractions.

If Levinas emphasizes the transcendence of ethical difference, the ways in which the Other precedes and goes beyond any egotistical desires, Arendt emphasizes otherness in terms of the necessary plurality of politics. In each case, if everyone were essentially the *Same*, if we were not singular individuals, there would simply be no possibility of any ethics or politics as such. Nor, of course, would anything new, any novel understanding, emerge from our encounters. The ethical and the political spaces, where the Others/others express something of themselves as themselves, in their singularity, emerge only through creative associations that concern themselves with sustaining such different/plural possibilities.

These ethical and political associations differ insofar as Levinas is concerned with the emergence of ethics as such, as a prior association between self and Other composed as a "fundamental structure of subjectivity."[13] The encounter with the face of the Other evokes a proximity that touches and troubles us before we can conceptualize its effects on us, a trace that does not allow "itself to be invested by the *archē* of consciousness"[14] and that dispossesses us, that is, draws us out of our self-possessive concerns. [...] In other words, ethics challenges the very idea of a sovereign individual with absolute authority to decide on what does and does not concern him or her. The fact that this relation is *pre*conscious also means that it necessarily transcends (lies beyond) its inscription into the linguistic categories within which consciousness is formulated and that denote the accepted (ontological) order of the world. "Anarchically, proximity is a relationship with a singularity, without the mediation of any principle or ideality."[15]

Arendt, on the other hand, is concerned with the emergence of politics as such, an association between self and others in what appears as a broader public realm, one where our relations to others are mediated through *words* as well as deeds. For her, words are an expression of others' individual characters, but this does not mean that their public persona encompasses everything there is to that person—just that this is how they choose to appear politically, and it is this political appearance that concerns her above all else. For her, *appearances matter* quite literally: that is, they have material (political) effects on others. But she does not fall into what Levinas would regard as the trap of treating the human individual as the pregiven (ontological) basis of political intersubjectivity. The political self, the individual who does more than just labor or work, is far from being a pregiven entity; indeed, individuals constitute themselves as themselves only within the possibilities offered by political space.

The "who" of Arendtian politics is not equivalent or reducible to either the "I" or the Other of Levinasian ethics, although she or he may (indeed must), if Levinas is right, have been first constituted through exposure to such ethical relations. That is, individuals are never *simply* self-interested, nor are their actions, insofar as they are individuals, *simply* motivated by their need to compete in a struggle for existence (although neither Levinas nor Arendt would in any way deny that people often act competitively and selfishly—see later discussion). The ethical self and the political self are composed within and through what might be termed an *intimate ecology of responsibility* to others/Others, a patterning of relations that the ethical/political self cannot avoid if she or he is to be some*one*.

Such responsibilities arise differently: for Levinas, one is held ethically responsible by and for the Other, by the face that *singles one out*, that addresses and contests one's identity. The experience of the face is one of being addressed by the Other, of passivity, and yet the "I" finds herself or himself bound by a responsibility for the Other that is absolute and infinitely demanding. This is an obligation that extends far beyond being responsible for my own actions toward the Other, even including a "responsibility for what is not my deed, or for what does not even matter to me."[16] For Arendt, responsibility [...] arises as a direct result of her argument that political action reveals who the individual is. Insofar as the act I perform is incontrovertibly mine, since it is this action that marks *my* political appearance before others, then I alone can be held responsible for its consequences—this responsibility cannot be passed to anyone else. Yet the consequences of acting into the political realm are inherently unpredictable and continue to cascade forward into the future. In other words, the events set in motion by my actions are potentially limitless, and so my responsibilities too extend far beyond those associated with what I consider to be their immediate or intended consequences. These responsibilities too are, in effect, infinite and can be redeemed only by the possibility of others, who also understand the vagaries of the human condition, offering their understanding and forgiveness.

Importantly, Levinas's emphasis on the passivity, presubjectivity, and inescapability of the ethical encounter with the Other leads him to postulate ethical responsibility as an obsession, a compulsion, an absolute and infinite obligation. This is because ethical responsibility concerns a "subjectivity prior to the Ego, prior to its freedom and non-freedom."[17] For Levinas, freedom is associated with consciousness and hence the self-possession of the individual[18]; it places a limit on responsibility in a way that is the antithesis of Arendt's perspective. Her emphasis on activity, emergent subjectivity, and the need to involve oneself politically—and to make judgments concerning, for example, the extent of that involvement—sees the initiation of such responsibility in more voluntaristic terms. [...] It is not easy to see how these two very different understandings are reconcilable, although at the very least, it provides another reason for recognizing the irreducibility of Levinasian ethics to Arendtian politics and highlights two different, yet potentially complementary, ways in which responsibility (for others) is ethically and politically articulated.

This also brings us to the issue of ontology: for both Levinas and Arendt, the singularity of the Other/other troubles the "given" ontology of the world. This is especially so because Levinas (rightly or wrongly) regards ontology as that dominant philosophical tradition which has concerned itself with making the world present to, and encompassed by, thought. Ontology considers all that there is, for example, of another person as being inscribed within the phenomenal world of appearances and hence as potentially appropriable for our self-possessive purposes. This is another reason why Levinas describes the Other as beyond *being* (ontology), as always exceeding that made present in appearances, knowledge, or language. The Other who faces us ethically retains a capacity to surprise us, to interrupt the workaday self-centered world that would otherwise proceed almost automatically, without our intrusion and theirs.

Leaving aside potential philosophical differences between Levinas's and Arendt's understanding of ontology, both agree on the singular importance of not taking appearances for granted. Ethics and politics as such constantly introduce possibilities that escape or transcend what were previously taken as the ordering first principles (*archē*) of the natural or social worlds. And for this reason, among others, Levinas and Arendt are extremely critical of attempts to naturalize ethics or politics, to treat ethics as something that can be read off from, for example, our biology (Levinas) or to treat human society as something that operates only according to pregiven structures and processes (Arendt). Ethical and political responsibilities cannot be derived from any fixed ontology of human behavior. Ethics as such is not reducible, for example, to a sociobiological understanding of altruism, to selfish genes. [...] Arendt too targets both naturalistic explanations of and justifications for the sociopolitical order and is especially critical of the systematization of political structures that try to predict and eradicate political uncertainties, to get society to run like a well-oiled machine at the cost of politics as such. And this, after all, is precisely what biopolitics attempts to do—to treat politics as no more than a process to be efficiently managed.

What is important here is that both Levinas and Arendt recognize the vital importance of the ethical and political *event* that interrupts what would otherwise be taken for granted, what is taken as being the ontological order of the ethical and political world. For Levinas,[19] "the face *enters* our world from an absolutely foreign sphere ... exterior to all order, to all world." [...] Arendt too regards politics as such as an expression of that initiating and constitutive power that interrupts the given order of things, referring to this capacity to set events into motion as the "natality" of action, its almost miraculous ability to make new beginnings, to intrude on and change forever what had, up until that moment, been taken as natural, social, or historical necessities. [...]

This leads to the third anarchic aspect of Levinas's and Arendt's understandings, since the ethical and political event is a beginning, the principle and point of origin (*archē*) of which cannot be fully identified, encapsulated, or enunciated in language. In Levinas's terms, it is a *saying* (addressed to one or more others) that always exceeds and troubles that which is *said*—that which language serves to fix as the ontology, the totalizing *logos*, of the spoken or written wor(l)d. Saying is the anarchic expressivity that informs the spoken word, what is said, but is not thereby defined by that word (just as the singular Other comes from beyond and informs our being but resists being appropriated by it). [...]

This links to Arendtian politics in at least two important ways. First, Arendt emphasizes how singular expressions can interrupt the supposedly fixed flow of history. These expressions might be seen as exemplifying a political *saying* that informs, but also destabilizes, the overarching narrative themes of an otherwise depoliticized history.[20] Second, she, like Levinas, emphasizes the importance of not reducing the (ethical or political) "as such" to just following rules or formulae. To accept this reduction is to replace politics with a kind of antipolitical and uncritical conformity with current norms, whatever they might be. This is typical of bureaucratic (and biopolitical) state regimes and in its most extreme forms is indicative of totalitarianism.[21] This inattentiveness to individual ethical and political responsibilities is precisely what Arendt believes facilitated the easy transition from bourgeois respectability to acquiescence with the inverted (im)morality that marked the Nazis' accession to power. [...]

Levinasian and Arendtian Politics

These comparisons seem to bring us a little closer to elucidating how an ethically informed ecological politics might be conceived. It should at least be clearer how following the paths between Leviansian ethics and Arendtian politics avoids the quasi–Platonic pitfalls that reduce ethics to moral first principles (*archē*) and then treat these as sovereign over an ontologically defined politics—a fixed moral/political ordering of the world. Strangely, though, these paths between Levinas and Arendt seem little followed, even where human politics is concerned.

The relative dearth of secondary material directly comparing Arendt and Levinas's work is unfortunate and baffling, especially considering the shared historical context of their writings. After all, their mature philosophies were both developed as a direct response to the rise of Nazism and its systematic reduction of Jews, Gypsies, and others first to bare life and then to dead matter in the "fabrication of corpses"[22] in the camps. (Both Arendt and Levinas were also responding directly to Heidegger's active political support for Nazism.) Their focus on the anarchic aspects of ethics and politics as such became necessary because of the absolute and catastrophic failure of what had passed for ethics and politics in the totalitarian state of Germany and beyond.[23]

Some might argue that this lack of comparative material also relates to real difficulties in relating Levinas's ethics to politics, especially the ambiguities that arise when trying to associate Levinas's philosophy with any particular governmental form or political ideology. But such difficulties should actually make an attempt to connect his ethics with politics as such a more obvious path [...]. Critchley,[24] who goes so far as to claim that "Levinasian ethics is not ethics for its own sake, but for the sake of politics, that is, for the sake of a transformed understanding of the organization of social life," belatedly suggests, at the conclusion of his *Ethics of Deconstruction*[25] that Arendt and Levinas might be fruitfully connected given their mutual interest in justice. [...] But even the tentative connections outlined here (their anarchic concern with singularity, ontology, the resistance to authoritative inscription, and the focus on complementary but irreducible aspects of individual responsibility) suggest that their philosophical, ethical, and political resemblances run much deeper than just a mutual concern with justice.

Levinas's own attempts to find a place for politics alongside ethics falter largely because he never really develops a clear idea of politics as such, associating politics, especially in his earlier writings, with an almost Hobbesian war of each against all and a social–Darwinian "struggle for existence," which he regards as unethical not only because of the way this was directly employed by Nazi ideologues but because it explicitly reduces human life to a matter of mere survival, to Agamben's bare life. To oversimplify, the trouble is that Levinas accepts de facto that politics has always been, and can only be, biopolitics. [...] Thus, at least in this (almost biologically) reductive sense, Levinas's understanding of politics is actually the very antithesis of Arendt's, and so the difficulty in connecting their thought is hardly surprising.

Arendt too recognizes that violence is a form of political action, an interruptive event, but specifically defines it as that which is employed to negate (constitutive) political power and is negated by it.[26] War and violence constitute the limit of politics, and the "justification of violence as such ... [is] no longer political but anti-political."[27] Both Arendt and Levinas often associate violence with attempts to enforce political authority over others, with establishing and policing a totalizing, sometimes an overarching totalitarian, social order that seeks to deny expressions of plurality and difference. [...] [E]ven given his jaundiced view of politics, Levinas sometimes finds himself arguing that there can be an "ethical necessity"[28] as well as a practical and even military necessity for the defense of the state. This seems difficult to reconcile with his view that "unfortunately for ethics, politics has its own justification," a justification that, taken to its extreme, creates a "direct contradiction between ethics and politics,"[29] where "politics' own justification," for Levinas, is that of the struggle for survival, and ethics is an infinite, irrevocable, responsibility to the Other.

This is why Arendt's much less restrictive and much more positive conception of politics, as a creative dimension exceeding bare life, where freedom and difference are manifested among "ordinary humanity,"[30] is so important. Certainly politics has, in Levinas's phrase, its own justification, but for Arendt, this is only in the sense that it is a means without end: its justification is certainly not success in the struggle for survival, nor are the freedoms it makes possible set in opposition to ethics.

As already intimated, and especially in his later work, Levinas develops a more complex account of the relation between ethics and politics in terms of justice. But Levinas's account of political justice is far from satisfactory because, as even he seems to accept, it works only to the extent that it does violence to, or at least compromises, his account of ethics. His account introduces an incorporeal "third" party behind self and Other, a "neighbor" who supposedly represents all others but can only do so in an abstract manner, in a relation that is not face to face and so, unlike the self's relation to the singular Other, requires linguistic mediation. The "third party looks at me in the eyes of the Other—language is justice."[31] If this third party was just a figure (of the ethical imagination or of speech) intended to remind the self that ethical responsibilities are not contained within a relation to one singular Other, then this would not be so problematic. But Levinas clearly intends it as much more telling than this. Indeed, he argues, "The epiphany of the face qua face opens humanity,"[32] which suggests that the third party *is* or represents humanity ("the whole of humanity that looks at us")[33] or at least the other humans within the individual's ethical/political community. The emphasis on universalization suggests the first, that of justice within a state, and the second: Levinas equivocates between or conflates the two as and when it suits his inclinations.

But how can this be so? How can the third party be more than just a figuration of difference unless the self's responsibilities to all Other humans (or all the other humans in the self's state) are essentially the *Same*, something, after all, that Levinas's entire ethical oeuvre denies and something that simultaneously resuscitates the anthropological machine. How can the third party stand in for all parties without replacing the asymmetrical relation between the self and the singular Other with a symmetrical relation to *all* others and without turning an anarchical ethical relation into a relation contained within a political (and conceptual/linguistic) totality, a totality that, not incidentally, rules out all ethical and political relations to anything other than the human?

Perhaps Levinas's desire to speak to a secular politics framed entirely by and within the notions of humanism and state sovereignty led him to take this route. But whatever his motives, he certainly proceeds to link the notion of justice associated with the ghostly absence/presence of the third party in every ethical relation with a universalizing form of state politics: "In the measure that the face of the Other relates us with a third party, the metaphysical relation of the I to the Other moves into the form of the We, aspires to a State, institutions and laws which form the source of universality."[34] And yet he knows that the consequence of treating all Others "according to universal rules, and thus in absentia," not in their singularity,[35] is that it necessarily deforms the ethical relation. For this reason, too, Levinas claims both that "politics left to itself bears a tyranny within itself"[36] and that "there is a certain measure of violence necessary in terms of justice."[37]

Even if we accept (as Levinas does and political anarchists certainly do not) the necessity of a state (qua a nation-state) rather than a polis in the broader sense of an associative political community, this seems both contradictory and (at least potentially) politically dangerous. If politics is, within itself, tyrannical and the state is a political totality, then if there is to be any justice, there has to be some way in which justice can be informed by ethics as such. But how can it be so informed without individuals engaging in a publicly expressed politics that is itself ethically motivated (and perhaps even publicly recognized as being ethically motivated), that is to say, without engaging in a politics that is not solely, or even primarily, about being concerned with a struggle for survival? [...]

In other words, although one's concern for justice may be, as Levinas claims is the case for ethics as such, beyond being—that is, it precedes and exceeds what is (ontologically) given—the question of what justice requires is not something determinable a priori or something that can be decided by one for all others (for that is, by definition, tyranny) but something that has to be approached through the in-between of politics understood as the public expression of numerous *differently* human individuals, those who, if Levinas is right, are themselves always constituted through the ethical call of the Other and thus have the possibility of not being simply self-serving. Even on its own terms, then, Levinasian ethics cannot inform political justice without the initial intervention of Arendtian politics, a politics that is, to some extent, always already ethical.

This does not collapse ethics into politics, or vice versa; they are not coextensive and their relations, although often co-constitutive, remain asymmetric. Ethics as such and politics as such remain anarchic in all the senses already mentioned. This understanding will not then automatically issue, as Levinas seemingly hoped, in a politics (or a political state) in the service of ethics—"politics must be controlled by ethics"[38]—nor, as Critchley apparently thinks, an ethics "for the sake of politics." Nor, even admitting that justice is necessary, will it naturally result in a given political form, still less a state form, that somehow universalizes or captures the essence of this (anarchic) relation. Instead, it brings us back to an earlier thesis: *If politics as such is a matter of pure means, a means without end, then ethics as such could be thought of in terms of being concerned with others as impure ends, that is, as beings of indefinable (infinite) value but finite worldly existence.* And these matters of ethical and political concern can be thought of in anarchic terms: as expressions of singularity, natality, saying, and responsibility.

Earthly Associations: Ethics and Politics

> Anarchy cannot be sovereign, like an *archē*. It can only dis-
> turb the state—but in a radical way, making possible
> moments of negation *without any* affirmation. The state
> then cannot set itself up as a whole. But, on the other hand,
> anarchy can be stated.
>
> —Emmanuel Levinas, *Entre Nous:*
> *Thinking-of-the-Other*

No doubt the relation between Arendtian politics and Levinasian ethics could be explicated in other ways, but it is necessary to focus here on the ecological implications of this anarchic understanding and to do so without Arendt's, and especially Levinas's, own humanist presuppositions. This is necessary for both an ethical and a political reason. First, Levinas's ethical thought concerning the specificity of the Other has anthropological limits. As we have seen, Levinas's metaphysical pre-suppositions about the special quality of the encounter with the human face preclude any straightforward extension or application of his theory to an ecological ethics. Second, this same metaphysics ensures that the ghost of the anthropological machine haunts his own failure to articulate a politics that might be more than matters of self-interest, survival (bare life), and the sovereignty of the nation-state.

To even begin to understand the ecological potential of ethics and politics as such, it is thus necessary to recognize that the words and deeds of environmentalists (among others) attest that ethical concerns for our (differently) nonhuman neighbors are both possible and politically important. Of course, those beholden to a modernist constitution founded on the separation of nature and politics may refuse to countenance such a possibility, but then, as already argued, ethics and politics as such concern themselves with creating constitutive associations and are not beholden to constitutionally imposed limits on their activities.

In any case, the best that could be hoped for, given a politics that accepted Levinas's metaphysical strictures on the ethical specificity of the human, is an extremely anthropocentric form of distributive environmental justice: a form of ethicopolitics that regards every nonhuman aspect of the natural world as a resource to be allocated by and for humans, hence, ultimately, reducing ecological politics to those political frames of reference that already exist. [...]

So an ecological politics has to be informed by an ethics that exceeds Levinas's humanist presuppositions, supplemented by a liberating Arendtian understanding of politics as such. And although Arendt, like Levinas, was almost entirely concerned with the *human* condition, although the "who" that appears in the political space is always (differently) human, there are no a priori restrictions on what or who these persons might be concerned to speak about or for. Although expressing that *amor mundi*—the love for the world that Arendt also felt—may have no constitutional place, there is nothing inherently apolitical about ecological concerns.

But this does suggest that we need to ask what kinds of ecological politics might express such concerns, raising questions about the relation of ethics and politics as such to (ecologically sensitive) forms of politics—about whether this "anarchy" is, as Levinas's quotation suggests, only a "negation without *any affirmation*" (whether, or in what sense, it might be nihilistic) and whether it can actually be stated both in terms of enclosing its saying within what is said and in terms of its being enclosed within and reduced to associations within current constitutional (state) forms.

Ecological politics is actually far from being nihilistic if this is understood in the sense of a total (and totalizing) rejection of everything present, of everything that has ever been said, of every moral norm, of every aspect of all ethical and political systems—it is not just a critique of all there is, in the name of nothing at all, although it certainly initiates a continual critique of all (ethically and politically) restrictive deployments of metaphysical absolutes. [...] Nor is it nihilistic in many other senses—not least because it is through such political engagement that we exercise our freedom, use our judgment, and appear as that singular individual who we are, before others. More important, and in Levinas's terms, less "egotistically," this politics is concerned with facing and sustaining ecological beings that are not congruent with, nor reducible to, my own self-possessive interests. [...] An ecological politics as such emerges through facing up to and recognizing our potentially infinite ethical responsibilities for Other (more-than-human) beings. It is difficult to think what could be less nihilistic than this, or more life-affirming. [...]

This ecological politics is informed by an ethics of responsibility before and beyond all else, before even the claims of justice. For justice can be couched in terms of a compromise between the (selfish) needs of all those (human) "citizens" concerned and metaethical formulae and/or constitutionally defined governmental practices designed to ensure that all (who count as citizens) are treated equally, processed as ethically and politically the *Same* in an abstract sense. Such a system is clearly exclusionary both of ethics as such and of those who cannot speak for themselves (at least in ways that the system could hear or accept). Leaving open the possibility of attending to the singularity of each ecological instance requires ethically informed political interventions, interventions already accepting some responsibility for more-than-human others as Others.

It is also important to recognize that even if justice is couched in terms of the apportioning of ethical responsibilities, to the extent that this could ever be applied *systematically* without the continual reappearance of politics as such to trouble its decisions, it would risk becoming dangerously biopolitical and even totalitarian. And without politics as such, even systems of ecological justice that explicitly recognize some ethical (or, perhaps more accurately, moral) obligations to the more-than-human world run this same risk. [...]

What is more, the understanding of ethical responsibility being developed here is anarchic and asymmetric from its inception. Both Arendt and Levinas emphasize the radical asymmetry of the associative relations among individuals: "the asymmetry of intersubjectivity."[39] The singular individuals of Levinasian ethics and Arendtian politics are, for example, in no way reducible to the sovereign, self-interested, and incorporeal abstraction that is *homo economicus*. Consequently, neither Arendt nor Levinas (at least when we leave aside the matter of the Third) is interested in what would be (un)ethical or (a)political communities that can only exist theoretically on the premise of sameness or equivalence—such as an idea(l) of an essential, shared, or universal human nature, one based only (or at all) on reciprocally beneficial exchange. Theirs are associations constituted in irreducible difference and plurality. And it is this asymmetry that opens the very possibility of an ecological politics that can envisage ecological communities of (differently) human and more-than-human beings. Only such ethical responsibilities *and* their political expression can constitute an ecological politics as such, one that recognizes the traces left by the diverse denizens of the world and where it is possible to speak and act concerning the more-than-human world.

This affirmation is already suggestive of certain political possibilities, but it still leaves unanswered the question of whether, or to what extent, an anarchic ethics and politics as such can be, in Levinas's words, "stated"—encompassed by what is said within, for example, a particular theory or political ideology and/or a particular state form.

Savage Democracy: Ecology in the Political Wilderness?

An obvious consequence of emphasizing the ways in which ethics and politics are constitutive of our ecological and human associations is that there cannot be any a priori or definitive answer as to how to found political constitutions, institutions, and ideologies on principles (*archē*) that (claim to) guarantee political stability or particular outcomes. Neither ethics nor politics begins with, requires, or can be contained within first principles, and the myriad forms and contents they take are inseparable from their expression and enactment. Yet this does not mean that an understanding of ethics and politics as such is without consequence in the sense that those who espouse such a perspective remain neutral about either the forms taken by government/governance or the content of ethicopolitical ideologies. Clearly, such an understanding is placed in opposition to those systems of government and thought that want to manage and suppress ethics and politics as such, that are dependent on reducing human life to bare life, and that seek to impose a monotheistic conception of the properly human and deny plurality and diversity or to replace ethical responsibility with moral rules and/or political responsibilities with automatic obligations. It is antitotalitarian and antibiopolitical, valuing singular expressive freedoms. In other words, it sets itself in opposition to many forms of government and ideology in their entirety. And, being against the principle of sovereignty in all its guises, it is, in its pure form, anarchist—although, as already argued, any claims to encapsulate such purity/innocence even (or perhaps especially) in a state of nature, are actually culturally conditioned myths.

This leaves open the possibility that some forms of government may be preferable to others, more amenable to sustaining (or at least less actively repressing) ethics and politics as such, more tolerant of difference and diversity, more concerned with leaving open possibilities for individual expression, and this is something only the purist would deny. But it is also to recognize that this *never* equates with a claim that ethics and politics as such are reducible to participation in the constitutional machinery of government. Indeed, ethics and politics as such most frequently take the form of extragovernmental community and social activism (and of a civil society very broadly understood) of one kind or another. The point is to recognize that constitutional questions are, as they were for Arendt, secondary questions: they come only after, and are dependent on, the enactment of ethics and politics as such (which again is not to say such questions are unimportant). This is why Arendt constantly emphasizes the natality of the political event, the totalitarian dangers inherent in replacing politics with *policy* or bureaucracy,[40] the vital importance of exercising individual ethical and political judgments in all circumstances,[41] and the need for civil disobedience in some.[42] She even specifically criticizes the U.S. Constitution,[43] which she otherwise regards as genuinely revolutionary in intent, for leaving precious little space for politics as such. [...]

It is also important to remember that this anarchic articulation of the relation between ethics and politics is not necessarily ecological in and of itself, just as the understandings of Levinas and Arendt are not necessarily ecological. [...] It only becomes ecological when understood in relation to the twisting and weakening (*Verwindung*) critique of the plots and metaphysical presuppositions of the anthropological machine and of the claim to human sovereignty over the natural world. It is here, in displacing and dissolving the anthropological centrality of the category of the properly or fully human in both ethics and politics, that ecology expresses a truly radical break with any and all previous political *archē*. But this critique is not the sole property of radical ecology. It is clearly articulable within, and even a vital constituent of, the political writings of many of those whose primary concerns are certainly not ecological, such as Arendt and Agamben. [...] And so there is "common ground" here where discussion and persuasion can take place, and once the incessant productions of the anthropological machine are stilled, the walls that exclude ecological ethics may crumble, be pulled apart, and fall, much like the Berlin Wall.

Such possibilities arise because radical ecology is an underdetermined association of ecology, ethics, and politics because of its natality and constitutive potential. And this potential also means that it resists being stated in the sense of being encapsulated within formulaic or programmatic party manifestos (even those of a Green Party). Any such attempt can only be indicative and provisional. [...] Such an understanding does not result in an ecologism,[44] a novel ideology to rival liberalism, socialism, Marxism, or anarchism. Radical ecology's concerns and involvements exceed any attempts to enclose it within and place it under a set of first principles, and it has no interest in asserting itself as a new ethicopolitical world order,[45] as an *archē*, or a new form of Green sovereignty. To say that radical ecology is not a specific political ideology is by no means to claim that it escapes ideology in general—as Althusser[46] famously declared, Marxism escaped ideology by aligning itself with the knowledge provided by the natural and (post–Marxist) social sciences—even if that science is, in this case, the supposedly "subversive science" of ecology. Radical ecology cannot pretend to provide a singular truth or to be value free—quite the contrary—although it too recognizes, as those favoring the term *ecologism* have also contended,[47] that ecological politics is relatively autonomous in terms of its concerns (it is certainly not reducible to any previous *ism*) and that there are "family resemblances" between its various elucidations.

While far from presenting a uniform political ideology, radical ecology is certainly not without critical and affirmative content. Critically, for example, in rejecting the claims of human sovereignty over the natural world and the subsequent and systematic reduction of that world to resource or standing reserve, radical ecology opposes the fundamental principles and global dominance of corporate capitalism. Capitalism's systematic commodification of the more-than-human world through its reduction to exchange value remains unquestioned and unquestionable because of the (originally theological) assumption of human sovereignty. Radical ecology is anticapitalist insofar as capitalism depends not only on the alienating expropriation of that "surplus" value that Marx argued was created by human labor but on the biopolitical stripping of all ethical possibilities from (differently) human relations to nature. But this also means that it is no less opposed to any Marxism that similarly reduces more-than-human singularities to just their human *use* values. Despite Marxism's radical pretensions, the core concept of use value deploys the same (anthropological) sovereign principle (*archē*) as capitalism; it is complicit in systematically and universally reducing nature to its value in serving human needs (however defined). [...]

But what, then, is affirmative about the attempt to sustain an anarchic, ecologically informed ethics and politics? And here, what is being asked, at least insofar as the answer expected is not a total(izing) vision of a political order deduced from first principles, is what *form* might ethics and politics take other than the constant critique of ruling principles and contemporary political structures. The assumption behind the question is that taking responsibility for the ethical and political effects of one's words and actions without some form of metaphysical and/or institutional regulation is somehow impossible, insufficient, or entirely negative. And yet ethics and politics as such are practiced every day, even in the most adverse of circumstances, often without ever having been formulated as such and without seeking or requiring the permission of some higher authority.

If arguing that ethics and politics as such pervade our social and ecological interactions is deemed insufficiently affirmative, this is because those asking this question usually require an answer that would fit their own expectations, that dismisses these mundane forms as having little or nothing to do with the founding of a new political order or espousing new political principles. The question represents the presumed necessity of securing a vision of how to found an alternative and faultless system in its totality, the seeming impossibility to escape "the belief that somehow or other such foundations ... [are] necessary, the belief that unless there are foundations something is lost or threatened or undermined or just in question."[48] This, then, is a question that mirrors those posed to atheists by those convinced that the authority of God must be replaced by some other overarching principle, preferably one guaranteed by the authority of a unitary institution—a secular equivalent of the one true Church. It takes the same form as the question posed to anarchists by political realists incapable of thinking that politics might be initiated, organized, and practiced outside of the state form (and this despite its relatively recent historical origins) and who demand to know what form an anarchist state would take and how it would guarantee its hegemony. It reflects the dissatisfaction moralists have with the anarchic aspects of [...] Levinas's ethics, which again seem to offer no permanence, no solid foundations, only a constant questioning—"Is this good (enough)?"—and a finite life facing infinite responsibilities.

Of course, there might also be a pragmatic aspect to this question, concerning how best to sustain ethics and politics as such in very different circumstances. But the fact that there are very different circumstances suggests that there can be no one universal answer. To provide such an answer is the function of an ideology like liberalism, Marxism, or anarchism. But since *isms* are not options, what seems lacking here is not an alternative set of principles to replace sovereignty but ethico-political concepts capable of articulating some of the possibilities that arise from affirming the value of ethics and politics as such, of provisionally expressing provisional (not authoritative, complete, or ultimate) political forms. And the danger in providing such a vocabulary is that it immediately becomes open to ideological abuse—it ceases to be treated as provisional. For this reason, these concepts must be envisioned in terms that (so far as is possible) resist the logocentrism that places words themselves in some position of absolute authority over the world, ethics, and politics, the use of language as a definitive expression of human "authority." *Provisionality* must recognize, in Levinas's terms, that saying is never fully encapsulated in the said and moreover that what is said should not be reified as if it were itself a principle (or essential) aspect of reality. [...]

The principle of sovereignty, even the sovereignty of the people, and especially the sovereignty of the people over the Earth, has to be rejected; otherwise we are in constant danger of replacing Arendt's political spaces of encounter—and of concern, discourse, persuasion, interpretation, and responsibility for others—with a symbol that reifies the people as an abstract ruling (constitutional) principle rather than an actual living (constitutive) plurality. And, as argued previously, this is precisely how the anthropological machine works. [...]

This ecopolitics is a politics of singular freedom and responsibility that is both antitotalitarian and antibiopolitical. It persists only where nature, no less than humanity, escapes being entirely managed and controlled and for as long as *diversity* (human and more-than-human) is expressed and sustained (it is never monocultural). It emerges first through face-to-face encounters (by no means limited to Other humans) and is therefore born of and sustained by relations of proximity that are both intimate and embodied, relations that can be expressed (if not defined) through our subsequent words and deeds. It recognizes the finitude (mortality) of Earthly existence, the unique and irreplaceable singularity of every life that touches us and is lost, and the infinite responsibility that dispossesses us, a responsibility we would face alone were it not for the potential forgiveness of our fellows. It is not based on any natural(ized) laws or beholden to any overarching universal principles. It resists the way that capital (and its lack) constantly threatens to turn people and places into shadows of themselves.

But beyond all this, an ecological ethics and politics of responsibility troubles and contests the key principle and supposed origin of all modern constitutional politics—the self-possessive principle of sovereignty, whether the sovereignty of the individual self, the word, God, the Good, the nation-state, the people, or human sovereignty over the natural world.[49] It does so because this often taken-for-granted and naturalized principle abrogates the constitutive power of others to itself and grounds its own powers in its ultimate ability to strip Others of their ethical and political possibilities, even of their very lives, and because ultimately it harbors the potential to turn the whole world into a realm of crisis and disaster.

NOTES

1. Mick Smith, *An Ethics of Place: Radical Ecology, Postmodernity and Social Theory* (Albany: State University of New York Press, 2001).

2. Hannah Arendt, *The Human Condition* (Chicago: University of Chicago Press, 1958), 12–13.

3. Giorgio Agamben, *Means Without End: Notes on Politics* (Minneapolis: University of Minnesota Press, 2000), 3.

4. *Ibid.*

5. Giorgio Agamben, *Homo Sacer: Sovereign Power and Bare Life* (Stanford: Stanford University Press, 1998).

6. Aristotle, *The Politics* (Cambridge: Cambridge University Press, 1988), 1253a, line 2.

7. *Ibid.*, 1253a, lines 25–27.

8. *Ibid.*, lines 16–17

9. Emmanuel Levinas, *Entre Nous: Thinking-of-the-Other* (London: Athlone Press, 1998).

10. For example, Levinas, *Entre Nous*, 99–102; Emmanuel Levinas, *Humanism and the Other* (Urbana: University of Illinois Press, 2003), 45–57; see also Jean Greisch, "The Face and Reading: Immediacy and Meditation," in *Re-Reading Levinas*, ed. Robert Bernasconi and Simon Critchley (Bloomington: Indiana University Press, 1991), 80; Silvia Benso, *The Face of Things: A Different Side of Ethics* (Albany: State University of New York Press, 2000); Miguel Abensour, "'Savage Democracy' and the 'Principle of Anarchy,'" *Philosophy and Social Criticism* 28, no. 6 (2002).

11. Jeffrey C. Isaac, *Arendt, Camus, and Modern Rebellion* (New Haven, CT: Yale University Press, 1992).

12. Hannah Arendt, *The Human Condition* (Chicago: University of Chicago, 1958). Quoted in Elisabeth Young-Breuhl, *Why Arendt Matters* (New Haven, CT: Yale University Press, 2006), 201.

13. Emmanuel Levinas, *Ethics and Infinity: Conversations with Philippe Nemo* (Pittsburgh: Duquesne University Press, 1985), 95.

14. Emmanuel Levinas, "Substitution," in *Emmanual Levinas: Basic Philsophical Writings*, ed. Adrian T. Peperzak, Simon Critchley, and Robert Bernasconi (Bloomington: Indiana University Press, 1996), 81.

15. *Ibid.*

16. Levinas, *Basic Philosophical Writings*, 95.

17. Levinas, *Humanism*, 51.

18. Levinas, "Substitution," 82.

19. Levinas, *Humanism*, 32.

20. Mick Smith, "Hermenutics and the Culture of Birds: The Environmental Allegory of Easter Island," *Ethics, Place and Environment* 8, no. 1 (2005a) 21–38.

21. Hannah Arendt, *The Origins of Totalitarianism* (New York: Harcourt Brace Jovanovich, 1975).

22. Theodor Adorno and Max Horkheimer, *Dialectic of Enlightenment* (London: Verso, 1973). Quoted in Giorgio Agamben, *Remnants of Auschwitz: The Witness and the* Archive (New York: Zone Books, 1999), 81.

23. Richard J. Bernstein, "Evil and Theodicy," in *The Cambridge Companion to Levinas*, ed. Simon Critchley and Robert Bernasconi (Cambridge: Cambridge University Press, 2002), 254.

24. Simon Critchley, introduction to *Parallax* 8, no. 3 (2002): 1.

25. Simon Critchley, *The Ethics of Deconstruction: Derrida and Levinas*, 2nd. ed. (Edinburgh: Edinburgh University Press, 1999), 237–38.

26. Hannah Arendt, *On Violence* (New York: Harcourt Brace & World, 1970).

27. Hannah Arendt, *On Revolution* (Harmondsworth, England: Penguin, 1965), 19.

28. Emmanuel Levinas, "Ethics and Politics," in *The Levinas Reader*, ed. Seán Hand (Oxford: Blackwell, 1989), 292.

29. *Ibid.*

30. George Kateb, "Political Action: Its Nature and Advantages," in *The Cambridge Companion to Hannah Arendt*, ed. Dana Villa (Cambridge: Cambridge University Press, 2000), 148.

31. Emmanuel Levinas, *Totality and Infinity* (Dordrecht: Kluwer, 1991), 213.

32. *Ibid.*

33. *Ibid.*

34. *Ibid.*, 300.

35. *Ibid.*

36. *Ibid.*

37. Levinas, *Entre Nous*, 105.

38. Emmanuel Levinas in William Paul Simmons, "The Third: Levinas's Theoretical Move from An-Archical Ethics to the Realm of Justice and Politics," *Philosophy and Social Criticism* 25, no.6 (1999): 92.

39. Levinas, *Entre Nous*, 105.

40. Arendt, *The Origins of Totalitarianism.*

41. Hannah Arendt, *Eichmann in Jerusalem: A Report on the Banality of Evil* (New York: Penguin, 1994).

42. Hannah Arendt, "Civil Disobedience," in *Crisis of the Republic* (San Diego: Harcourt Brace, 1973).

43. Arendt, *On Revolution*, 232.

44. Andrew Dobson, *Green Political Thought* (London: Routledge, 1995); Brian Baxter, *Ecologism: An Introduction* (Edinburgh: Edinburgh University Press, 1999).

45. Luc Ferry, *The New Ecological Order* (Chicago: University of Chicago Press, 1992).

46. Louis Althusser, *Philosophy and the Spontaneous Philosophy of the Scientists and Other Essays* (London: Verso, 1990).

47. Mark J. Smith, *Ecologism: Towards Ecological Citizenship* (Buckingham: Open University Press, 1998).

48. Chantal Mouffe, *The Return of the Political* (London: Verso, 2005), 15.

49. Mick Smith, "Suspended Animation: Radical Ecology, Sovereign Powers, and Saving the (Natural) World," *Journal for the Study of Radicalism* 2, no. 1 (2008): 1–23.

Affirmation versus Vulnerability

On Contemporary Ethical Debates

ROSI BRAIDOTTI

At the end of postmodernism, politics is in decline, whereas ethics triumphs in the public debate. This is not in itself a progressive move as once again the charge of moral and cognitive relativism is moved against any project that shows a concerted effort at displacing or decentering the traditional, humanistic view of the moral subject. This attitude asserts the belief in the necessity of strong foundations, such as those that a liberal view of the subject can guarantee. Doxic consensus is set: without steady identities resting on firm grounds, basic elements of human decency, moral and political agency, and ethical probity are threatened. In opposition to this belief, which has little more than longstanding habits and the inertia of tradition on its side, I want to argue in this essay that a posthumanistic and nomadic vision of the subject can provide an alternative foundation for ethical and political subjectivity.

This argument is framed by a larger dispute, which I will not explore here—that of the thorny relationship between poststructuralist ethics in continental philosophy, on the one hand, and the dominant, mostly Anglo-American traditions of moral philosophy on the other. Todd May[1] argued persuasively that moral philosophy as a discipline does not score highly in poststructuralist philosophy or in French philosophy as a whole. This is no reason, however, to move against it the lazy charges of moral relativism and nihilism. One only has to look across the field of French philosophy—Deleuze's ethics of immanence,[2] Irigaray's ethics of sexual difference,[3] Foucault's attempt to self-style the ethical relationship, Derrida's and Levinas's emphasis on the receding horizons of alterity—to be fully immersed in ethical concerns. It is the case that ethics in poststructuralist philosophy is not confined to the realm of rights, distributive justice, or the law; it rather bears close links with the notion of political agency, freedom, and the management of power and power relations. Issues of responsibility are dealt with in terms of alterity or the relationship to others. This implies accountability, situatedness, and cartographic accuracy. A poststructuralist position, therefore, far from thinking that a liberal individual definition of the subject is the necessary precondition for ethics, argues that liberalism at present hinders the development of new modes of ethical behavior.

The proper object of ethical enquiry is not the subject's moral intentionality, or rational consciousness, as much as the effects of truth and power that his/her actions are likely to have upon others in the world. This is a kind of ethical pragmatism, which is conceptually linked to the notion of embodied materialism and to a non-unitary vision of the subject. Ethics is therefore the discourse about forces, desires, and values that act as empowering modes of being, whereas morality is the established sets of rules. Philosophical nomadism shares Nietzsche's distaste for morality as sets of negative, resentful emotions and life-denying reactive passions. Deleuze joins this up with Spinoza's ethics of affirmation to produce a very accountable and concrete ethical line about joyful affirmation.

There is no logical reason why Kantians should have a monopoly on moral thinking. In moral philosophy, however, one touches Kantian moral universalism at one's peril. From the Habermasian school and its American branch—Benhabib,[4] Young, and Fraser[5]—to the hard-core Kantianism of Martha Nussbaum,[6] a general rejection of poststructuralist theories in general and ethics in particular has taken place. Lovibond[7] expresses her concern with the loss of moral authority that is entailed by a non-unitary vision of the subject and reasserts the necessity of a Kantian agenda as the only source of salvation after the debacle of postmodernism.

I want to take the opposite road and attempt to read poststructuralist philosophy in its own terms rather than reduce it to the standards of a system of thought—in this case the Kantian tradition—that shares so few of its premises. There are serious advantages to the anti-representational slant of contemporary poststructuralist philosophy, in that it entails the critique of liberal individualism and its replacement by an intensive view of subjectivity. The ethics of nomadic subjectivity rejects moral universalism and works towards a different idea of ethical accountability in the sense of a fundamental reconfiguration of our being in a world that is technologically and globally mediated. One of the most pointed paradoxes of our era is precisely the clash between the urgency of finding new and alternative modes of political and ethical agency, on the one hand, and the inertia or self-interest of neoconservatism on the other. It is urgent to explore and experiment with more adequate forms of non-unitary, nomadic, and yet accountable modes of envisaging both subjectivity and democratic, ethical interaction. Two crucial issues arise: the first is that, contrary to the panic-stricken universalists, an ethics worthy of the complexities of our times requires a fundamental redefinition of our understanding of the subject in his/her contemporary location and not a mere return to a more or less invented philosophical tradition. Second, an alternative ethical stance based on radical immanence and becoming is capable of a universalistic reach, if not a universalistic aspiration. It just so happens to be a grounded, partial form of accountability, based on a strong sense of collectivity and community building. In what follows I want to argue for the relevance of a Deleuzian approach to this urgent ethical project.

The following main discursive alignments can be seen at present in poststructuralist ethical thought. Besides the classical Kantians,[8] we have a Kantian-Foucauldian coalition that stresses the role of moral accountability as a form of bio-political citizenship. Best represented by Nicholas Rose[9] and Paul Rabinow,[10] this group works with the notion of "Life" as *bios*, that is to say as an instance of governmentality that is as empowering as it is confining. This school of thought locates the ethical moment in the rational and self-regulating accountability of a bio-ethical subject and results in the radicalization of the project of modernity.

A second grouping takes its lead from Heidegger and is best exemplified by Agamben.[11] It defines *bios* as the result of the intervention of sovereign power, as that which is capable of reducing the subject to "bare life," that is to say *zoē*. The latter is, however, contiguous with Thanatos or death. The being-aliveness of the subject (*zoē*) is identified with its perishability, its propensity and vulnerability to death and extinction. Biopower here means Thanatos-politics and results in the indictment of the project of modernity.

Another important cluster in this brief cartography of new ethical discourses includes the Levinas-Derrida tradition of ethics, which is centered on the relationship between the subject and Otherness in the mode of indebtedness, vulnerability, and mourning.[12] I have enormous respect for this school of thought, but the project I want to pursue takes as the point of reference *bios-zoē* power defined as the nonhuman, vitalistic, or post-anthropocentric dimension of subjectivity. This is an affirmative project that stresses positivity and not mourning.

The last discursive coalition, to which this project belongs, is inspired by the neo-vitalism of Deleuze, with reference to Nietzsche and Spinoza.[13] Biopower is only the starting point of a reflection about the politics of life itself as a relentlessly generative force. Contrary to the Heideggerians, the emphasis here is on generation, vital forces, and natality. Contrary to the

Kantians, the ethical instance is not located within the confines of a self-regulating subject of moral agency, but rather in a set of interrelations with both human and inhuman forces. These forces can be rendered in terms of relationality (Spinoza), duration (Bergson), immanence (Deleuze), and, in my own terms, ethical sustainability. The notion of the nonhuman, inhuman, or posthuman emerges therefore as the defining trait of this new kind of ethical subjectivity. This project moves altogether beyond the postmodern critique of modernity and is especially opposed to the hegemony gained by linguistic mediation within postmodernist theory.

Transformative Ethics

At the core of this ethical project is a positive vision of the subject as a radically immanent, intensive body, that is, an assemblage of forces or flows, intensities, and passions that solidify in space and consolidate in time, within the singular configuration commonly known as an "individual" self. This intensive and dynamic entity is rather a portion of forces that is stable enough to sustain and undergo constant though nondestructive fluxes of transformation. It is the body's degrees and levels of affectivity that determine the modes of differentiation. Joyful or positive passions and the transcendence of reactive affects are the desirable mode. The emphasis on "existence" implies a commitment to duration and conversely a rejection of self-destruction. Positivity is built into this program through the idea of thresholds of sustainability. Thus, an ethically empowering option increases one's *potentia* and creates joyful energy in the process. The conditions that can encourage such a quest are not only historical; they concern processes of transformation or self-fashioning in the direction of affirming positivity. Because all subjects share in this common nature, there is a common ground on which to negotiate the interests and the eventual conflicts.

It is important to see that this fundamentally positive vision of the ethical subject does not deny conflicts, tension, or even violent disagreements between different subjects. The legacy of Hegel's critique of Spinoza is still looming large here, notably the criticism that a Spinozist approach lacks a theory of negativity, which may adequately account for the complex logistics of interaction with others. It is simply not the case that the positivity of desire cancels or denies the tensions of conflicting interests. It merely displaces the grounds on which the negotiations take place. The Kantian imperative of not doing to others what you would not want done to you is not rejected as much as enlarged. In terms of the ethics of *conatus*, in fact, the harm that you do to others is immediately reflected in the harm you do to yourself, in terms of loss of *potentia*, positivity, self-awareness, and inner freedom. Moreover, the "others" in question are non-anthropomorphic and include planetary forces. This move away from the Kantian vision of an ethics that obliges people, and especially women, natives, and others, to act morally in the name of a transcendent standard or universal rule is not a simple one. I defend it as a forceful answer to the complexities of our historical situation; it is a move towards radical immanence against all Platonizing and classical humanistic denials of embodiment, *mater*, and the flesh.

What is at risk, however, in nomadic ethics is the notion of containment of the other. This is expressed by a number of moral thinkers in the continental tradition, such as Jessica Benjamin[14] in her radicalization of Irigaray's horizontal transcendence, Lyotard in the "differend"[15] and the "unattuned," and Butler[16] in her emphasis on "precarious life." They stress that moral reasoning locates the constitution of subjectivity in the interrelation to others, which is a form of exposure, availability, and vulnerability. This recognition entails the necessity of containing the other and the suffering and the enjoyment of others in the expression of the intensity of our affective streams. An embodied and connecting containment as a moral category could emerge from this, over and against the hierarchical forms of containment implied by Kantian forms of universal morality.

The objection that a Spinozist ethics fails to account for the interaction with the Other is predictable, and it is connected, on the one hand, to the issue of the negotiations of boundaries, limits, and costs and, on the other, to affectivity and compassion. The nomadic view of ethics takes place within a monistic ontology that sees subjects as modes of individuation within a common flow of *zoē*. Consequently there is no self-other distinction in the traditional mode but variations of intensities, assemblages set by affinities and complex synchronizations. Bio-centered egalitarianism breaks the expectation of mutual reciprocity that is central to liberal individualism. Accepting the impossibility of mutual recognition and replacing it with mutual specification and mutual codependence is what is at stake in a nomadic ethics of sustainability. This is against both the moral philosophy of rights and the humanistic tradition of making the anthropocentric Other into the privileged site and inescapable horizon of otherness.

If the point of ethics is to explore how much a body can do in the pursuit of active modes of empowerment through experimentation, how do we know when we have gone too far? How does the negotiation of boundaries actually take place? This is where the non-individualistic vision of the subject as embodied and hence affective and interrelational, but also fundamentally social, is of major consequence. Your body will thus tell you if and when you have reached a threshold or a limit. The warning can take the form of opposing resistance, falling ill, or feeling nauseous, or it can take other somatic manifestations, like fear, anxiety, or a sense of insecurity. Whereas the semiotic-linguistic frame of psychoanalysis reduces these to symptoms awaiting inter-pretation, I see them as corporeal warning signals or boundary markers that express a clear message: "Too much!" One of the reasons why Deleuze and Guattari are so interested in studying self-destructive or pathological modes of behavior, such as schizophrenia, masochism, anorexia, various forms of addiction, and the black hole of murderous violence, is precisely to explore their function as thresholds or boundary-markers. This assumes a qualitative distinction between, on the one hand, the desire that propels the subject's expression of his/her *conatus*—a neo–Spinozist perspective is implicitly pos-itive in that it expresses the essential best of the subject—and, on the other hand, the constraints imposed by society. The specific, contextually deter-mined conditions are the forms in which the desire is actualized or actually expressed.

Bodily entities are not passive, but rather dynamic and sensitive forces forever in motion, which "form unities only through fragile synchronization of forces."[17] This fragility concerns mostly the pitch of the synchronization efforts, the lines of demarcation between the different bodily boundaries, and the borders that are the thresholds of encounter and connection with other forces, the standard term for which is "limits." Because of his monistic understanding of the subject, Spinoza sees bodily limits as the limits of our awareness as well, which means that his theory of affectivity is connected to the physics of motion. Another word for Spinoza's *conatus* is therefore self-preservation, not in the liberal individualistic sense of the term but rather as the actualization of one's essence, that is to say, of one's ontological drive to become. This is neither an automatic nor an intrinsically harmonious process, insofar as it involves interconnection with other forces and consequently also conflicts and clashes. Negotiations have to occur as stepping stones to sus-tainable flows of becoming. The bodily self's interaction with his/her envi-ronment can either increase or decrease that body's *conatus* or *potentia*. The mind as a sensor that prompts understanding can assist by helping to discern and choose those forces that increase its power of acting and its activity in both physical and mental terms. A higher form of self-knowledge by under-standing the nature of one's affectivity is the key to a Spinozist ethics of empowerment. It includes a more adequate understanding of the intercon-nections between the self and a multitude of other forces, and it thus under-mines the liberal individual understanding of the subject. It also implies, however, the body's ability to comprehend and to sustain physically a greater number of complex interconnections, and to deal with complexity without being overburdened. Thus, only an appreciation of complexity and of increas-ing degrees of complexity can guarantee the freedom of the mind in the awareness of its true, affective, and dynamic nature.

This is expressed by Spinoza in terms of achieving freedom through an adequate understanding of our passions and consequently of our bondage. Coming into possession of freedom requires the understanding of affects or passions by a mind that is always already embodied. The desire to reach an adequate understanding of one's *potentia* is the human being's fundamental desire or *conatus*. An error of judgment is a form of misunderstanding (the true nature of the subject) that results in decreasing the power, positivity, and activity of the subject. By extension, reason is affective, embodied, and dynamic; understanding the passions is our way of experiencing them and making them work in our favor. In this respect, Spinoza argues that desires arise from our passions. Because of this, they can never be excessive, given that affectivity is the power that activates our body and makes it want to act. The human being's built-in tendency is toward joy and self-expression, not toward implosion. This fundamental positivity is the key to Deleuze's attachment to Spinoza.

Lloyd argues that Spinoza's treatment of the mind as part of nature is a source of inspiration for contemporary ethics. Spinozist monism acts "as a basis for developing a broader concept of ethology, a study of relations of individual and collective and being affected."[18] Clearly, it is a very non-moralistic understanding of ethics that focuses on the subject's powers to act and to express their dynamic and positive essence. An ethology stresses the field of composition of forces and affects, speed and transformation. In this perspective, ethics is the pursuit of self-preservation, which assumes the dissolution of the self: what is good is what increases our power of acting, and this is what we must strive for. This results not in egoism but in mutually embedded nests of shared interests. Lloyd calls this "a collaborative morality."[19] Because the starting point for Spinoza is not the isolated individual but complex and mutually depended co-realities, the self-other interaction also follows a different model. To be an individual means to be open to being affected by and through others, thus undergoing transformations in such a way as to be able to sustain them and make them work toward growth. The distinction activity/passivity is far more important than that between self and other, good and bad. What binds the two are the ideas of interconnection and affectivity as the defining features of the subject. An ethical life pursues that which enhances and strengthens the subject without reference to transcendental values, but rather in the awareness of one's interconnection with others.

About Pain and Vulnerability

This vision of ethics involves a radical repositioning or internal transformation on the part of subjects who want to become minoritarian in a productive and affirmative manner. It is clear that this shift requires changes that are neither simple nor self-evident. They mobilize the affectivity of the subjects involved and can be seen as a process of transformation of negative into positive passions. Fear, anxiety, and nostalgia are clear examples of the negative emotions involved in the project of detaching ourselves from familiar and cherished forms of identity. To achieve a post-identity or non-unitary vision of the self requires the disidentification from established references. Such an enterprise involves a sense of loss of cherished habits of thought and representation and thus is not free of pain. No process of consciousness-raising ever is.

The beneficial side effects of this process are unquestionable, and in some way they compensate for the pain of loss. Thus, the feminist questioning and in some cases rejection of gender roles triggers a process of disidentification with established forms of masculinity and femininity, which has fueled the political quest for alternative ways of inhabiting gender and embodying sexuality.[20] In race discourse, the awareness of the persistence of racial discrimination and of white privilege has led, on the one hand, to the critical reappraisal of blackness[21] and, on the other, to radical relocation of whiteness.[22]

In a Spinozist vein, these are transformative processes that not only rework the consciousness of social injustice and discrimination but also produce a more adequate cartography of our real-life condition, free of delusions of grandeur. It is an enriching and positive experience which, however, includes pain as an integral element. Migrants, exiles, and refugees have first-hand experience of the extent to which the process of disidentification from familiar identities is linked to the pain of loss and uprooting. Diasporic subjects of all kinds express the same sense of wound. Multilocality is the affirmative translation of this negative sense of loss. Following Glissant,[23] the becoming-nomadic marks the process of positive transformation of the pain of loss into the active production of multiple forms of belonging and complex allegiances. What is lost in the sense of fixed origins is gained in an increased desire to belong in a multiple rhizomic manner that transcends the classical bilateralism of binary identity formations.

The qualitative leap through pain, across the mournful landscapes of nostalgic yearning, is the gesture of active creation of affirmative ways of belonging. It is a fundamental reconfiguration of our way of being in the world, which acknowledges the pain of loss but moves further. This is the defining moment for the process of becoming-ethical: the move across and beyond pain, loss, and negative passions. Taking suffering into account is the starting point; the real aim of the process, however, is the quest for ways of overcoming the stultifying effects of passivity, brought about by pain. The internal disarray, fracture, and pain are the conditions of possibility for ethical transformation. Clearly, this is an antithesis of the Kantian moral imperative to avoid pain or to view pain as the obstacle to moral behavior. Nomadic ethics is not about the avoidance of pain; rather it is about transcending the resignation and passivity that ensue from being hurt, lost, and dispossessed. One has to become ethical, as opposed to applying moral rules and protocols as a form of self-protection. Transformations express the affirmative power of life as the vitalism of *bios-zoē*, which is the opposite of morality as a form of life insurance.

The awakening of ethical and political consciousness through the pain of loss has been acknowledged by Edgar Morin[24] in his account of how he relinquished Marxist universalism to embrace a more "situated perspective"[25] as a European. He describes his "becoming European" as a double affect. The first concerns the disappointment with unfulfilled promises of Marxism. The second involves compassion for the uneasy, struggling, and marginal position of postwar Europe, squashed between the USA and the USSR. The pain of this awareness that Europe was ill loved and a castaway results in a new kind of bonding and a renewed sense of care and accountability. This produces a postnationalistic redefinition of being a European in a minoritarian mode, which defines the European space-time location as a zone of mediation and transformation.[26]

The sobering experience—the humble and productive recognition of loss, limitations, and shortcomings—has to do with self-representations. Established mental habits, images, and terminology railroad us back toward established ways of thinking about ourselves. Traditional modes of representation are legal forms of addiction. To change them is not unlike undertaking a disintoxication cure. A great deal of courage and creativity is needed to develop forms of representation that do justice to the complexities of the kind of subjects we have already become. We already live and inhabit social reality in ways that surpass tradition: we move about, in the flow of current social transformations, in hybrid, multicultural, polyglot, post-identity spaces of becoming.[27] We fail, however, to bring them into adequate representation. There is a shortage on the part of our social imaginary, a deficit of representational power, which underscores the political timidity of our times.

The real issue is conceptual: how do we develop a new post-unitary vision of the subject and ourselves, and how do we adopt a social imaginary that does justice to the complexity? How does one work through the pain of disidentification and loss? Given that identifications constitute an inner scaffolding that supports one's sense of identity, how do changes of this magnitude take place? Shifting an imaginary is not like casting away a used garment but more like shedding an old skin. It happens often enough at the molecular level, but in the social it is a painful experience. Part of the answer lies in the formulation of the question: "we" are in this together. This is a collective activity, a group project that connects active, conscious, and desiring citizens. It points towards a virtual destination—post-unitary nomadic identities, floating foundations, etc.—but it is not utopian. As a project it is historically grounded, socially embedded, and already partly actualized in the joint endeavor, that is, the community, of those who are actively working toward it. If this is utopian it is only in the sense of the positive effects that are mobilized in the process: the necessary dose of imagination, dreamlike vision, and bonding without which no social project can take off.

Steps Towards an Ethics of Affirmation

The ethics of affirmation, with its emphasis on moving across the pain and transforming it into activity, may seem counterintuitive. In our culture people go to great lengths to ease all pain, but especially the pain of uncertainty about identity, origin, and belonging. Great distress follows from not knowing or not being able to articulate the source of one's suffering, or from knowing it all too well, all the time. People who have been confronted by the irreparable, the unbearable, the insurmountable, the traumatic and inhuman event will do anything to find solace, resolution, and also compensation. The yearning for these measures—solace, closure, justice—is all too understandable and worthy of respect. Nowadays, this longing is both supported and commercially exploited by genetics and its application to the tracking of racial and territorial origins.

The ethical dilemma was already posed by Jean-François Lyotard in *Le Differend* and, much earlier, by Primo Levi about the survivors of Nazi concentration camps: the kind of vulnerability human beings experience in the face of events on the scale of high horror is something for which no adequate compensation is even thinkable, let alone applicable. There is an incommensurability of the suffering involved for which no measure of compensation is possible—a hurt or wound beyond repair. This means that the notion of justice in the sense of a logic of rights and reparation is not applicable in a quantifiable manner. For Lyotard, in keeping with the poststructuralist emphasis on the ethical dimension on the problem, ethics consists in accepting the impossibility of adequate compensation and living with the open wound. On the contrary, contemporary culture has taken the opposite direction: it has favored, encouraged, and rewarded a public morality based on the twin principles of claims and compensation, as if financial settlements could provide the answer to the injury suffered, the pain endured, and the long-lasting effects of the injustice. Cases that exemplify this trend are the compensation for the Shoah in the sense of restitution of stolen property, artworks, and bank deposits. Similar claims have been made by the descendants of slaves forcefully removed from Africa to North America,[28] and more recently compensation for damages caused by Soviet communism, notably the confiscation of properties across eastern Europe, from Jewish and other former citizens.

The ethics of affirmation is about suspending the quest for both claims and compensation, resisting the logic of retribution of rights and taking instead a different road. In order to understand this move it is important to depsychologize the discussion of affirmation. Affectivity is intrinsically understood as positive: it is the force that aims at fulfilling the subject's capacity for interaction and freedom. It is Spinoza's *conatus*, or the notion of *potentia* as the affirmative aspect of power. It is joyful and pleasure-prone, and it is immanent in that it coincides with the terms and modes of its expression. This means concretely that ethical behavior confirms, facilitates, and enhances the subject's *potentia*, as the capacity to express his/her freedom. The positivity of this desire to express one's innermost and constitutive freedom (*conatus*, *potentia*, or becoming) is conducive to ethical behavior, however, only if the subject is capable of making it endure, thus allowing it to sustain its own impetus. Unethical behavior achieves the opposite effect: it denies, hinders, and diminishes that impetus or is unable to sustain it. Affirmation is therefore not naive optimism or Candide-like unrealism. It is about endurance and transformation. Endurance is self-affirmation. It is also an ethical principle of affirmation of the positivity of the intensive subject—its joyful affirmation as *potentia*. The subject is a spatio-temporal compound which frames the boundaries of processes of becoming. This works by transforming negative into positive passions through the power of an understanding that is no longer indexed upon a phallogocentric set of standards, but is rather unhinged and therefore affective.

This sort of turning of the tide of negativity is the transformative process of achieving freedom of understanding through the awareness of our limits, of our bondage. This results in the freedom to affirm one's essence as joy, through encounters and minglings with other bodies, entities, beings, and forces. Ethics means faithfulness to this *potentia*, or the desire to become. Deleuze defines the latter with reference to Bergson's concept of "duration," thus proposing the notion of the subject as an entity that lasts, that endures sustainable changes and transformation and enacts them around him/herself in a community or collectivity. Affirmative ethics rests on the idea of sustainability as a principle of containment and tolerable development of a subject's resources, understood environmentally, affectively, and cognitively. A subject thus constituted inhabits a time that is the active tense of continuous "becoming." Endurance has therefore a temporal dimension: it has to do with lasting in time—hence duration and self-perpetuation. But it also has a spatial side to do with the space of the body as an enfleshed field of actualization of passions or forces. It evolves as affectivity and joy, as in the capacity for being affected by these forces to the point of pain or extreme pleasure, which come to the same thing; it means putting up with hardship and physical pain.

The point, however, is that extreme pleasure or extreme pain—which may score the same on a Spinozist scale of ethology of affects—are of course not the same. On the reactive side of the equation, endurance points to the struggle to sustain the pain without being annihilated by it. It also introduces a temporal dimension about duration in time. This is linked to memory: intense pain, a wrong, a betrayal, a wound are hard to forget. The traumatic impact of painful events fixes them in a rigid, eternal present tense out of which it is difficult to emerge. This is the eternal return of that which precisely cannot be endured and returns in the mode of the unwanted, the untimely, the unassimilated or inappropriate/d. They are also, however, paradoxically difficult to remember, insofar as remembering entails retrieval and repetition of the pain itself.

Psychoanalysis, of course, has been here before.[29] The notion of the return of the repressed is the key to the logic of unconscious remembrance, but it is a secret and somewhat invisible key which condenses space into the spasm of the symptom and time into a short circuit that mines the very thinkability of the present. Kristeva's notion of the abject[30] expresses clearly the temporality involved in psychoanalysis—by stressing the structural function played by the negative, the incomprehensible, the unthinkable, the other of understandable knowledge. Deleuze calls this alterity "Chaos" and defines it ontologically as the virtual formation of all possible form. Lacan, on the other hand—and Derrida with him, I would argue—defines Chaos epistemologically as that which precedes form, structure, and language. This makes for two radically divergent conceptions of time and negativity. That which is incomprehensible for Lacan, following Hegel, is the virtual for Deleuze, following Spinoza, Bergson, and Leibnitz.

This produces a number of significant shifts: from negative to affirmative; from entropic to generative; from incomprehensible, meaningless, and crazy to virtual waiting to be actualized; from constituting constitutive outsides to a geometry of affects that require mutual synchronization; from a melancholy and split to an open-ended weblike subject; from the epistemological to the ontological turn in poststructuralist philosophy.

This introduces a temporal dimension into the discussion that leads to the very conditions of possibility of the future, to futurity as such. For an ethics of sustainability, the expression of positive affects is that which makes the subject last or endure. It is like a source of long-term energy at the affective core of subjectivity.[31] Nietzsche has also been here before, of course. The eternal return in Nietzsche is the repetition, yet neither in the compulsive mode of neurosis nor in the negative erasure that marks the traumatic event. It is the eternal return of and as positivity.[32] This kind of ethics addresses the affective structure of pain and suffering but does not locate the ethical instance within it, be it in the mode of compassionate witnessing[33] or empathic co-presence. In a nomadic, Deleuzian-Nietzschean perspective, ethics is essentially about the transformation of negative into positive passions, that is, about moving beyond the pain. This does not mean denying the pain but rather activating it, working it through. Again, the positivity here is not supposed to indicate a facile optimism or a careless dismissal of human suffering.

What is positive in the ethics of affirmation is the belief that negative affects can be transformed. This implies a dynamic view of all affects, even those that freeze us in pain, horror, or mourning. Affirmative nomadic ethics puts the motion back into emotion and the active back into activism, introducing movement, process, and becoming. This shift makes all the difference to the patterns of repetition of negative emotions.

What is negative about negative affects is not a value judgment (any more than it is for the positivity of difference), but rather the effect of arrest, blockage, and rigidification that come as a result of an act of violence, betrayal, or trauma—or which can be self-perpetuated through practices that our culture simultaneously chastises as self-destructive and cultivates as a mode of discipline and punishment: all forms of mild and extreme addiction, differing degrees of abusive practices that mortify and glorify the bodily matter, from binging to bodily modifications. Abusive, addictive, or destructive practices do not merely destroy the self but harm the self's capacity to relate to others, both human and nonhuman others. Thus, they harm the capacity to grow in and through others and become others. Negative passions diminish our capacity to express the high levels of interdependence, the vital reliance on others, which is the key to a non-unitary and dynamic vision of the subject. What is negated by negative passions is the power of life itself as the dynamic force, vital flows of connections and becomings. This is why they should not be encouraged, nor should we be rewarded for lingering around them too long. Negative passions are black holes.

An ethics of affirmation involves the transformation of negative into positive passions: resentment into affirmation, as Nietzsche put it. The practice of transforming negative into positive passions is the process of reintroducing time, movement, and transformation into a stifling enclosure saturated with unprocessed pain. It is a gesture of affirmation of hope in the sense of affirming the possibility of moving beyond the stultifying effects of the pain, the injury, the injustice. This is a gesture of displacement of the hurt, which fully contradicts the twin logic of claims and compensation. This is achieved through a sort of depersonalization of the event, which is the ultimate ethical challenge. The displacement of the ego-indexed negative passions or affects reveals the fundamental senselessness of the hurt, the injustice, or the injury one has suffered. "Why me?" is the refrain most commonly heard in situations of extreme distress. This expresses rage as well as anguish at one's ill fate. The answer is plain: for no reason at all. Examples of this are the banality of evil in large-scale genocides like the Holocaust[34] and the randomness of surviving them (think of Primo Levi who could not endure his own survival). There is something intrinsically senseless about the pain or injustice: lives are lost or saved for all and no reason at all. Why did some go to work in the WTC on 9/11 while others missed the train? Why did Frida Kahlo take the tram that crashed so that she was impaled by a metal rod, and not the next one? For no reason at all. Reason has nothing to do with it. That is precisely the point.

Contrary to the traditional morality that follows a rationalist and legalistic model of possible interpretation of the wrongs one suffered to a logic of responsibility, claim, and compensation, affirmative ethics rests on the notion of the random access to the phenomena that cause pain (or pleasure). This is not fatalism, and even less resignation, but rather *amor fati*. This is a crucial difference: we have to be worthy of what happens to us and rework it within an ethics of relation. Of course, repugnant and unbearable events do happen. Ethics consists, however, in reworking these events in the direction of positive relations. This is not carelessness or lack of compassion, but rather a form of lucidity that acknowledges the impossibility of finding an adequate answer to the question about the source, the origin, the cause of the ill fate, the painful event, the violence suffered. Acknowledging the futility of even trying to answer that question is a starting point.

Edouard Glissant[35] provides a perfect example of this productive ethics in his work on race and racism. An ethical relation cannot be based on resentment or resignation but rather on the affirmation of positivity. Every event contains within it the potential for being overcome and overtaken; its negative charge can be transposed. The moment of the actualization is also the moment of its neutralization. "Every event is like death, double and impersonal in its double," argues Deleuze.[36] The free subject, the ethical subject, is the one with the ability to grasp the freedom to depersonalize the event and transform its negative charge. The focus thus shifts to asking the adequate questions. Adequateness, both the logic of claim and compensation, lies at the heart of the ethical stance. This requires a double shift: of the pain itself—from the frozen or reactive effect to proactive affirmation—and of the line of questioning—from the quest for the origin or source to a process of elaboration of the kind of questions that express and enhance a subject's capacity to achieve freedom through the understanding of its limitations.

What is an adequate ethical question? One that is capable of sustaining the subject in his/her quest for more interrelations with others, that is, more

Life, motion, change, transformation, and *potentia*. The adequate ethical question provides the subject with a frame for interaction and change, growth, and movement. It affirms life as difference-at-work. An ethical question has to be adequate in relation to how much a body can take, which is the notion of sustainability. How much can an embodied entity take in the mode of interrelations and connections; that is, how much freedom of action can we endure? That is the question. It assumes, following Nietzsche, that humanity does not stem from freedom but rather that freedom is extracted out of the awareness of limitations.

Ethics is about freedom from the weight of negativity, freedom through the understanding of our bondage. A certain amount of pain, the knowledge about vulnerability and pain, is actually useful. It forces one to think about the actual material conditions of being interconnected and thus being in the world. It frees one from the stupidity of perfect health and the full-blown sense of existential entitlement that comes with it. Paradoxically, it is those who have already cracked up a bit, those who have suffered pain and injury, who are better placed to take the lead in the process of ethical transformation. Because they are already on the other side of some existential divide, they are anomalous in some way—but in a positive way, for Deleuze.[37] Their anomaly deterritorializes the force of habit and introduces a powerful element of productive difference. They know about endurance, adequate forces, and the importance of Relations.

Marxist epistemology and feminist standpoint theory have always acknowledged the privileged knowing position of those in the "margins." Postcolonial theory displaces the dialectics of center-margin and locates the force of discursive production. Affirmative ethics is on the same wavelength: only those who have been hurt are in a position not to return the violence and hence make a positive difference. In order to do so, however, they have to become-minoritarian, that is, transcend the logic of negativity (claim and compensation) and transform the negative affect into something active and productive. The center being dead and empty of active force, it is on the margins that the processes of becoming can be initiated. It is also crowded on the margins.

The figure of Nelson Mandela—a contemporary secular saint—comes to mind, as does the world-historical phenomenon that is the Truth and Reconciliation Commission in post-apartheid South Africa. This is a case of repetition that engenders difference and does not install the eternal return of revenge and negative affects, a massive exercise in transformation of negativity into something more livable, more life enhancing. Christianity has tried to be here before. It has had an important input in the work of Cornell West, bell hooks, and other spiritually-minded activists today, especially in reconstituting a sense of community and mutual responsibility in places devastated by hatred and mutual suspicion. Affirmative nomadic ethics is profoundly secular and it refuses simply to turn the other cheek. It proclaims the need to construct collectively positions of active, positive interconnections and relations that can sustain a web of mutual dependence, an ecology of multiple belongings.

It is a case of extracting freedom from the awareness of limits. For the affirmative ethics of sustainability, it is always already a question of life and death. Being on the edge of too-muchness, or of unsustainability, surfing on the borders of the intolerable, is another way of describing the process of becoming. Becoming marks a qualitative leap in the transformation of subjectivity and of its constitutive affects. It is a trip across different fields of perception, different spatiotemporal coordinates. Mostly it transforms negativity into affirmative affects: pain into compassion, loss into a sense of bonding, isolation into care. It is simultaneously a slowing down of the rhythm of daily frenzy and an acceleration of awareness, connection to others, self-knowledge, and sensorial perception.

Ethics includes the acknowledgment of and compassion for pain, as well as the activity of working through it. Any process of change must do some sort of violence to deeply engrained habits and dispositions which got consolidated over time. Overcoming these engrained habits is a necessary disruption, without which there is no ethical awakening. Consciousness-raising is not free of pain. The utterance: "I can't take it anymore!" far from being an admission of defeat, marks the threshold and hence the condition of possibility for creative encounters and productive changes. This is how the ethical dimension appears through the mass of fragments and shreds of discarded habits that are characteristic of our times. The ethical project is not the same as the implementation of ruling standards of morality. It rather concerns the norms and values, the standards and criteria that can be applied to the quest for sustainable, that is to say for newly negotiated, limits. Limits are to be rethought in terms of an ethics of becoming, through a non–Hegelian notion of "limits" as thresholds, that is to say points of encounter and not of closure, living boundaries and not fixed walls.

The joint necessity for both the pursuit of social change and in-depth transformation, as well as for an ethics of endurance and sustainability, is important to stress because critical and creative thinkers and activists who pursue change have often experienced the limits or the boundaries like open wounds or scars. The generation that came of age politically in the seventies has taken enormous risks and has enjoyed the challenges they entailed. A lot was demanded and expected from life and most ended up getting it, but it was not only a joy ride. An ethical evaluation of the costs involved in pursuing alternative visions, norms, and values is important in the present context where the alleged "end of ideology" is used as a pretext for neoliberal restoration that terminates all social experiments. It is necessary to find a way to combine transformative politics with affirmative ethics so as to confront the conceptual and social contradictions of our times. Sustainable affirmative ethics allows us to contain the risks while pursuing the original project of transformation. This is a way to resist the dominant ethos of our conservative times that idolizes the new as a consumerist trend while thundering against those who believe in change. Cultivating the ethics of living intensely in the pursuit of change is a political act.

NOTES

1. Todd May, *The Moral Theory of Poststructuralism* (University Park: Pennsylvania State University Press, 1995).
2. Gilles Deleuze, "L'immanence: une vie…," *Philosophie* 47, no. 1 (1972).
3. Luce Irigaray, *L'éthique de la différence sexuelle* (Paris: Minuit, 1984). English translation: *An Ethics of Sexual Difference*, trans. Carolyn Burke and Gillian Gill (Ithaca: Cornell University Press, 1993).
4. Seyla Benhabib, *The Claims of Culture: Equality and Diversity in the Global Era* (Princeton: Princeton University Press, 2002).
5. Nancy Fraser, "Multiculturalism and Gender Equity: The U.S. 'Difference' Debates Revisited," *Constellations* 3, no. 1 (1996).
6. Martha Nussbaum, *Cultivating Humanity: A Classical Defense of Reform in Liberal Education* (Cambridge: Harvard University Press, 1999).
7. Sabina Lovibond, "The End of Morality," *Knowing the Difference: Feminist Perspectives in Epistemology*, ed. Kathleen Lenno and Margaret Whitford (New York: Routledge, 1994).
8. See Habermas's recent work on human nature, 2003.
9. Nicholas Rose, "The Politics of Life Itself," *Theory, Culture, and Society* 18, no. 6 (2001).
10. Paul Rabinow, *Anthropos Today* (Princeton: Princeton University Press, 2003).
11. Giorgio Agamben, *Homo Sacer: Sovereign Power and Bare Life* (Stanford: Stanford University Press, 1998).
12. Simon Critchley, *The Ethics of Deconstruction* (Edinburgh: Edinburgh University Press, 1992).
13. Keith Ansell-Pearson, *Viroid Life: Perspectives on Nietzsche and the Transhuman Condition* (New York: Routledge, 1997); Keith Ansell-Pearson, *Germinal Life: The Difference and Repetition of Deleuze* (New York: Routledge, 1999).
14. Jessica Benjamin, *The Bonds of Love: Psychoanalysis, Feminism and the Problem of Domination* (New York: Pantheon Books, 1988).
15. Jean François Lyotard, *Le Différend* (Paris: Minuit, 1983).
16. Judith Butler, *Precarious Life* (London: Verso, 2004).
17. Genevieve Lloyd, *Part of Nature: Self-knowledge in Spinoza's Ethics* (Ithaca: Cornell University Press, 1994), 23.
18. Lloyd, *Part of Nature*, 18.
19. *Ibid.*, 74.
20. Rosi Braidotti, *Metamorphoses: Towards a Materialist Theory of Becoming* (Cambridge: Polity Press, 2002).
21. Paul Gilroy, *Against Race: Imaging Political Culture Beyond the Color Line* (Cambridge: Harvard University Press, 2000).
22. Braidotti, *Metamorphoses*.
23. Édouard Glissant, *Poétique de la Relation* (Paris: Gallimard, 1990). English translation: *Poetics of Relation*, trans. Betsy Wing (Ann Arbor: University of Michigan Press, 1997).
24. Edgar Morin, *Penser l[apost]Europe* (Paris: Gallimard, 1987).
25. Donna Haraway, *Modest Witness* (New York: Routledge, 1997).

26. Étienne Balibar, *Politics and the Other Scene* (London: Verso, 2002).

27. Braidotti, *Metamorphoses*.

28. Paul Gilroy, *Against Race*.

29. Jean Laplanche, *Life and Death in Psychoanalysis* (Baltimore: Johns Hopkins University Press, 1976).

30. Julia Kristeva, *Pouvoirs de l'horreur* (Paris: Seuil, 1980). English translation: *Powers of Horror*, trans. Leon Roudiez (New York: Columbia University Press, 1982).

31. Elizabeth Grosz, *The Nick of Time* (Durham: Duke University Press, 2004).

32. Ansell-Pearson, *Germinal Life*.

33. Zygmunt Bauman, *Postmodern Ethics* (Oxford: Blackwell, 1993); Zygmunt Bauman, *Globalization: The Human Consequences* (Cambridge: Polity Press, 1998).

34. Hannah Arendt, *Eichmann in Jerusalem: A Report on the Banality of Evil* (New York: Viking Press, 1963).

35. Glissant, *Poétique de la Relation*.

36. Gilles Deleuze, *Logique du sens* (Paris: Minuit, 1969). English translation: *The Logic of Sense*, trans. M. Lester and C. Stivale (New York: Columbia University Press, 1990), 152.

37. Deleuze, *Logique du sens*.

Index